THE COMPLETE BOOK OF

SPORT FISHING

THE COMPLETE BOOK OF SPORT FISHING

KEN SCHULTZ

Photographic acknowledgments
Front cover: Main photograph: Adela Ward Battin
Below left: Bob Stearns
Below: Shimano Reels

Back cover: Bob Stearns

All other photographs supplied by
World Angling Services/Ken Schultz

The publishers would like to dedicate this book to Captain Joseph Masone and the crew of the Debra.

An Imprint of BDD Promotional Book Company, Inc.
666 Fifth Avenue
New York, N.Y. 10103

First published in the Unites States of America in 1989
by The Mallard Press

ISBN 0792-45021-3

Produced by Mandarin Offset
Printed in Hong Kong

CONTENTS

FOREWORD

To the extent that any book can be called "complete," as angling is in a constant state of change, *The Complete Book of Sport Fishing* is as current as any volume can be, or as any author can make it; and therein lies its true value. Ken Schultz is not only an expert in the angling arts but, as associate fishing editor of *Field & Stream*, he has for sixteen years been responsible for accurate reporting to more than ten million readers each month. And, wearing two literary hats, he writes a syndicated newspaper column for the Gannett News Service resulting in almost daily contact with a fish of some kind.

The bulk of angling literature encompasses countless titles on singular subjects, often didactic treatments on salmon, trout or black bass fishing – all valuable in their own right – but few authors have the professional experience to describe a broad range of sport fishing. As a reference, especially for beginners, Ken Schultz not only provides dimension to the art but detailed instruction in the pursuit of our popular freshwater and saltwater gamefish. It comes as a great bonus that his book is lavishly illustrated as photos can add practical scope by instant recognition of the tackle used, the type of water being fished, the type of boat required if not in a wading situation, even the clothing worn in that particular angling season. And any instructional text profits by line drawings which here the author has selected with an eye to the fundamentals of technique.

Ken Schultz not only lives in the historical angling country of the Catskill Mountains but he also travels extensively throughout North America and many foreign lands from the Arctic to the tropics, peregrinations that I consider essential to in-depth writing. An author cannot provide meaningful perspective without experiencing the whole spectrum of fishing possibilities. Those lures, baits and methods that are successful for a particular species of fish are not always universal, and knowing the options is important once the angler ventures from home waters – which we all do, sooner or later. In *The Complete Book of Sport Fishing* you will find the panoply that ensures thrills and enjoyment to the degree that the writen word can teach.

I have been in the angling writing game for a half century and one thing I've learned is that my peers, friends, and even small children often have little nuggets of wisdom to offer about catching fish that somehow escaped me. Indeed, the learning process goes on forever. Ken's book is a goldmine of "nuggets" which is reason enough for this volume to be on every shelf.

A.J. McClane

EQUIPMENT

COMBINATOR

RODS

It's debatable what type of fishing equipment is most important to an angler. A rod is certainly very important, yet it's the most ignored and perhaps most abused tackle item. Rods need little maintenance, especially if used only in freshwater; and unless something breaks (like a reel seat or guide or ferrule), a rod is never serviced. Reasonable neglect is fine as long as you've got the right rod for your needs.

There is no one rod that will fill all needs. There's a reason why there are fly, spinning, bait casting, spin casting, surf, trolling, boat, flipping, popping, noodle, and downrigger rods, to name just some of the possibilities. Obviously a fly fisherman can't do justice to fly fishing without the right type of rod, but neither can the same type of spinning rod be used adequately in stream trout fishing as in trolling for trout with downriggers. If a rod is to be used for a variety of fishing applications, there is necessarily some compromise to be made.

Different species, special applications, and regional preferences lead to a proliferation in rods that anglers who do a variety of fishing will need. Therefore, it's important to get the right type, length, and style of rod at the outset. One of the most misunderstood facets of rod selection is that of action.

Action

This refers to the point where a rod flexes along its length.

The closer it flexes to the tip, the quicker the action. To determine action, take a fishing rod in your hand, hold it parallel to the floor and waist high, and snap it from side to side in a continuous motion. As you look at the rod you'll see a flexing point. If the flex is in the third of the rod closest to the butt, it's a slow-action product; in the middle third it's a medium action; in the tip third it's a fast action; close to the tip is an extra-fast action. Fast, medium, and slow are the primary actions, though there is also ultralight and medium-heavy.

These terms also refer to the size of line and lures that rods are capable of handling properly. This, in turn, can be related to species of fish and their respective sizes and fighting abilities. A light spinning rod, for instance, would normally be used with 4- to 8-pound-test line and small lures. Such a rod could be used in fishing for white bass or bonefish, but not for stripers or tuna.

Taper

Action is also related to taper. In a 'fast' taper rod, the diameter of the tip section is much thinner than that of the butt section. A 'slow' taper signifies a gradual lessening in diameter from butt to tip. A fast taper rod has good hook-setting strength, exhibits more bend in the tip section than in the butt, and has more sensitivity. A slow taper rod has a more uniform bend throughout and is relatively limber.

Rods differ greatly by type, function, material, and action. A fast-taper rod, such as the graphite product used by this steelhead angler, has a sensitive tip but is strong enough to subdue large fish.

Limberness

This is a quality that many anglers seek in a rod, yet this may not be good. A limber (meaning very pliable and soft), whippy rod can make the casting of light lures very easy. It is also a lot of fun to use for small, scrappy fish. But it can be a hindrance in the use of heavy lures, or such items as diving plugs and plastic worms, or for fighting large and strong fish.

In many cases a stiff-tipped rod, though it doesn't cast as well, provides better strike detection and hook-setting performance than a limber rod. Some surface plugs and light floating diving lures, however, are best worked on a soft-tipped rod (one that has strength in the mid section, but a soft tip).

Power

Rods are also referred to in terms of power by some manufacturers, who use a numerical system for grading purposes, with high numbers denoting greater power. Power describes how much effort is required to bend a rod. A light-power rod is one that requires little effort to bend. The more effort, the greater the power.

Composition

Fishing rods are made of different materials as well as mergers of materials. The latter are known as composites. Fiberglass, graphite, boron, and Kevlar are the principal materials that are used by major manufacturers in rod construction, with the latter two primarily relegated to composite use. There are several different grades of fiberglass and graphite. In general, fiberglass is an economical material and one that withstands a lot of abuse. Graphite is stronger and more sensitive. Graphite rods are preferred by most avid anglers for superior casting, hook-setting, and fish-playing attributes.

One-piece and multi-piece rods

Most dedicated fishermen also prefer one-piece rods because they have a better feel and transmit activity better than multi-piece rods, especially in the ferrule area, and are less prone to breakage. But modern ferrules, which are designed to be part of the rod blank, make multi-piece rods less undesirable than in the past, and especially satisfactory where you must use such rods (for storage, travel, etc.).

Locking and unlocking ferrules is occasionally a problem, however. To connect them, place the female section over the male section while the guides on both sections are a little out of alignment. Twist both sections until the guides are aligned.

Don't align the guides and jam the two pieces together; you can damage the fit of the ferrules with direct pressure. To disassemble, twist the sections apart; don't pull directly in opposite directions.

Guides

Check to see that a rod you're thinking of buying has the proper number and spacing of guides. Guides should be spaced so that the fishing line closely follows the curvature of the rod. On rods on which the guides face upward, such as level-wind or spin-casting rods, the line should not touch the blank of the rod when the rod is bent over. If it does, the rod doesn't have enough guides. If the line goes from guide to guide at a sharp angle, the rod needs more or better spaced guides. Generally, there should be a minimum of five guides plus a tip top on any rod; certain rods have more than a dozen guides.

One-piece fiberglass rods are preferred for all-purpose saltwater fishing and may be referred to as boat or bay rods. This medium-heavy rod was used in trolling for bluefish.

Balancing tackle

Rods and reels ideally should be matched to each other, and this matching is referred to as 'balanced tackle.' This term means nothing more than that the rod and reel should complement each other and be suited for use together. You wouldn't use a small ultralight reel with a medium-action rod. Nor would you use a big reel capable of holding 200 yards of 10-pound line with a rod meant for 4-to 8-pound line. Filling that big reel with 6-pound line isn't a solution either, because it isn't so designed, and you'd still have a reel that is too large for comfortable use with that particular rod.

Length

The length of rod to select is a matter of preference at times, of necessity at others. Longer rods are usually easier to cast, except in tight quarters; they help achieve long-distance casts; and they are helpful in hook-setting. Surf fishing, trolling, casting from shore, and fishing for large fish are circumstances that require long rods. The average length of a light- to medium-action spinning rod is 6 feet. Long rods are generally those over $6^{1/2}$ feet long, except in fly fishing, where rod lengths virtually start at 7 feet.

Buying a rod

When fishermen go into a store to look at rods, they must determine what is suitable for their fishing needs. They should already have an idea what type of fishing they will be doing, with what line strengths and lure of sizes, and under what conditions, in order to make an intelligent choice.

Assuming that you have some idea what your applications will be and what your needs are, you'll have to 'try out' a prospective rod to the best of your ability. Don't judge by cosmetics or the composition of the reel handle. Wiggling the rod and flexing it is highly subjective and of dubious value, though you can check the action somewhat this way. By carefully putting the tip of the rod on a carpeted floor or up against the ceiling, you can flex it enough to see the shape of the rod when pressure is applied and know if it has uniform bending. The best option is to put a reel on the rod (preferably the one you're going to use with it) and tie on a lure or practice casting plug. Now you can simulate the feel and casting performance. If it's possible, take the outfit outside where you can make a few casts (you may have to leave some collateral behind).

Spinning tackle is among the most universally popular fishing equipment, particularly in freshwater. Balanced, light-action tackle provides good sport and can be used for a variety of applications.

Categories of rods

Bait-casting Used with level-wind or bait-casting reels, which sit on top of the rod handle and face the angler, this tackle provides excellent casting accuracy for the skillful user. Most bait-casting rods are one-piece models, though larger, heavier-duty ones may have a telescoping butt, and are generally stiffer than spinning rods. Guides are usually small to medium size, and newer models sport a blank that runs through the handle, which may be straight or with a pistol grip.

Spin-casting These rods are similar to bait-casting types but have larger guides to accommodate the use of spin-casting reels. Reels mount a little higher on the rod seat. Spin-casting rods usually aren't as stiff, with a lighter action for use with light lines and lures.

Spinning Used with open-faced spinning reels that mount underneath the rod, this tackle is very popular for wide usage. Guides are big to accommodate the large spirals of line that come off the reel spool when casting. Handles are straight, with fixed or adjustable sliding (top and bottom rings) reel seats.

Fly Fly rods are long and rather limber; unlike other tackle, they use a large-diameter, heavy line to cast a very light object. Guides are small, and rod length varies from 7 to 12 or 14 feet, although most fly rods used in North America are $7^{1/2}$- to 10-footers. Fly rods are rated for casting a specific weight line; a fly reel usually sits at the bottom of the handle, but some rods have extension butts for leverage in fighting big fish. An 8-to $8^{1/2}$-foot rod suited for a No. 7 line is probably the most popular all-around version.

Surf These long rods are used for casting great distances from the beach into the surf and come in both spinning and level-wind versions. Length varies

Above: Bait casting tackle is preferred by many anglers who cast and retrieve fairly large lures and fish where there is substantial cover.

from 7 to 14 feet, though most are in the 8- to 10-foot range with long two-handed handles. They are heavy, in order to cast objects weighing 2 to 4 ounces, and guides are large.

Boat-and-bay A lot of different rods fall into this category. These are usually workhorse products with beefy two-handed handles that accommodate level-wind reels. They are generally stiff, heavy-action rods, with longer ones used in pier fishing and shorter ones in boat work.

Big-game These rods, meant for subduing the largest creatures of the sea, have the sturdiest construction. Generally short, they feature a roller guide on the tip top or throughout the blank, and sport an extra-heavy-duty handle with a gimbal-mount butt for insertion into rod holders. These rods are rated according to the class of line (and reel size) they are suited for.

Others Travel or pack rods are found in bait, spin, or fly versions and are multi-piece products (some also have telescoping butt sections). Ice fishing rods are usually very short rods with a soft tip for use around holes in the ice. Flipping rods are long (7 to 8 feet), heavy-action rods with telescoping butts that are used for making short casts in close quarters to heavy cover when largemouth bass fishing. Noodle rods are whippy 12-to 14-foot rods with guides that curve around the rod blank; they are primarily used in stream steelhead and salmon fishing for presentation and fish-fighting advantages, and sometimes in trolling. Downrigger rods are 8- to 9-foot slow-action products that are primarily found in level-wind versions and take a long, deep bend for use when trolling with downriggers. Some other rods are made for special applications, and many manufacturers make rods designed for particular species of fish or for use with certain lures or baits (crankbait rods, for example, or mooching rods).

Below: This four-piece pack-style fly rod extends to nine feet and is capable of providing good casting and fish playing, but when encased in its small tube, can be readily transported anywhere.

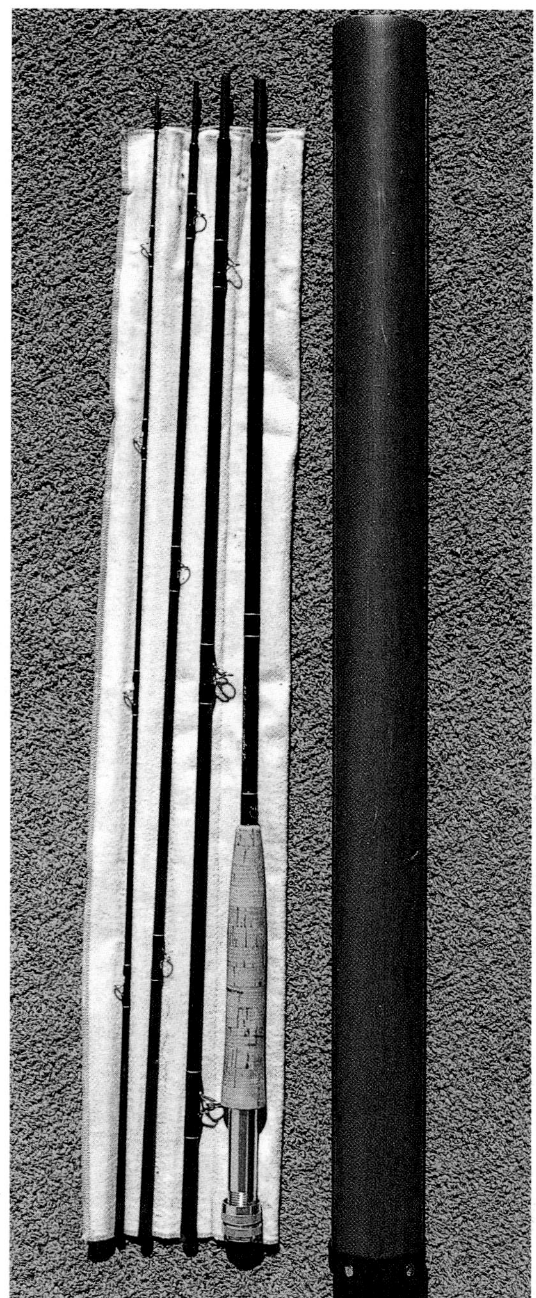

REELS

Reels are an integral component of fishing and generally get more attention than rods or line, although the matters of gear ratio and drag are not well understood by a lot of people.

Gear ratio

This refers to the number of times line is wrapped around the reel spool each time the handle is turned. A ratio of 5 to 1, for example, means that for each revolution of the handle, line is wrapped around the spool five times. On a bait-casting reel this means how many times the spool revolves per handle revolution. On a spin-casting reel it means how many times the head revolves around the stationary spool per handle revolution. On a spinning reel it means how many times the complete bail assembly revolves around the stationary spool per handle revolution.

Drag

The purpose of the drag function is to let line slip from the reel at varying pressures when force is applied to the line. It serves as a shock absorber, or clutch. The looser it is set, the less force is required to strip line off. If the drag is set properly, a strong-pulling fish may be able to take line from the spool by applying less pressure than would be required to break the line or knot. Thus, the drag acts as insurance, as a buffer between you and the fish. Properly set line drag is most useful when playing strong, hard-fighting fish; when using light line; and when reacting to sudden surges by fish.

The most accurate way to set the drag is to bring line off the spool through the rod guides and attach it to a reliable spring scale. Keep the rod up as if you were fighting a fish and have someone pull on the scale to watch the dial so you know at what amount of pressure the drag began to slip. Lighten or increase tension accordingly. Many anglers set the drag tension at between 30 and 50 percent of the breaking strength of the line for normal fishing conditions, raising it in heavy cover. If you think about drag tension in terms of the breaking strength of your line, you'll realize that 50 percent of 12-pound line is still 6 pounds of pressure, and few fishermen exert 6 or more pounds of pressure even when setting the hook. Most anglers would be fooled if they were to pull line off their drag and guess the tension setting.

Spinning reels

These are the most popular type of reel in general use, in both freshwater and saltwater fishing applications. Let's review components.

Spools It used to be that spinning reel spools, which hold line, fit inside the bail housing; that often led to line tangling around the shaft under the spool. Today it's hard to find new reels so designed. The skirted spool, which shrouds the shaft and slips over the bail housing, has successfully curbed tangling. Better reels sport line-capacity information printed on the outside of the spool. Most reels now feature pop-off (versus screw-type) spools, which aids spool changing without affecting the drag setting.

Bail mechanisms The traditional way to prepare to cast a spinning reel was to utilize two hands, one to open the bail arm and the other to grab the line. That is still the predominant method, but some reels sport a bail-opening lever or trigger that makes one-handed casting of spinning reels (since you grab line and press the bail-opening trigger with one finger) a reality.

The bail is closed by either internal or external tripping devices. The latter, in which the bail is tripped closed when you turn the reel handle, is the traditional method, but has yielded to quiet spring-loaded internal tripping, which is preferred by most anglers. The bail assembly of better-quality reels may also be closed by hand without turning the reel handle.

Drag By tightening or loosening the drag adjustment mechanism, you increase or decrease tension on the spool shaft. The drag mechanism on spinning reels has improved significantly since the late 1970s. The popularity of light monofilament line made it necessary to have a forgiving reel, one that would yield line when strong fish applied extreme pressure. Multiple-disc, spring-loaded systems that could be set reliably at various adjustments evolved.

There are two types of spinning reel drag systems: top-mounted and stern-mounted. Stern-mounted drag-adjustment knobs have become popular of late, though there are many fishermen who feel that a smoother operation is achieved with top-mounted models. The newest innovation in reel drags has been the pre-strike adjustable drag, which can be fixed at one level for setting the hook, and another for playing fish. This idea has been around in big-game saltwater reels for a long time, but it remains to be seen whether anglers casting for more diminutive game can adjust to this and find it functional.

Anti-reverse The anti-reverse switch keeps the spool from turning backward, which is useful in most fishing applications, and especially significant when the drag is utilized. Silent anti-reverse, which does away with the bothersome clicking sound that used to be made by older reels, is a welcome change in the modern products.

The function of the anti-reverse is to keep the reel handle from turning backward while a hooked fish is running away. If the anti-reverse on your reel is not on and a fish runs off, you can either hold the handle still and let the fish pull out line against the drag, or you can leave the handle alone and let the handle spin as the fish runs off. The latter works fine as long as you don't get your knuckles or fingers in the way of the spinning handle. If you keep the anti-reverse on, you can keep your hand off the handle while the fish is pulling against the drag.

Gear ratios Spinning reels have featured moderate- and high-speed retrieves for a long time. A high speed would be roughly 5 to 1 or greater. High-speed retrieves are beneficial when you need to reel in a lure quickly to make another cast, or when playing big strong fish.

Weight Light weight is desirable in a reel, particularly if you expect to use it continuously for long hours of fishing. Many of the latest reels feature all or partial graphite construction, or graphite/titanium components that help decrease overall weight. This makes reels easier for anyone, especially youths and women, to use, and easier for all-day casting.

Spin-casting reels

Few avid or experienced anglers use this tackle, and it is generally overlooked by many anglers and ignored in most literature. Although young children are primary users of spin-casting tackle, beginning anglers of all ages as well as casual fishermen are also drawn to it.

Characteristics The reason is simplicity of use, as well as low cost. The spin-casting reel was originally designed to sit on the offset type of rod handle used by bait-casting-tackle users in the past. It was also designed to have the handle on the right side of the reel, to be cranked with the right hand, similar to bait-casting reels.

Today, some of that has changed, but the basic method of operation for spin-casting reels remains the same. The reel sports a nose cone through which line passes. There is no bail arm, as in spinning reels, but some type of internal pin (stationary or revolving) that picks up the line as it is retrieved through the hole in the nose

Spinning reels are used by fishermen of all ages and skills. New features and components have made them increasingly functional, though light-action models receive foremost use.

WORLD
ANGLING
SERVICES

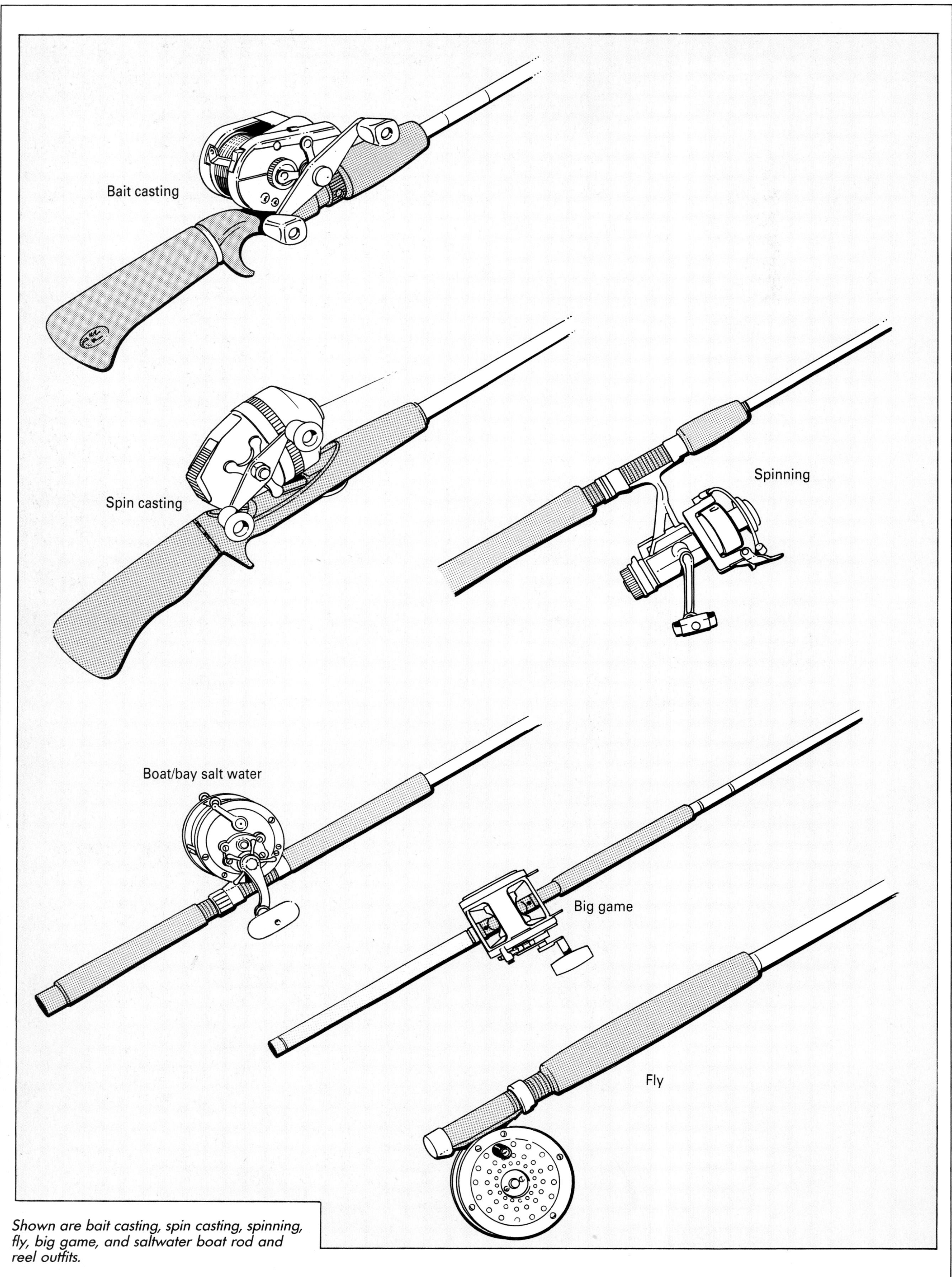

Shown are bait casting, spin casting, spinning, fly, big game, and saltwater boat rod and reel outfits.

Spin casting reels are also referred to as closed-face reels because of their conical spool cover. While generally popular, they are not preferred by most avid anglers.

cone and directed around a concealed spool. Few spin-casting reels have anti-reverse, like spinning reels, and their spools remain stationary. To cast, you depress a trigger or button at the base of the reel, and release the button when the lure or bait reaches its target.

Some spin-casting reels are of better quality than others, of course, and sport features that make them more suitable to achieving casting distance, or eliminating line twist, or retrieving fast. Some even have interchangeable right- or left-hand retrieves, and some sit under the reel and feature a casting trigger on top of the reel, so there are good-quality products to be had.

Disadvantages There are some drawbacks to spin-casting tackle that keep experienced fishermen from using it, as well as anglers in pursuit of large and hard-fighting fish. One of these is a generally low line capacity and the fact that with the spool concealed under the cone (which is readily but not often removed) there is a tendency to let line get so low as to hinder the ability to play a fish that takes a lot of line or to having little left to cast. Line twist often builds up unseen on the spool, usually because the handle has been cranked while the drag is slipping, and it isn't difficult to develop a twisted nest as a result.

The drag may slip when a decent fish is played because the reel lacks power, and this can be observed at times even when simply reeling in a lure that dives deep and takes a lot of pressure to retrieve. Lures that work best at high speeds of retrieve are often not compatible with spin casting reels because those reels usually have a relatively low gear ratio. Another drawback is the shorter casting range usually experienced with spin casting; this results from internal friction as the line comes off the spool and immediately passes through the hole in the cone.

For many fishermen, however, the most serious deficiency of spin-casting tackle is the fact that casting accuracy is harder to achieve. It is easier to make consistently accurate lure placement with bait-casting or spinning equipment. Nonetheless, many anglers do use this tackle, primarily in situations where accuracy and distance are not critical, and where species of fish are usually small. The predominant usage is in freshwater.

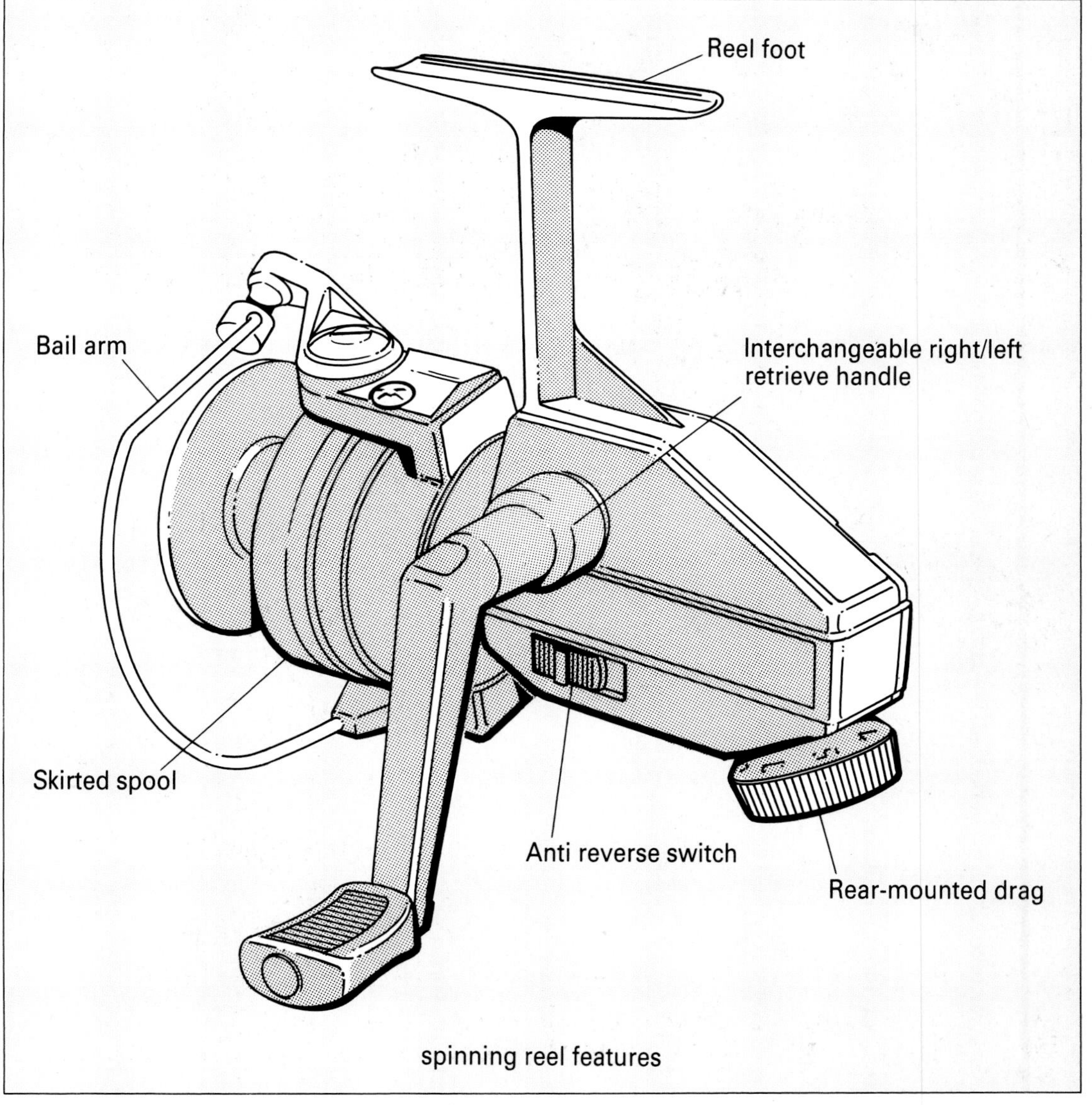

spinning reel features

The basic features of most modern spinning reels are similar.

Bait casting reels have shed their former hard-to-use image.

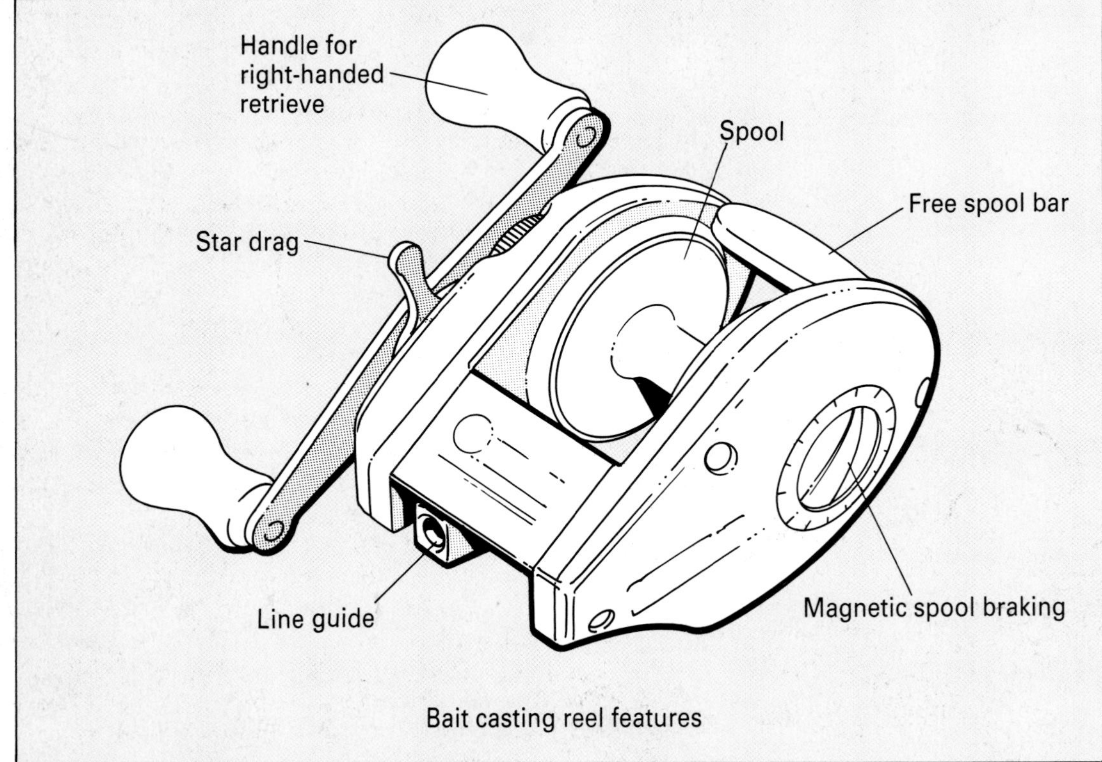

Bait casting reel features

Bait-casting reels

For years, fishing with these reels was such a chore that few people wanted to have anything to do with them. Today, the situation is markedly changed. Not only is bait-casting tackle functional, it is probably more functional for many fishing situations than other types of gear, and is unquestionably preferred by many anglers, particularly those who use medium to heavy line strengths and fish for large species. Technological innovations and advances in recent years have really made bait-casting reels very sophisticated, functional, and of the highest quality.

Most of the features outlined below are becoming standard on the more expensive and top-of-the-line bait-casting reels, although less expensive mid-range models have features like high-speed retrieve, magnetic cast control, narrow spool, and one-handed casting.

It should be noted that bait-casting reels are often referred to as 'level-wind reels', as are larger such reels which aren't suitable for casting, but used mainly for trolling, jigging, and bait fishing in saltwater or for very large species of fish. The larger level-winds don't sport all of the features of their smaller brethren, and are less expensive, but they do store more line, are very durable, and usually have smooth drag systems. Let's review features.

Size Many of the latest reels feature all or partial graphite construction, or graphite/titanium components that help decrease overall weight. This makes reels easier to use for all-day casting. Narrow spools with modest line capacity have become popular with anglers whose fishing circumstances don't dictate a lot of reserved line on the reel, and this helps bring weight down.

Cast control The cast control is an important feature on bait-casting reels that serves to prevent backlashes caused by spool overruns. Essentially it is a spool-braking device. Most of the latest and best bait casters now augment or override their standard cast control operation with magnetic spool braking. Magnets on the sideplate of the reel are adjustable and allow a precise range of pressure on a reel. Gradients from zero (no magnetism) to 10 (the most) allow you to adjust spool braking pressure according to the situation and your casting ability. In theory you can take your thumb off the revolv-

Bait casting reels used to be difficult to cast, but the advent of magnetic spool braking has changed that and such reels are viewed as providing good accuracy.

Fly reels generally do little more than store fly line, although they must be capable of storing sufficient backing when pursuing fish that make long runs.

ing spool and cast without applying thumb pressure and not have a backlash. This can be overridden on most reels.

Gear ratios Fast retrieve ratios are another aspect of modern reels that have become standard. In the past few years some bait-casting reels have sported retrieval ratios as high as 7 to 1. A fast retrieval ratio can be an aid when working a lure, recovering slack line, or fighting a fish, and it requires less handle-cranking effort by the angler, but it can be a detriment when trying to work hard-pulling deep-diving lures.

Free-spool Older bait-casting reels sported a free-spool button on the side of the reel. Many newer reels have one-handed casting releases in the form of a bar between sideplates or a push-button on the sideplate, and they allow you to release the spool for casting by using the thumb on the hand that holds the reel. With other reels you have to use a finger on your non-casting hand to reach over and depress the spool-release button before casting.

Left-retrieve Another thing that has happened currently to bait-casting reels is the emergence of high-quality left-hand-retrieve reels. The majority of bait-casting reels sport a right-hand retrieve, meaning that if you cast right-handed, you must switch the rod from your dominant hand to your left hand after casting, holding the rod and reel (and retrieving lures and playing fish) with your left hand while reeling with your right. This is contrary to how right-handed anglers use spinning and spin-casting tackle and requires some adjustment. Several manufacturers produce high-quality left-retrieve reels; a few have models that are convertible.

Flipping feature This is a knob that allows you to instantly strip off line by depressing the free-spool mechanism without having to turn the handle to engage gears. This makes it easy to strip line off without having to stop and engage gears. When this feature isn't utilized, the reel functions as a normal bait-casting reel.

Direct drive Some reels now have an optional direct-drive switch, used by anglers who don't want to use their drag, but who wind in reverse, or back-pedal the handle.

Lever drags A few new bait-casting reels sport a lever drag, a system that originated with big-game ocean reels.

The strongest and largest fish require stout tackle. This angler is using a 50-pound-class big-game outfit attached to a shoulder harness.

Reels usually get more attention than rods, but their features complement each other, especially when trying to subdue active, strong fighters like this bonefish.

Lever drags have dual drag settings locked-down strong for hook setting, and normal for fish playing.

Fly reels

Fly reels primarily store line for fly casting and don't sport many features as other types of reels do. Single-action and automatic fly reels usually have a modest drag, mainly to prevent fly line from bunching off when it is stripped quickly during casting. Small reels are used with light fly rods and have minimal line capacity. For big fish that will take a lot of line, larger reels are employed.

Saltwater reels

Spinning and bait-casting reels are employed in saltwater for many species of fish, but when pursuing big species, fishing in very deep water, fishing in the surf, trolling for big game, and so forth, a variety of heavier-duty reels are used. These are sturdy products, corrosion-resistant, and capable of holding a lot of line. Level-wind reels and revolving spool reels are favored, although large spinning reels are used in some situations. Big game reels are a distinct category, being ruggedly built for punishing use. These usually sport a pre-set strike drag and lever-controlled drag settings, and may have ring clamps for the attachment of a fighting harness and/or clamps to fasten the reel tightly to the rod handle.

LINE

Because modern fishing line is so superior to its predecessors, and because anglers seldom catch fish large enough to severely stress their line, many of them take fishing line for granted. Fishing line is vital equipment, however, and you should know some basic facts about line and about how its features influence angling.

Composition of lines

Today, for uses other than fly fishing, there are essentially nylon monofilament, cofilament, braided Dacron, lead-core, and wire lines.

Wire and lead-core lines sink fast, are only applicable for trolling, and are used by relatively few fishermen. Braided Dacron, which is technically a multifilament line (strands are woven together), accounts for a small percent of all line sold in North America.

Monofilament means a single strand of line but the term has become synonymous with the word 'nylon'. Monofilament line sales account for most fishing line sold. Nylon monofilament has become extremely popular with anglers for all types of fishing since its refinement and premium introductions in the 1950s, and with advances in spinning and bait-casting tackle. Nylon monofilaments can be separated into several classes.

Cofilament fishing line first became available in late 1985. It is comprised of two filaments merged in the manufacturing process into one unit. There is just one cofilament line presently on the market, and its filaments exist in a sheath/core relationship.

Characteristics

Materials and manufacturing processes create the characteristics of fishing line and determine how it performs in fishing applications. The characteristics of any fishing line include some degree of the following: breaking strength, stretch, knot strength, memory, uniformity, and resistance to abrasion. Color is an additional feature, though not one that affects basic performance.

Breaking strength – how many pounds of pressure are applied to the line before it breaks – is akin to durability, and is most prominent in the minds of anglers. Because nylon monofilament absorbs water, its performance changes the moment it becomes wet. Wet breaking strength is always less than dry breaking strength; 15 percent

Above: Fishing line is the vital link between you and the fish, and is a more important piece of equipment than most anglers realize.

Below: Braided Dacron line, which this fisherman is using, has little stretch, but nylon monofilament lines stretch considerably.

Line gets really tested when fish surge close to the boat, and when the angler has to apply pressure to direct a hard-fighting fish.

less is about average.

In this regard there are two classifications of line: 'test' and 'class.' Class line is guaranteed to break under the labeled strength in a wet condition. Test lines generally break at or above (nearly always above) the labeled strength in a wet condition, and there can be great variation in how far above the labeled strength they actually break. Anglers fishing with a class 12-pound line, for example, are using a line that will break at slightly less than 12 pounds in a wet state, while those fishing with a good-quality test 12-pound line are using a product that will probably break between 13 and 14 pounds in a wet state. Some break much higher, however. Usually, the greater the breaking strength, the larger the diameter.

Knot strength Line strength is affected by knots, which generally weaken it. It is important to tie reliable fishing knots to get the maximum strength possible from fishing line. Knots that are tested in a wet condition are weaker than when in a dry condition. Manufacturers claim that their technological processes produce molecular formations that result in specific knot strength abilities for their line. Since the same knots are tied with various levels of expertise by different individuals, this is hard to verify when comparing knots tied by one angler to those tied by another. Nonetheless, if you are tying known knots carefully and uniformly, and they are not holding, it could be the knot strength of the line (its ability to withstand weakening when knotted) is deficient.

Abrasion resistance Another less obvious characteristic of fishing line is its abrasion resistance. Some lines endure abrasion much better than others, either due to greater diameter or to the molecular composition of the line itself. Lack of abrasion resistance is one of Dacron's shortcomings; Dacron doesn't compare favorably in this respect to even the poorest nylon monofilaments, and the poorest of these do not compare to premium nylon monofilaments or to cofilament line.

Stretch Where Dacron shines is in its negligible stretch. Braided Dacron stretches a little simply by virtue of the fact that the braids have some give in them and pull tighter together when extreme tension is applied. Premium nylon monofilaments have between 15 and 25 percent stretch in a wet state. High-stretch lines cast well, but hinder hook setting (particularly in the case of an inattentive angler who forgets to keep all of the slack out of the line when setting the hook) and playing fish. The less stretch there is in a line the better the hook-setting ability and the more control you have over a fish, although you increase the chance of breaking the line. Having some amount of stretch allows for mistakes in fighting fish, inadequate drag setting, or countering sudden close-to-the-angler

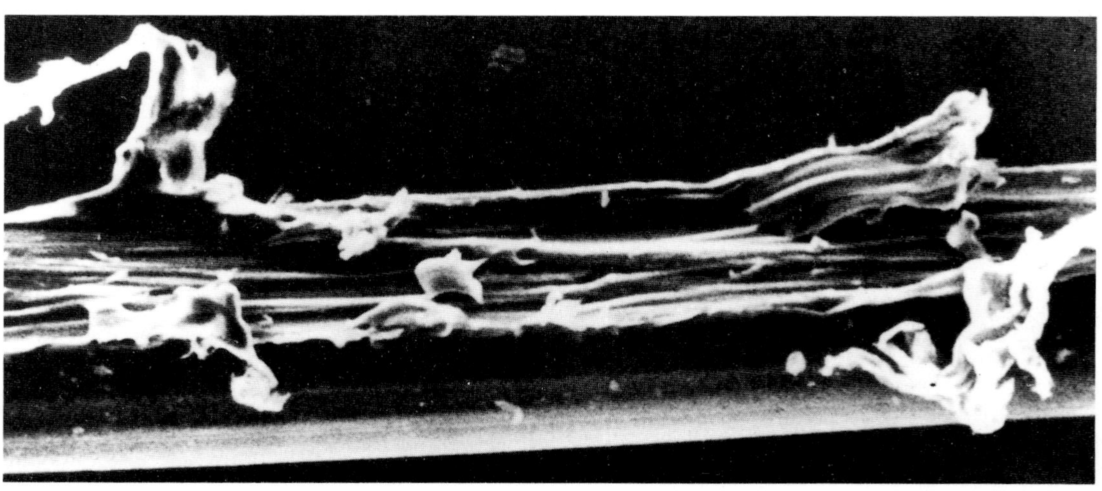

A slight nick in fishing line, shown in this magnified photograph, can greatly weaken it; check line periodically and cut off abraded sections.

surges by strong fish. Stretch, then, is both good and bad for fishing.

Nylon monofilament manufacturers have long tried to develop a product that doesn't alter its characteristics from a dry to a wet state and thus has comparably little stretch, or to manufacture a line that has little stretch in a wet state without affecting other properties. The present cofilament line, and the new tri-polymer monofilaments, for example, have much less wet-condition stretch than equivalent-strength nylon monofilament line. For experienced fishermen looking for top performance, these lines provide better hook-setting ability, more control in playing a fish, a better ability to feel what a lure or bait is doing, and a greater ability to detect strikes, than other lines.

Good quality lines are capable of returning to their normal state after severe pressure (and stretching) is applied, and to maintain basic strength. Stretch should not be a permanent condition, although lines that have experienced particularly severe stress warrant close examination and possibly replacement.

Memory Nylon monofilament and cofilament lines form a memory when placed in a certain position (such as being spooled) for an extended period of time. Lines with less memory are said to be limp, and are more castable than stiff lines. Stiffness contributes to spooling and twist problems, and makes casting difficult. Castability is also affected by water absorption and line diameter. Wet lines cast better than dry lines. The greater the diameter of line the harder it is to cast.

Lines with special qualities As the result of technological advances, manufacturers are now starting to tailor lines to specific applications. For example, there is now a strong flat line just for bait-casting reels which casts like much lighter line. There is also a line that is fluorescent above the water, but nonfluorescent, and thus less visible, below the water. Another new nylon monofilament is 15 percent thinner than comparable strength lines because it absorbs less water.

Line twist problems

How to use and care for line is important in order to get the most out of it. Spinning tackle users and light line anglers experience a lot of difficulty with line, and often this is a result of improper use rather than poor line quality. Probably the greatest problem that most fishermen experience in relation to line is twisting. Line twist can occur as a result of improper spooling, improperly playing a fish, having too loose a drag, using certain lures without a swivel, fishing in swift current, and using a poor-running lure.

Moderately twisted line is not difficult to cure if you are in a boat or near running water. Nylon monofilament and cofilament line will untwist itself if you let a long length of it out behind your boat or down current, with absolutely nothing attached to the end of it, and drag it along for a few minutes. Reel the line back in and you're ready to attach terminal gear and fish.

The best performance of your line and reel is achieved when that reel has been spooled to within 1/8- to 3/16-inch of the edge. This allows good casting distance and accuracy and permits better drag functioning.

You can put twist in the line by improperly spooling it, however. Nylon line has a memory factor, and it returns to its 'memoried' state after being used. Line spooled onto bait-casting, level wind or conventional reels is fairly free of twisting problems as a result of spooling. This is because the line is wound straight onto the reel arbor in a direct, level, overlapping manner.

Line spooling problems

Spinning reels and spin-casting reels pose line spooling problems because these systems actually put a slight twist in the line as it rotates off the bail arm and onto the arbor. If the line is of poor quality, and/or if it already has a fair degree of manufacturer-instilled coiling, and the angler improperly spools it onto his spinning reel, the result can be twisting, curling, coiling line that will cause no end of trouble unless run out behind the boat and rewound. The tricks to successful spooling are watching how the line comes off both sides of the manufacturer's spool; taking line off the side with the less apparent coiling; and applying moderate pressure on the line before it reaches the reel. After spooling new line on a reel, especially a spinning reel, it is also a good idea to soak the reel spool for a few minutes in warm water to help reduce coiling.

Fly line

Of the four standard types of fishing tackle – spinning, spin casting, bait casting, and fly casting – only fly casting

Fill a spinning reel by taking line off the side of the supply spool with the least coiling or twisting, and apply moderate tension on line while filling reel.

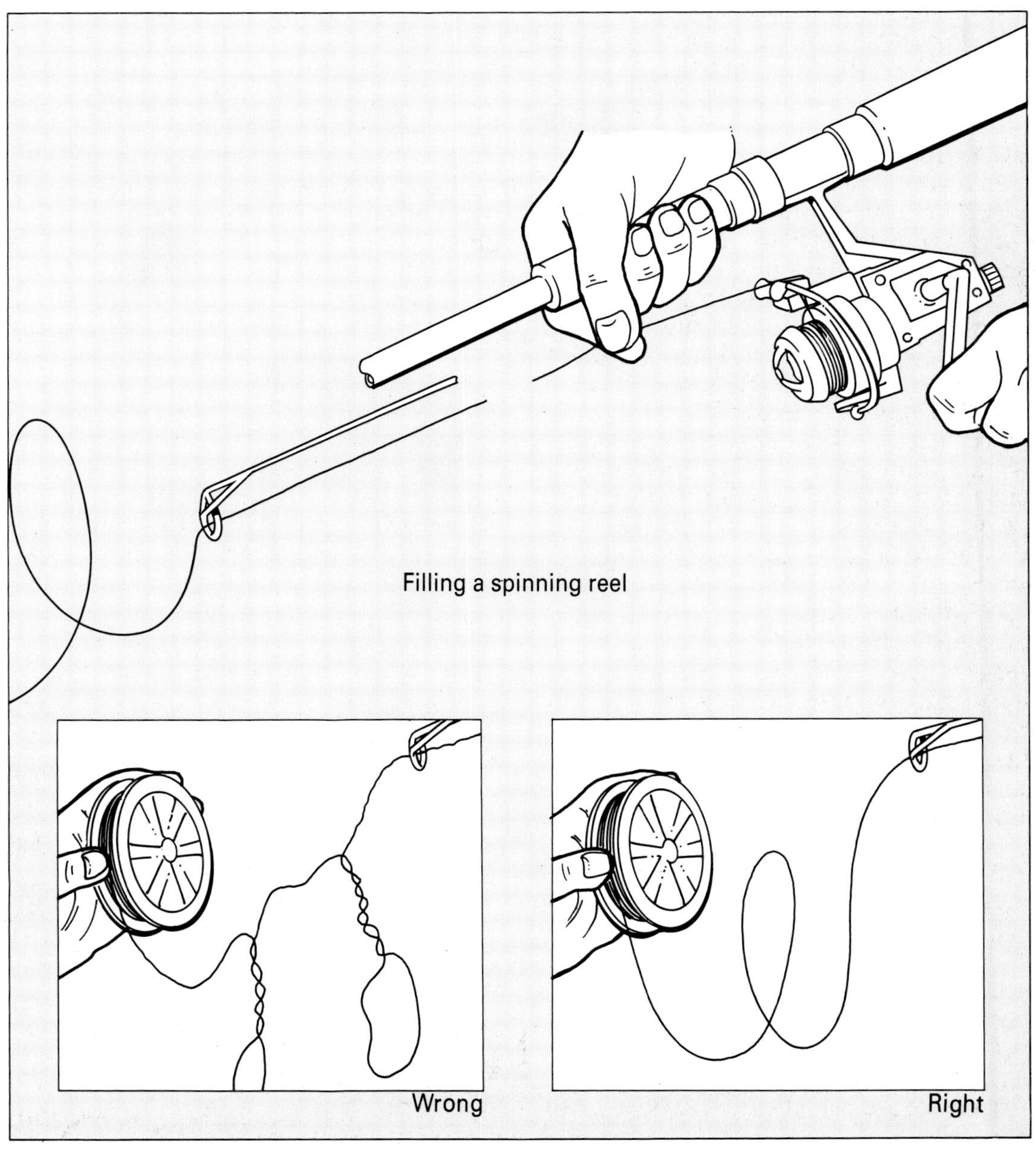

Fly line, such as the floating line used by this freshwater fisherman, is used to cast nearly weightless lifelike objects.

stands out as being considerably differently from the others. In those, a heavy lure carries a light line; how you fish is predominantly determined by the lure's action, weight, and physical characteristics.

In fly casting the object is to toss an extremely light lure, such as some type of fly, using a fairly heavy line. The line carries the fly, and is largely responsible for the depth and manner in which it is fished. Fly lines have to be matched to the rods that are used to cast them. Thus, fly lines take on an important dimension in fly fishing.

Fly lines are labeled according to size, function, and taper, all of which must be married to do the job required for the fishing circumstances.

Size varies according to the density, or weight, of the line. The heavier the line, the more difficult it is for the average person to cast. Most heavy lines (sizes 10 through 14) are used to cast large, bulky objects, and when angling for big fish in fairly demanding conditions. Sizes 5 through 8 are most popular nationally.

Function Essentially there are floating, sinking, and floating/sinking lines. A floating line (designated by the letter F) is for surface or near-surface fishing, and is often the first line possessed by a fly fisherman, particularly a trout angler who uses dry flies. A sinking line (S) is used only for fishing below the surface. There are different types of sinking lines, each of which varies according to how fast they sink. Their use is based upon fishing conditions (a slow-sinking line, for instance, might be used in shallow, gently-flowing water; a fast-sinking line would be necessary when you want to get your presentation down to fish near the bottom in a deep, swift-flowing river). Floating/sinking (F/S) lines possess a floating

Shown are several prominent types of fly lines, with business end to the right.

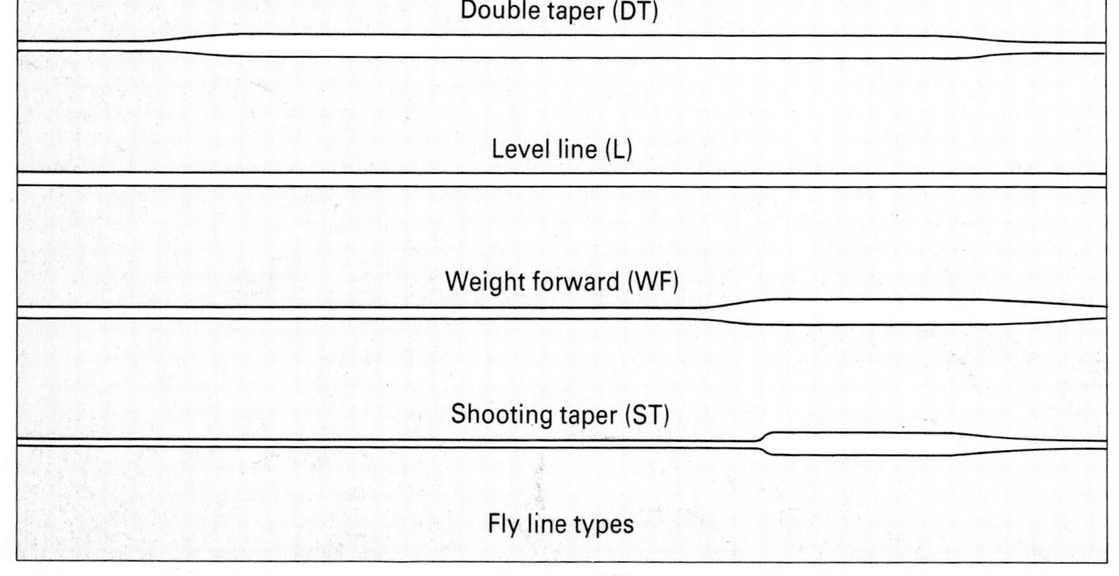

body and a sinking tip section.

Taper Fly lines are further characterized by their taper. A level line (signified by the letter L) is the same weight and diameter throughout, and essentially has no taper to it. A double taper (DT) line has the same taper at both ends, and is used primarily in short- to medium-range casting. A weight-forward (WF) line, which is tapered only at the business end, is used in distance casting, and sports a lighter and smaller diameter back section that eases casting and aids distance achievement.

There are also bass bug and saltwater tapers, which have a weight-forward portion that facilitates casting of large and wind-resistant flies and popping bugs; shooting tapers (ST), which are also meant for distance casting and which should be employed with a monofilament, rather than Dacron, reel backing (the line that is tied to the reel arbor, then to the back of the fly line); and special-purpose lines.

Those unfamiliar with fly fishing should realize that flies are not tied directly to fly line. A monofilament leader, of varying length, connects fly line and fly, and aids the presentation and appearance of the artificial.

To determine fly line features simply read the letters and numbers on the outer packaging. A product labeled DT5F would be a double-tapered size 5 floating line. A product labeled WF8S would be a weight-forward size 8 sinking line.

Colors

Most sinking lines are dark colored, and most floating lines are light colored. Dark green and white have traditionally been the favorites, but floating lines in yellow, orange, lime green, and fluorescent colors are available, mostly as an aid to angler visibility for casting and fishing control, and with no bearing on casting performance.

Knots

Many fishermen are under the mistaken impression that their knots are good because those knots have never failed them. They don't realize, however, that they rarely test their tackle to its fullest or make the greatest demands on a knot. It's when you get to light tackle use, angling for very large and hard-fighting fish, and fishing under shock-loading circumstances, that you prove a knot, and these times are precisely when less-than-perfect knots fail. Furthermore, even the best knots don't perform adequately unless they are tied properly and uniformly time after time. Attention to detail is rewarded with superior knot performance.

Follow these pointers to ensure good knot tying:

- Keep twists, spirals, and all tying steps uniform so that when you draw your knot closed, it is neat and precise.
- Snug knots up tightly with even, steady pressure. Watch for evidence of slippage and re-tie the knot if necessary. Don't pop the knot to tighten it.
- Wet the line as an aid to drawing it up smoothly.
- Don't nick a knot with clippers or knife when you cut off the protruding tag end.
- If your knot breaks repeatedly when you tighten it, check your hook eye or lure connection for rough spots that are cutting the line.
- Check the end of the line and clip off a damaged section.
- Use plenty of line to complete tying steps without difficulty.
- When using double lines keep them as parallel as possible and avoid twisting them as the knot is being tied.
- Test your knots occasionally with a scale to see if you are getting the performance you need. You can do this by tying wet line to the hook of a reliable spring scale. Have someone wrap the unknotted line around his hand several times, using a towel or cloth to keep from getting cut. While your accomplice pulls on the line, you hold and watch the scale, noting at what amount of pressure the line or knot breaks. If the line broke, your knot held; if the knot broke, check your tying.

There are many knots that anglers use, some of which accomplish the same thing, some of which have specific applications. There are terminal knots, for tying line to lure or hook eye; line-to-line knots; knots to create double line leaders; and loop knots.

Recommended knots The Improved Clinch is perhaps the most popular of all fishing knots, and is an excellent knot. Other highly rated knots include the Palomar, Uni, Albright Special, and Bimini Twist.

The Improved Clinch Knot can give 100 percent strength if tied properly, and is perhaps the most popular terminal tackle knot in use. The Palomar is a runner-up in popularity and is extremely reliable, though a little tough to carry out where large lures are used. The basic Uni Knot has many uses, but is especially valuable for tying two lines of similar diameter together. The Albright Special is a superior knot for joining light and heavy line. The Bimini Twist creates a double length of line that is especially valuable as a leader for big-game fishing and with ultralight lines. There are many other knots that exist, and you might want to look into these by checking the literature of line manufacturers.

Even spirals in this properly formed Improved Clinch Knot should result in a strong, non-slipping knot.

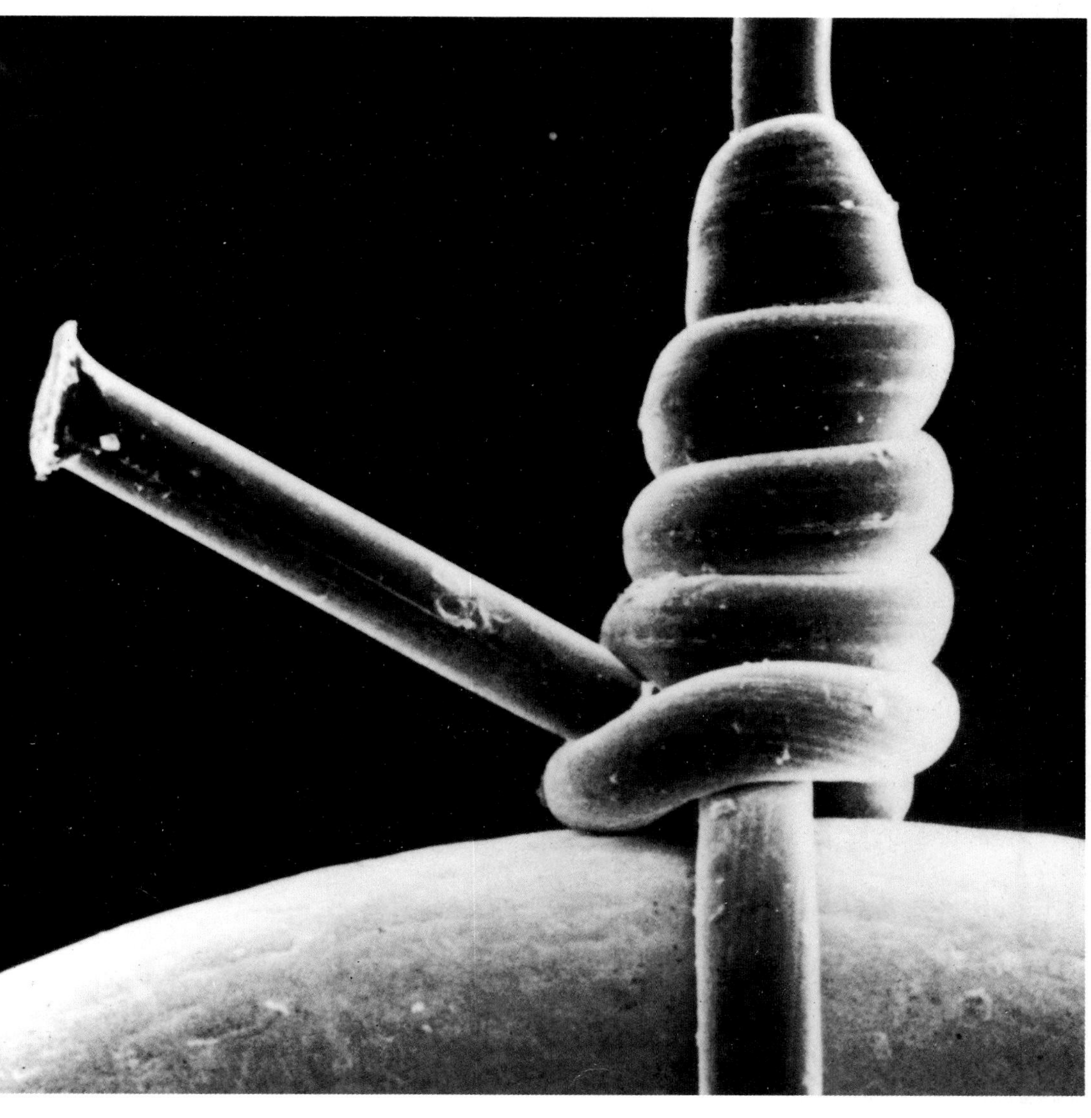

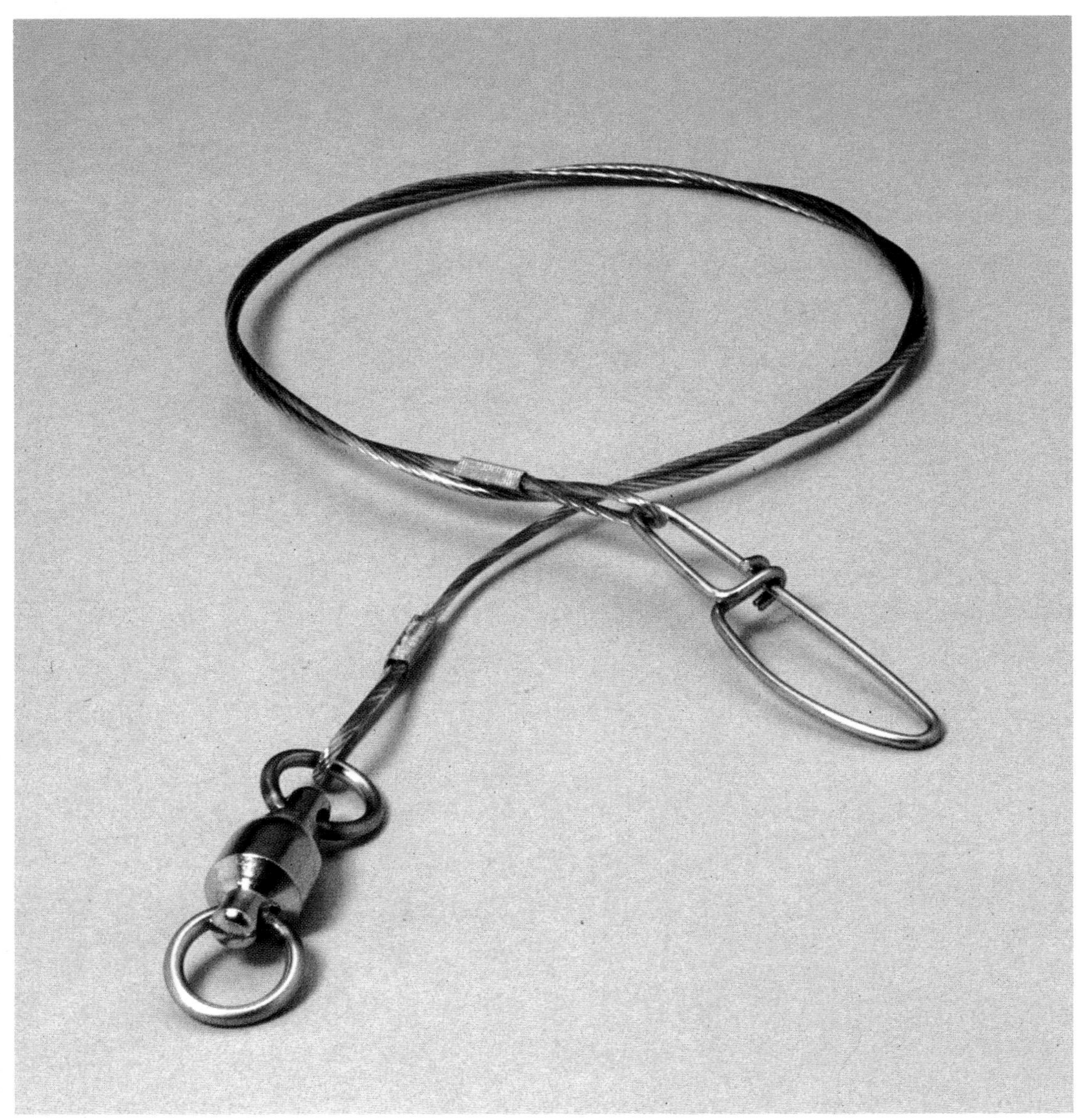

Wire leaders have application in some freshwater fishing and many saltwater fishing situations, and short ones like this are primarily used when casting.

Leaders

There are occasions when it is advantageous or important to use some kind of leader when fishing. In fly fishing, it is a necessity to use nylon monofilament leaders of varying lengths (up to 9 feet). These come in pre-manufactured knotless tapered versions, or are constructed by the angler in knotted lengths of different strength line. The stronger, or butt, end of the leader is tied to the fly line, and the fly is attached to the light end. Lengths and strengths vary with fish and conditions.

Leaders may also be used in non-fly fishing situations, where either a lighter or heavier nylon monofilament line (the latter is called a 'shock' tippet or leader) is attached to another fishing line, either to make a more subtle presentation (light leader) or to provide more near-the-lure strength (strong leader). The connecting knot must be strong enough to maintain the strength of the weaker line, and must also be able to pass through rod guides smoothly.

In big game fishing a double length of main line is formed with the appropriate knot and that is connected to a long, hand-fashioned wire leader. Short wire leaders, usually pre-made and of varying strengths, are used for casting or trolling for various toothy creatures in saltwater and freshwater.

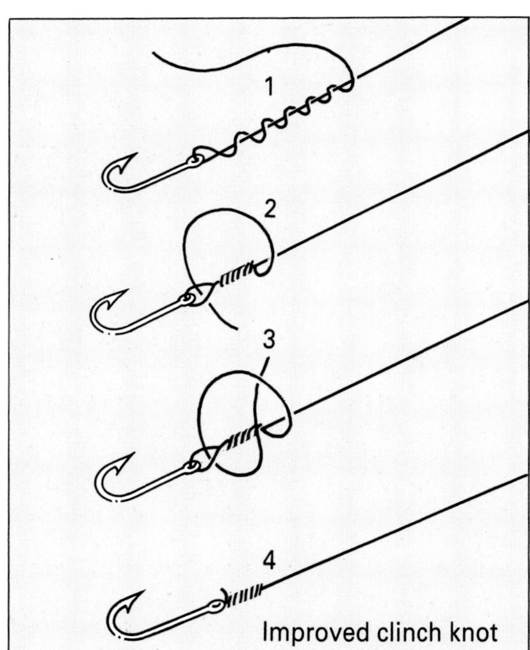

To form an Improved Clinch Knot, (1) pass the line through the hook eye, then make six turns around the standing line; (2) thread end through the loop ahead of the eye; (3) back end through the newly created large loop; (4) moisten the knot and line and tighten. Use six turns for line up to 12-pound-test, five for 14- to 17-pound line, and four spirals for 20-pound and over.

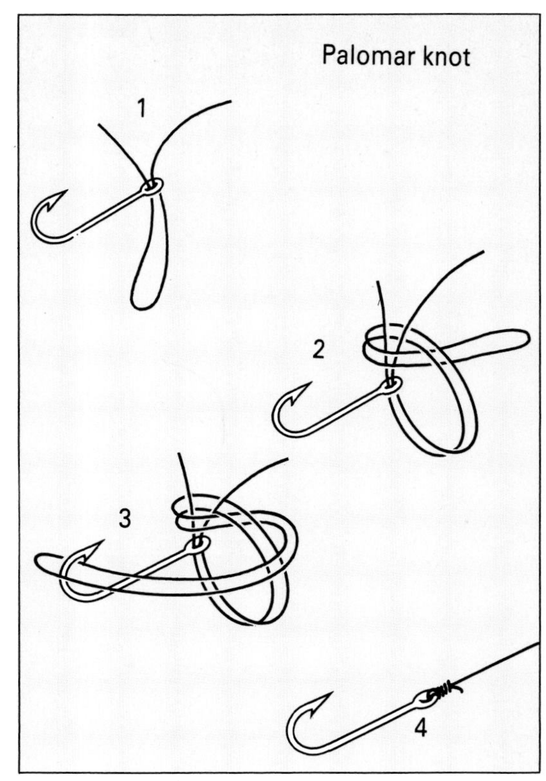

To form a Palomar Knot, (1) double about 6 inches of line and pass the loop through the eye of the hook; (2) tie an overhand knot in the doubled line; (3) pass the loop over the entire hook; (4) moisten the knot, pull on both ends, tighten, and clip the tag end. Use a greater length of line when tying on large lures.

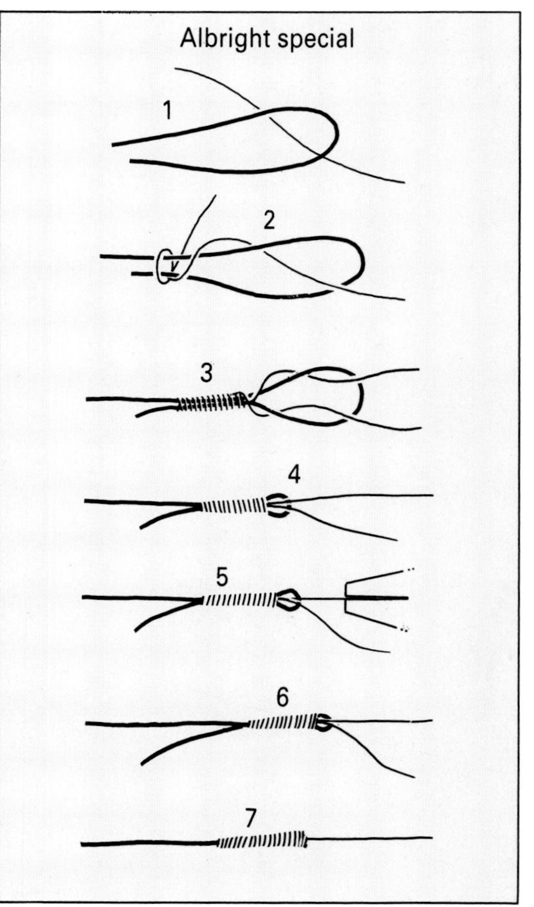

To form an Albright Special, (1) make a loop in the heavier line and pass 8 inches of lighter line through it; (2) tuck the light line between thumb and forefinger of your left hand; (3) wrap light line back over itself and the loop ten times; (4) pass standing end of light line through the loop; (5) pull gently on the tag ends; (6) pull firmly on the standing lines; (7) clip tag ends.

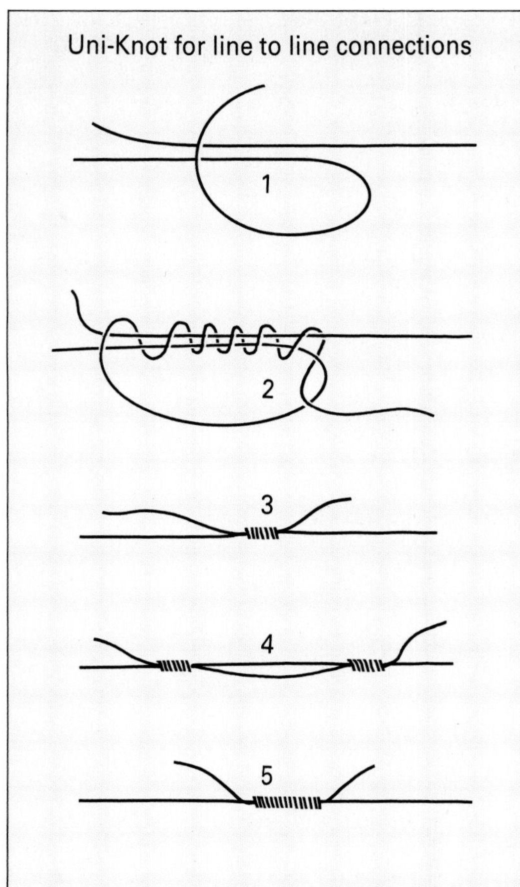

To form a Uni Knot to join two lines, (1) overlap both lines about 6 inches. Hold these in the middle of the overlap with your left hand while making a circle with the line to the right. (2) Bring the tag end around the double length six times. (3) Pull snugly. (4) Repeat in reverse on the other side. (5) Pull the two sections away form each other to draw the knot tight.

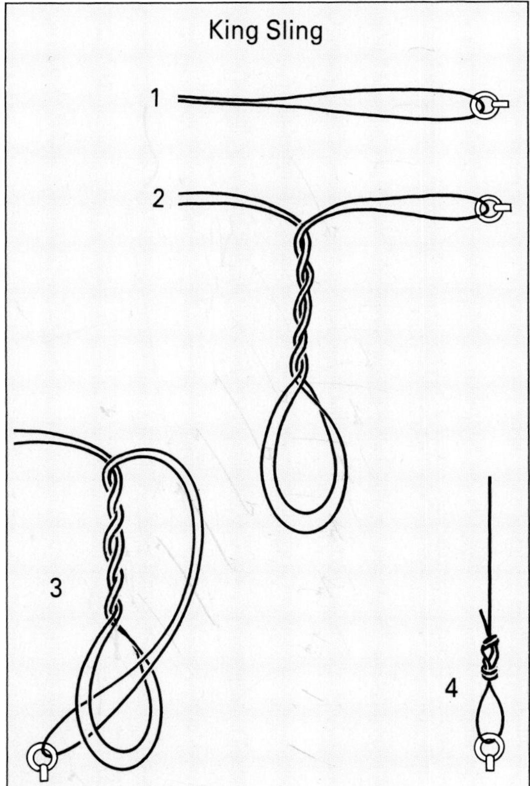

To form a King Sling Knot, which creates a loop ahead of a lure, (1) insert end of line through line-tie eyelet or split ring and double back about 10 inches; (2) bring the doubled line around to form a loop and spiral the lure four times around the doubled line above the loop; (3) bring the lure down and through the loop; (4) tighten it by pulling from both ends.

Knots to form double-line leaders

Bimini twist

The Bimini twist creates a long length of doubled line that is stronger than the single strand of the standing line. It is most often used in offshore trolling, but is applicable in light tackle trolling in both fresh and salt water.

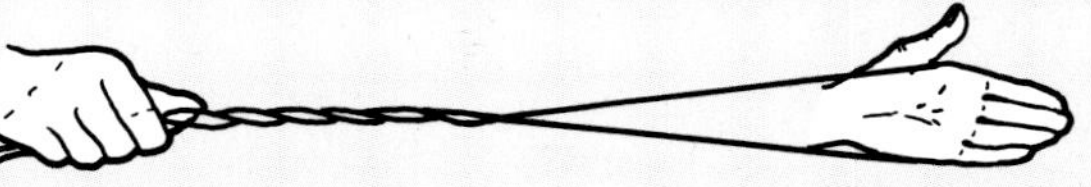

1. Measure a little more than twice the footage you'll want for the double-line leader. Bring end back to standing line and hold together. Rotate end of loop 20 times, putting twists in it.

2. Spread loop to force twists together about 10 inches below tag end. Step both feet through loop and bring it up around knees so pressure can be placed on column of twists by spreading knees apart.

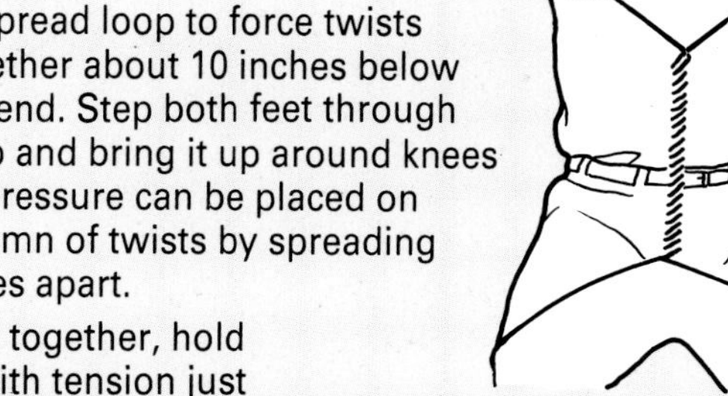

3. With twists forced tightly together, hold standing line in one hand with tension just slightly off the vertical position. With other hand, move tag end to position at right angle to twists. Keeping tension on loop with knees, gradually ease tension of tag end so it will roll over the column of twists, beginning just below the upper twist.

4. Spread legs apart slowly to maintain pressure on loop. Steer tag end into a tight spiral coil as it continues to roll over twisted line.

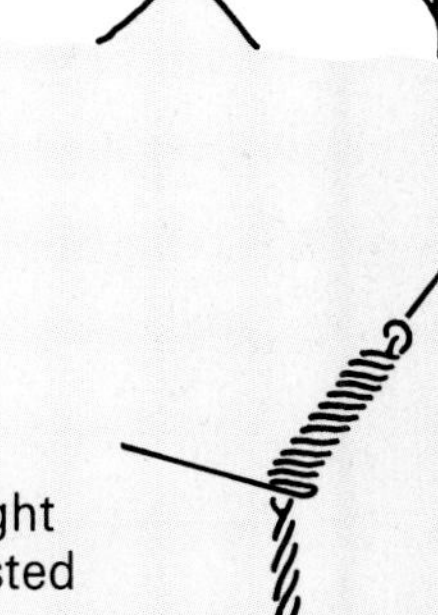

5. When spiral of tag end has rolled over column of twists, continue keeping knee pressure on loop and move hand which has held standing line down to grasp knot. Place finger in crotch of line where loop joins to prevent slippage of last turn, take half-hitch with tag end around nearest leg of loop and pull up tight.

6. With half-hitch holding knot, release knee pressure but keep loop stretched out tight. Using remaining tag end, take half-hitch around both legs of loop, but do not pull tight.

7. Make two more turns with the tag end around both legs of the loop, winding inside the bend of line formed by the loose half-hitch and toward the main knot. Pull tag end slowly, forcing the three loops to gather in a spiral.

8. When loops are pulled up nearly against main knot, tighten to lock knot in place. Trim end about ½ inch from knot. These directions apply to tying double-line leaders of around 5 feet or less. For longer double-line sections, two people may be required to hold the line and make initial twists.

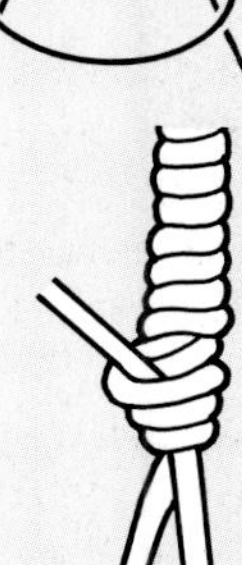

To form a Bimini Twist by yourself (with long leaders, two people do the tying):

(1) Start by measuring a little more than twice the footage needed to form a double line leader. Bring the end back to the standing line and hold together. Rotate end of loop twenty times, putting twists into it.

(2) Spread loop to force twists together about 10 inches below tag end. Step both feet through loop and bring it up around knees so pressure can be placed on column of twists by speading knees apart.

(3) With twists forced tightly together, hold standing line in one hand with tension just slightly off the vertical position. With other hand, move tag end to position at right angle to twists. Keeping tension on loop with knees, gradually ease tension of tag end so it will roll over the column of twists, beginning just below the upper twist.

(4) Spread legs apart slowly to maintain pressure on loop. Steer tag end into a tight spiral coil as it continues to roll over twisted line.

(5) When spiral of tag end has rolled over column of twists, continue keeping knee pressure on loop and move hand which has held standing line down to grasp knot. Place finger in crotch of line where loop joins knot to prevent slippage of last turn; take half-hitch with tag end around nearest leg of loop and pull up tight.

(6) With half-hitch holding knot, release knee pressure but keep loop stretched out tight. Using remaining tag end, take half-hitch around both legs of loop, but do not pull up.

(7) Make two more turns with the tag end around both legs of the loop, winding inside the bend of the line formed by the loose half-hitch and toward the main knot. Pull tag end slowly, forcing the three loops to gather in a spiral.

(8) When loops are pulled up nearly against main knot, tighten to lock knot in place, and trim end off.

LURES

One might wonder why we speak of lures in the plural rather than in the singular, since clearly the intent here is to attract a fish to strike. The reason is quite simple: there are many fish and they eat many different things, inhabit different environs, possess different habits, and require different styles of fishing. Lure use differs accordingly. A stream trout, for example, which feeds primarily on insects and small fish, wouldn't be attracted to a lure that was 7 inches long and imitated a large baitfish. Yet such a large lure would be appropriate for a barracuda that prowls the inshore saltwater environs and that seldom would be attracted to a floating fly or a small spinner. This is a generality, of course, as many specific kinds of lures do overlap in the species for which they are applicable.

The range of lure types and colors that are used by sport fishermen varies greatly, with some overlap between species and between freshwater and saltwater.

All lures, however, are meant to imitate some form of natural food, either mimicking them closely, as in the case of flies or minnow-style plugs, or in a purely suggestive manner, as in the case of jigs or spinners or spoons. Fish strike lures for many reasons. Hunger is a prime motivation, but not the only one. Instinctive reflex, aggravation, competition, and protection are some others. Fish refuse to strike lures at times for many reasons as well. No lure, no matter how appealing it is to the human eye, will catch fish of itself. How the angler uses it – in other words, where he puts it and how skillfully he retrieves it – are key factors in its success, although some kinds of lures are inherently better than others due to their design, swimming action, and appearance.

The angler who knows his quarry, and matches his lure selection to the habits of that fish and the prevailing conditions, is the one who is most consistently productive. The angler who is completely familiar with the characteristics of each lure he uses, and can make it work to its maximum designed ability, is the angler who will score when the chips are down. Therefore, the more you know about your lures and the fish you seek and the better you understand the conditions in which you seek them, the better prepared you will be to make a knowledgable lure selection.

There are several distinct lure categories and so many representatives within each category that there are enough lures to fill up an encyclopedia if writing about them all. All lures are designed to perform a specific function, however, and we can review lures in a general manner according to type or category.

Spinners

Probably no type of lure is sold in such quantity and with such international reception as the spinner. Essentially a spinner is a lure sporting a blade that revolves around a metal shaft, with a single or treble hook at the rear of the shaft. It has flash, action, and vibration, is relatively simple to use, and imitates small fish or emerging aquatic insects. It may not be the best lure to use for all species, or to use in any circumstance, but in the right size and fished in the appropriate place, it is a lure that will catch most species of freshwater fish. The basic small spinner style is of foremost appeal in angling for trout and salmon, which probably see more spinners (in 1/30- to 1/4-ounce sizes) than all other species of fish combined. Smallmouth bass, panfish, pike, and muskies (large bucktail versions for the last named) are also favorite freshwater quarries for the spinner angler. Spinners usually aren't thought of as being saltwater lures, but they

do account for some redfish, snapper blues, stripers, and other near-shore fish each season.

Variations of the standard spinner are incredibly popular in various places for different styles of fishing. For instance, millions of long-shafted spinners, with a lead weight and single hook for impaling a live worm, are sold each year to walleye fishermen. Simpler versions of these are known as 'June Bug spinners'.

A fairly snag-free lure with one or two spinners attached to a lead-bodied hook and shaped in an open safety-pin arrangement is known as a spinnerbait, and is a very popular lure for largemouth and smallmouth bass, pickerel, northern pike, and muskellunge, all of which are cover-oriented species. A similar shape lure, but equipped with a large, cupped propeller-like blade made of metal or plastic, is known as

A spinner, with or without hair on the hook, is one of the foremost freshwater lures.

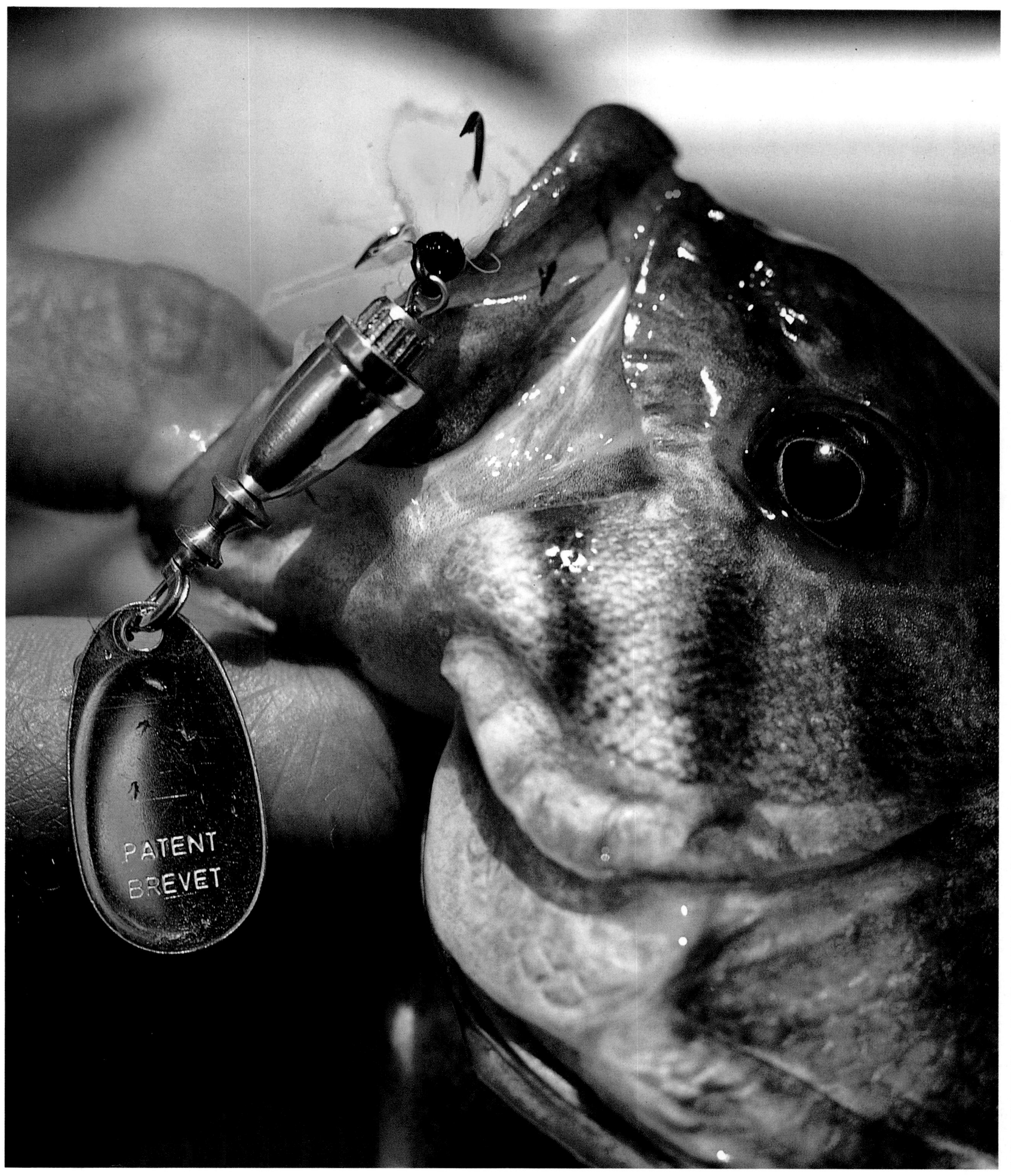

a buzz bait, and is very popular for surface fishing for the same species of freshwater fish.

Spinning blades have been attached to plugs, plastic worms, jigs, and even to lead-bodied sinking lures (called 'tailspinners'), and are found in varied shapes, materials, and colors. Sizes for all of these lures vary. Some sink faster than others, some blades revolve with more vibration, and some are often adorned with a trailer hook or curled tail piece of soft plastic.

Spoons

Spoons, too, are extremely popular lures. They are international in appeal and at some time or another will likely catch nearly any species of fish, although they are more preferable for some species than for others and are predominantly used in freshwater.

Invented in the early part of this century by J. T. Buehl in New York, this lure started as simply a utensil with hooks attached to it. Today, there are spoons of all sizes, shapes, and styles. Most spoons are metal and generally slender, with a slight curvature that provides swimming action when retrieved.

There is an assortment of thick-bodied spoons used in both casting and trolling. These range from tiny 1/32-ounce versions used for panfish and trout to objects 9 inches long weighing several ounces and used for large lake trout, muskies, and saltwater fish. Wafer-thin spoons which are too light to be cast are used in trolling where some device (weighted line, sinkers, downrigger, etc.) is employed to get the lure down to the desired trolling depth.

Weedless versions are used for fishing in freshwater locales where there is vegetation and sport a weedguard wire protector over the hook. Weedless spoons usually have a single hook.

Jigging spoons are made of either metal or lead. The former are usually long and somewhat slender while the latter are usually short and broad. These are used for casting to (and rapidly retrieving through) schools of surface-breaking fish, since great casting distance can be achieved, and in vertically jigging in deep water. Varied species of both freshwater and saltwater fish are targets for vertical jigging, and these lures may range from 1/4-ounce in weight to many ounces, with 3/4- to 2-ounce sizes being most popular.

Jigs

If there's one type of lure that cuts across the species lines, it's a jig. Jigs are a pre-eminent North American style of lure, and do not enjoy quite the international use that spinners or spoons do. There is no mystery about the basic jig, however. It is simply a piece of lead with a hook in it.

A trolling spoon fished behind a downrigger weight caught this chinook salmon.

Right: In freshwater or saltwater, some form of jig will catch nearly any species of fish.

The lead can be shaped in a host of ways, and is made in weights from 1/64 of an ounce to several ounces. It is useful in freshwater and saltwater for nearly every species of gamefish, and it is adorned with bait, rubber skirts, pork rind, plastic imitations of worms or fish or other food. Its successful use depends largely upon skillful manipulation by the angler.

There are so many good hair- or plastic-bodied jigs available these days that there's really no good reason why fishermen don't have a decent selection of these lures, some or several of which can be pressed into duty at any time for a particular fish or angling circumstance. Many of the same 1/8-ounce marabou or soft-plastic curl-tail jigs that catch smallmouth bass, for example, can also be employed to catch walleye, bluegill, yellow perch, trout, white bass, and some saltwater species (bonefish, snappers, and redfish, for example), and they can contribute to the unintended catch of such fish as pike or pickerel. The same jigs that catch amberjack in saltwater will catch large, deep-lake trout in freshwater, or striped bass. Maybe the preferred colors will differ; sometimes they don't. But there is a lot of crossover value. When you consider this, plus the fact that jigs are also inexpensive enough that you don't fret much over losing one (which you do fairly often, especially when using light tackle), it seems

that carrying along a few jigs ought to be as routine as filling your fishing reel with line.

Just as there are many types of lead-headed jigs, so are there many body styles. Hair jigs, sporting bucktail or marabou, are old favorites; soft-plastic-bodied jigs, featuring curltail, grub, fishtail, and paddletail configurations are very popular. There are also various pork-rind or soft-plastic frog-like products that adorn the jigs used in casting and flipping by black bass anglers. Jigs tipped with natural or dead bait, including earthworms, minnows, leeches, chunks of fish flesh, or other items have merit for many saltwater and freshwater fish.

Plugs

There is some type of plug that will catch virtually every gamefish of importance to anglers. Plugs come in all sizes, shapes, colors, and performance functions, in straight as well as in jointed versions, and are made of plastic, wood, and urethane foam. Floating/diving, sinking, and surface are the three categories into which plugs are divided.

Floating/diving plugs sit on the surface of the water at rest and dive to

Minnow-shaped plugs are popular lures, but there are many types and sizes of plugs that are productive. This walleye was caught on a deep-running plug.

various depths when retrieved or trolled. The extent to which they dive usually depends primarily upon the size and shape of their lip, and the location of the line-tie on the nose or lip of the plug.

Perhaps most popular among floating/diving plugs are minnow-shaped versions with small lips, which are designed to be fished very shallow, and which double as surface lures. Other floating/diving plugs are more bulbous or elongated (and referred to as 'crankbaits' by many freshwater anglers) and are strictly meant for below-surface retrieving or trolling duties. Some models have BBs inside that allow them to rattle when being retrieved and thus have a greater noise-making value. Their running depth may vary from 1 to 25 feet deep, and accordingly are classified as shallow, medium, or deep divers. The larger bodied plugs, which may be 6 to 9 inches long, are used in freshwater for such large species as pike, musky, and striped bass, and in saltwater for bluefish, barracuda, jacks, and wahoo, among others. These lures generally reach greater depths when trolled than when cast, and are usually fished close to the bottom. In saltwater these lures are trolled more than they are cast.

Sinking plugs are simply lures that do not float, but which are weighted to sink when they enter the water and will sink as far as the angler allows. These are often allowed to sink to a specific depth by counting roughly a foot of depth per second of descent, and then are retrieved. These are primarily used in freshwater.

Surface lures are perhaps the most popular plug in terms of preference, but generally the least regularly useful. Popping or chugging plugs, which feature a concave head, have many applications. In saltwater they will attract such species as bluefish, jacks, and stripers and in freshwater they are primarily used for largemouth and smallmouth bass. Wobbling surface plugs are characterized by their to-and-fro undulating action as the result of a wide lip or wings and are primarily used in freshwater.

There are several types of lures of the so-called stick bait genre that are popularly used, especially in freshwater. Certain types will walk enticingly on the surface from side to side if retrieved adroitly, while others are more like a jerk bait that gets repeatedly tugged forward. The noisier versions are those with a propeller on the rear or at both ends of the lure. These are primarily used for largemouth and smallmouth bass and sometimes stripers or white bass. The walking plugs are also effective on snook in saltwater. With these lures, success is often proportionate to the retrieval skill of the fisherman.

Flies

While there are so many types of flies – or light objects that are cast with a fly rod and fly line but which may not technically represent a fly –they can roughly be separated into several categories: dry flies, wet flies, nymphs, streamers and bucktails, and poppers.

Dry flies are relatively diminutive objects that float on the surface and represent specific insects that are found floating on the surface of streams, rivers, ponds, and lakes. Stiff hackle and tail feathers are tied on a lightweight hook to float the fly. Wet flies are very much like dries; they are also relatively diminutive objects that sink upon entering the water and represent drowned insects found in freshwater environs. The hackle on these flies is tied back and the body is dense to help sink the fly. Nymphs are also sinkers, but they are tied more precisely with wing cases and thorax to imitate the larval stage of aquatic insects. The choice of which type and then which pattern to use is dependent upon natural conditions and the kind of insect that fish (primarily trout) are feeding on at any given time.

Streamer flies and bucktails are meant to imitate baitfish and are tied on long-shanked hooks. Bucktails are tied with deer hair or other fur, streamers primarily with feathers. They are fished below the surface, and variations are used in both freshwater and saltwater, with the longer and brighter versions used for saltwater work. Poppers, also called popping bugs, are used in both environs as well, although the major use is in freshwater for bass and panfish. These objects float and are primarily made from balsa wood.

There are other 'flies' that are cast by fly fishermen that don't quite fit into categorical peg holes. These include many steelhead and salmon flies, some of which are quasi-streamers and some egg-sack imitations; foam-bodied spiders; and mylar-bodied fish imitations.

Soft plastics

Perhaps the single-most popular one-species lure is the plastic worm, which

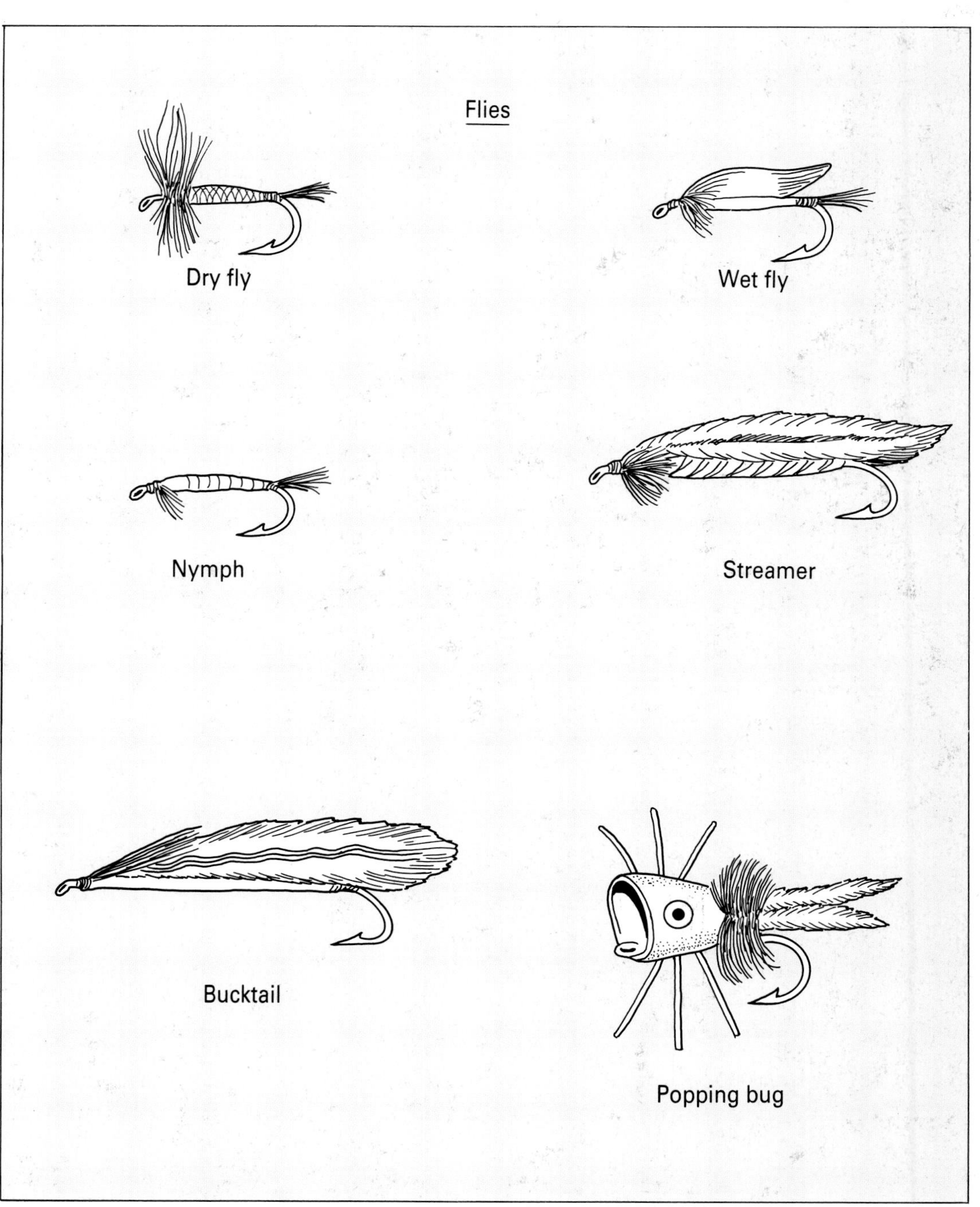

There are many categories of flies, as well as sizes and colors, and the selection of which is appropriate in a given circumstance can be a science in itself.

is essentially used for largemouth bass. Immensely popular from late spring through fall in all areas of the country, the plastic worm is like a jig in that its effectiveness is directly related to the angler's fishing abilities, and unlike a spoon or spinner in that it doesn't look very much like a readily identifiable and prominent food item (although snakes are a bass food in some places). But it is the foremost artificial for largemouth bass, especially in southern states, and, like other popular lures, has proven itself through time.

Colors, sizes, and tail configurations vary. Some worms are impregnated and/or coated with flavoring elements. The most popular size is about 6 inches long. There are several rigging methods, with the Texas rig, in which a hook is embedded in the worm in such a manner as to make it weedless, being most prominent. Rigged in this manner, plastic worms are noted for their ability to be fished effectively in all types of cover.

Besides worms, however, soft plastic baits include salamander, frog, crayfish, and minnow imitations, as well as an assortment of small to large bodies that are used to grace the hooks of other lures, primarily jigs. These come with a host of tail configurations, colors, etc., and are effectively employed in freshwater for many species of fish, and in saltwater for bottom species and fish that are caught by jigging.

Other lures

There are a number of lures common to either freshwater or saltwater usage that should be noted. Offshore saltwater trollers commonly use a large plug as a lure or teaser (no hook but meant to attract fish to a trailing rigged bait). The large ones, referred to as 'Kona Head style' trolling plugs, range in size from 7 to 13 inches long, with colorful vinyl or plastic skirts and a blunt head that causes the lure to dip and pop across the surface. Smaller versions, with feather or plastic skirts and bullet-shaped heads, are trolled as squid imitations. Another predominantly trolling lure for saltwater is the surgical tube rig, which features a swiveling rubber tube with a hook at a tapered end. It varies in length, and is used for bluefish, stripers, and barracuda. A popular trolling plug for salmon in the Great Lakes and West Coast waters is a plastic cut-plug lure that weaves wildly and is predominantly used in conjunction with a downrigger. There are others, too, many of which are rather specialized or localized in use.

Right: Plastic worms, shown here in the steps for creating a weedless Texas rig, are highly favored by largemouth bass fishermen.

Below: Saltwater trolling lures include a plastic squid imitation (a), feathered jigs (b and d), and long blunt-nosed Konahead plug.

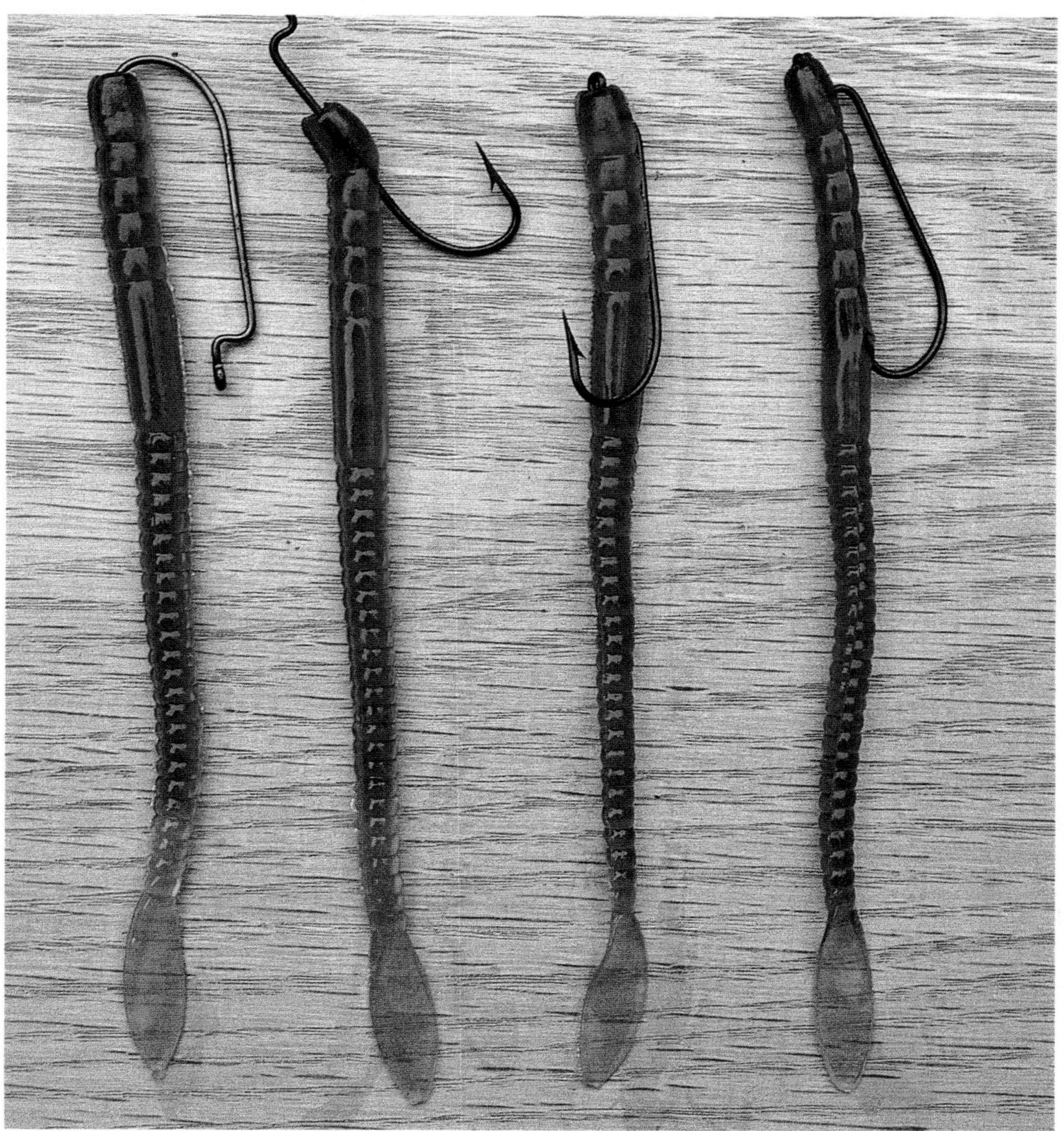

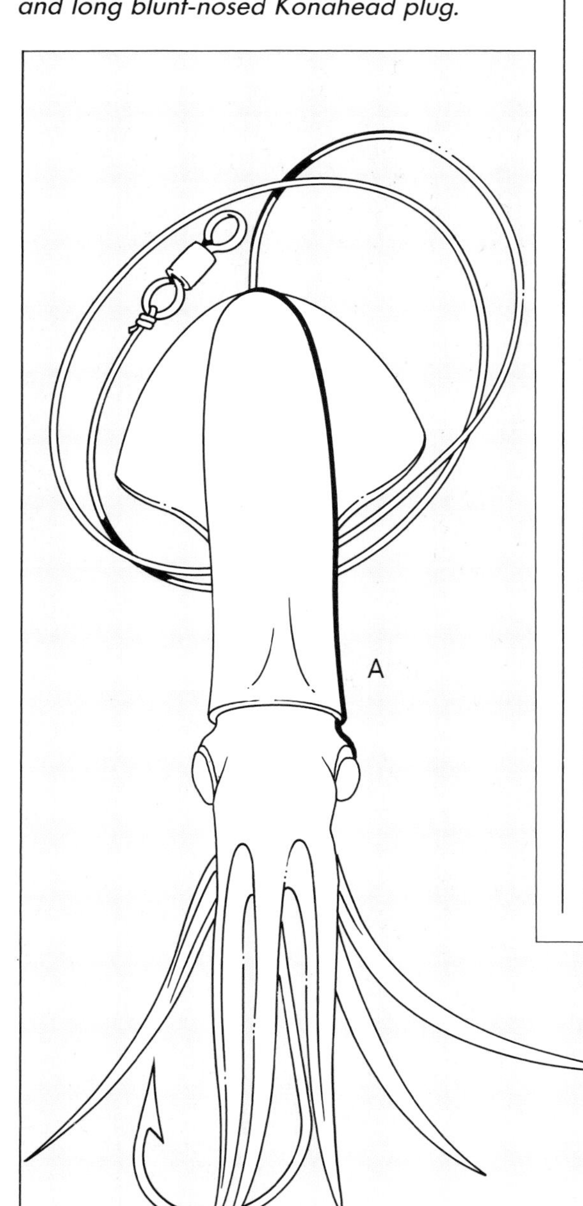

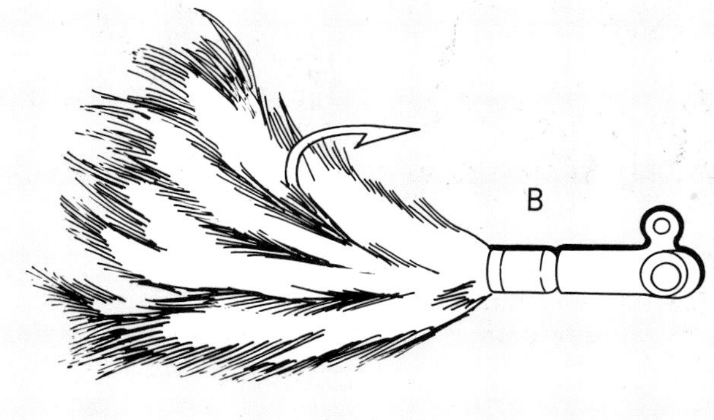

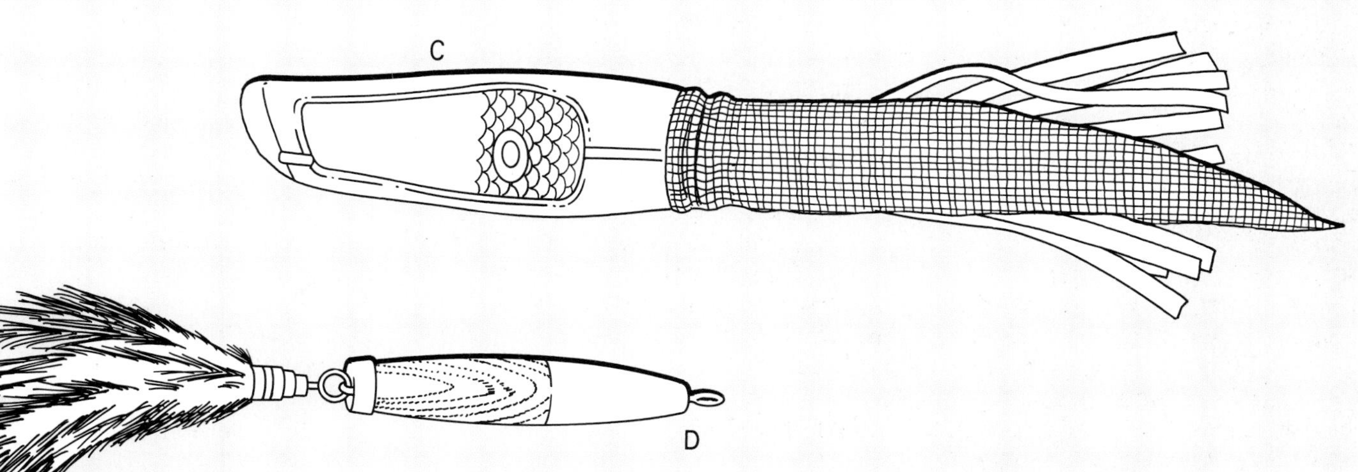

Bait

Bait is used popularly in both fresh-water and saltwater in North America, but not proportionately as much as in other areas of the world. Freshwater bait seldom tends to be in the form of small processed items, as in European angling. Such tidbits as maggots and larvae may be used to grace small jigs for ice fishing, but aren't used often by themselves, although corn kernels, baby marshmallows, and cheese are often fished for stocked trout. In freshwater as well saltwater, North American bait generally tends to be more natural, and larger, because the quarry are mostly all meat eaters and of larger size. There are many natural baits, used alive or dead, to catch game fish in North America.

Types of freshwater bait

Earthworms/nightcrawlers These are used in whole or in parts, on one or more bait hooks, and are tipped onto jig hooks, crawled behind spinner harnesses, and weighted and fished under a bobber. They are especially used in fishing for such panfish as bluegills and perch, as well as walleye, bullheads, stream trout, and river steelhead, primarily with a No. 6 or 8 hook.

Crayfish Also known as 'crawfish' or 'crawdads', and fished in both hardshell and softshell versions (the latter preferred but not always available), crayfish are hooked through the tail with a long-shanked hook. They are primarily used for smallmouth bass fishing. Tails and pieces of the tail are used for other fish, however, most notably for steelhead drift fishing.

Minnows/shiners There are numerous species and sizes of baitfish (including dace, Arkansas shiner, golden shiner, chub, and fathead minnow) used primarily as live bait for a host of large and small fish. Smaller bait may also be hooked through the lips to adorn the hook of a jig or jig/spinner combination. Small minnows are used for crappies, ice fishing, bass, walleye, and trout. Very large shiners are popularly used in Florida for big largemouth bass, and large baitfish (including suckers) are fished for such species as pike, muskellunge, and lake trout.

Leeches These are more popular in the Midwest than elsewhere, and used whole primarily for walleyes and smallmouth bass. They are rigged similarly to worms, and when cast or trolled are hooked through the sucker with a No. 6 or 8 hook.

Waterdogs Also known as 'mud puppies', these salamanders are not available everywhere, but are used for a variety of gamefish, including striped bass.

Crickets, grasshoppers, and hellgrammites These delectables are used for many small fish. Hellgrammites attract stream trout and smallmouth bass; grasshoppers and crickets are good for various panfish species as well as crappie and stream trout. Hellgrammites should be hooked under the collar with a No. 6 or 8 hook, and the others through the body with a long-shanked light-wire hook.

Frogs Live frogs are quite popular in some Canadian and northern U.S. locales and rather ignored most everywhere else. The prime quarry is bass, followed by pike. They can be hooked through the lips or thigh of the leg.

Salmon eggs Salmon eggs are very popularly used for drift fishing for trout and salmon. Rainbow trout and steelhead, in particular, are major quarries. These are fished singly with small salmon egg hooks, or as a group in an unwrapped cluster or in a nylon mesh spawn bag. Imitation eggs and egg sacks are quite popular as well.

Herring Included here are such fragile baitfish species as alewives, which are also called 'sawbellies' and found in northern climes where they are popularly used alive for trout in lakes; shad (primarily gizzard but also the threadfin variety), which are found in southern U.S. climes and fished live or as dead or cut-up bait; and herring, which are coastal, river-run fish used alive or dead for stripers and various

Crayfish, shown here next to floating/diving plugs meant to imitate them, populate many freshwater environments, and are a prime forage.

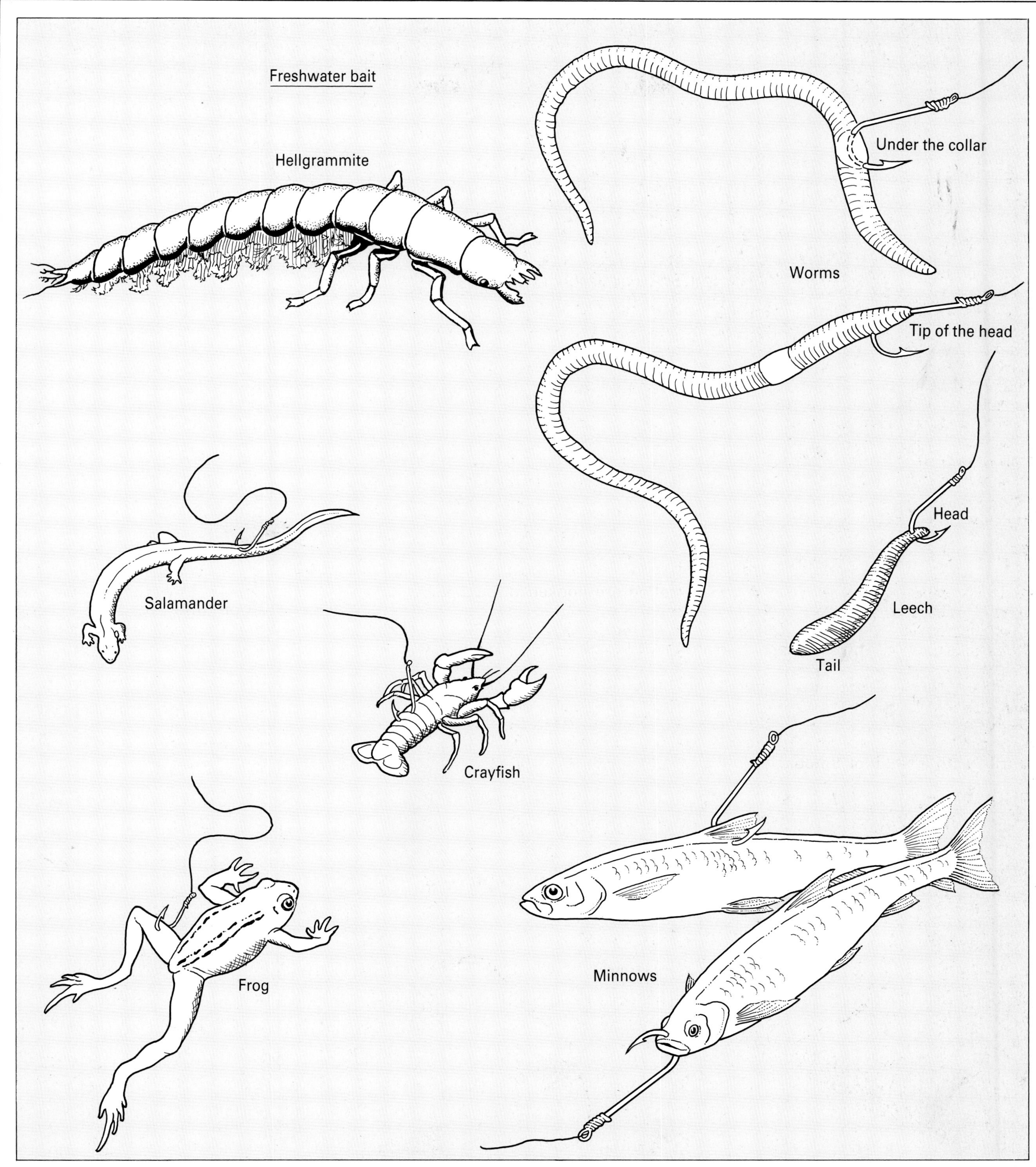

Although worms and minnows are most popular, other natural items are also used in freshwater fishing.

catfishes on the East Coast and for salmon on the West Coast.

Others There are other morsels used as bait for various freshwater fish. Where catfish are concerned, the list of items practically knows no bounds, and includes numerous stink bait concoctions as well as chicken liver (many prefer to use frozen liver). Some miscellaneous baits include doughballs, for carp; caddis larvae, for stream trout; mayflies, for trout, crappies, etc.; bluegills, for striped bass (which is legal in some states and not in others); grass shrimp, for panfish; perch eyes, for tipping on a jig when ice fishing for yellow perch; ciscoes, whitefish, and other large species fished alive for northern pike; and chunks or strips of fish meat, for tipping on a jig, especially for lake trout, or behind a spoon for pickerel or pike, or in some instances dead-bait bottom fishing for assorted species.

Most live baits are hooked through the head or lips (tail for crayfish) for casting and free-lining, but through the midsection for stillfishing with or without a bobber.

Types of Saltwater bait

Marine worms Sandworms, clamworms, bloodworms, and the like are used whole or in parts, on one or more hooks, or behind a spinner rig for stillfishing, trolling, or drifting for a variety of small inshore fish, as well as blackfish, flounder, and others.

Eels Eels are a hardy bait, primarily used in inshore drift fishing and casting. They are fished on jigs as well as threaded onto a leadered rig.

Shrimp/crabs/crayfish Live shrimp are a highly popular bait for a wide variety of coastal fish. They can be hooked through the top of the head for live-lining, or threaded on a bait hook or jig head. Live blue crabs are also used for many species of fish; smaller versions take tarpon and permit, while larger ones are fished deep for snapper, grouper, redfish, and others. They are

Various baits play an important role in saltwater fishing.

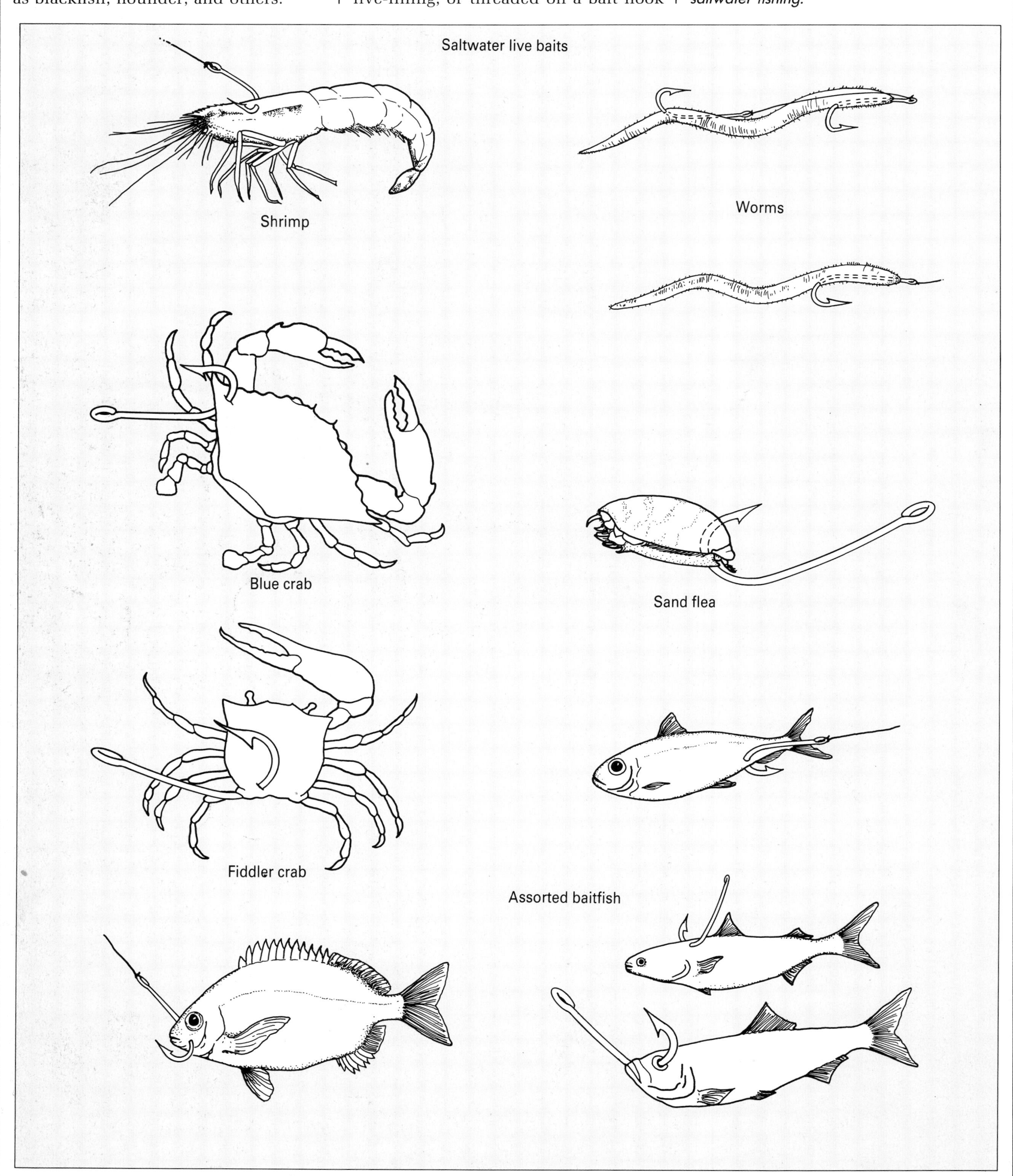

hooked through the tip of the shell, often with claws removed. Fiddler crabs, found abundantly in many tidal areas, are used for snappers, groupers, sheepshead, and other fish. Saltwater crayfish, which are quite large, are used in southern marine waters for cubera snapper and large groupers.

Assorted live fish You name the fish, and if it is the right size, it can probably be used as live bait for some other saltwater fish. Depending on locale and availability, of course, such species as pinfish, blue runner, anchovy, menhaden, grunts, sardines, pilchards, mackerel, and herring are favored. As in

Right: Large herring like this are fished live for landlocked striped bass, and as cut bait for stripers and catfish.

Below: A cigar minnow, hooked through the head, is about to be used for drifting or bottom fishing in saltwater.

igloo

Saltwater anglers chum for a range of fish species. Ground bait or small whole dead fish is ladled overboard periodically to attract small fish and in turn larger predators. A hooked piece of bait or live fish is drifted among the chum.

freshwater, these fish are hooked through the lips or back, sometimes with a double-hook setup, or through the eyes (soft-fleshed fish).

Offshore baits An assortment of natural baits are used in offshore trolling situations for billfish, tuna, dolphin, wahoo, king mackerel, and so forth. Squid, balao, mullet, mackerel, and bonito are the main baits, usually fished whole, but sometimes in strips. Many of these baits are purchased frozen, then thawed in water and rigged with wire and thread on stainless steel hooks and wire leaders.

Chum A good deal of chumming, which is the use of bait to attract fish to a particular spot, is done in saltwater, especially for tuna, shark, and bluefish. It is done inshore as well as offshore, however, by small private boat anglers as well as party and charter boat fishermen. Some chumming is very messy and elaborate, some clean and simple. Chum may be parts of freshly-caught fish ladled overboard piece by piece, or it may be a ground-up mixture of assorted small fish that is ladled overboard by the cupful or left hanging in the water by the boat. It is used as a means of catching live bait and larger predators, and is employed in judicious quantities to bring, and keep, game fish in the neighborhood of your boat.

Others Other morsels used for various saltwater fish include sand fleas, which are used by surf and pier anglers for pompano; dead baits, including clams, mussels, snails, fish chunks/strips/heads, used for drifting or stillfishing; cut plug baits, used for mooching (trolling with cut herring for Pacific Northwest salmon) or bottom fishing (as in stillfishing with mullet for Gulf Coast tarpon); and octopus chunks for drift fishing or stillfishing.

Tips on fishing with bait

It's worth remembering that most bait, whether used in freshwater or saltwater, has to be presented properly to be effective. Where live bait is used, liveliness is vital. Many fish, especially in freshwater, aren't interested in dull or dead bait, so it's important to keep your bait as fresh and vigorous as possible. Change live bait whenever the current offering seems to be losing its vitality, and make sure that it acts naturally. A crayfish that rolls instead of crawls, for example, or a minnow that doesn't swim, lessens your chance of success.

It is helpful to hold your line when live-lining bait. When fishing with a float or bobber it's easy to tell if a fish is mouthing your live offering. But that isn't the case when letting bait run freely. Then, it is often difficult to know if a fish has picked up your offering or if your bait is hung on brush, rock, or grass. Keep a light hold on your line to detect gentle strikes, and when in doubt, pull ever-so-softly on the line. If it moves off vigorously, you've got a fish.

Unless a fish has savagely attacked your bait offering and run off with it, wait to set the hook. Don't be in a rush to set the hook when live bait angling. A fish needs time to consume its quarry. Often it takes the bait crosswise in its mouth and swims a short distance away before swallowing the fish. By waiting a short time, and by not putting tension on the line during this period, you stand a better chance of hooking the fish.

One of the inherent problems of fishing with bait, however, is that fish tend to be deeply hooked and hard to release in good condition if it is necessary to release them (which, because of tighter management and increased size limits, it is often necessary to do).

There is a good chance that a fish released with a hook in it will survive. Clip the line off above the hook. In freshwater the hook will deteriorate within a few weeks if it is not stainless steel or cadmium/tin, and within days in saltwater. If the fish is not bleeding profusely, and if you have been careful to handle it as little as possible, it should survive.

Note the flow-through live bait container attached to these freshwater bait fishermen's boat. Keep bait lively and changing to fresh bait frequently is one of the keys to success.

TERMINAL GEAR

Fishermen may pay attention to their rods, reels, and line, but with the exception of lures and bait, they often take terminal tackle for granted.

Hooks

Whether used on lures, with flies, or alone for baitfishing, hooks are a vital part of sportfishing gear. Although the integral parts of a hook are essentially the same, styles are determined by the way in which their features vary, which in turn influences use. Variations in features include forging for extra strength; turned up or down eyes (the former is preferred on short-shanked heavily dressed flies while the latter is preferred by some for its line of hook penetration); and sliced shanks (used to retain bait or plastic worms and keep them from sliding down the hook), keel shanks (used with some plastic worm rigs and with large streamer flies), and humped shanks (for cork-bodied popping plugs).

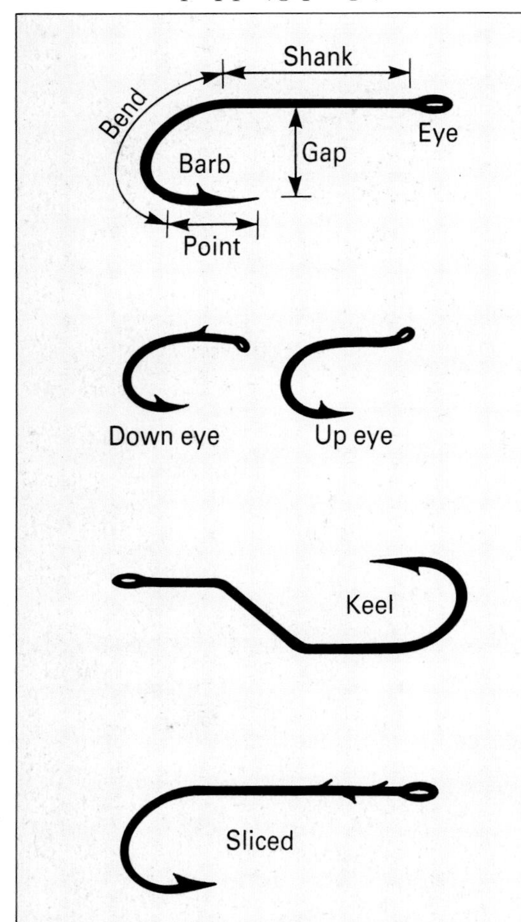

Hook sizes range from as large as 14/0, used in saltwater, to as low as 24 for freshwater fly fishing. Size is determined by the gap, which is the distance between the hook point and the shank. Gap width may differ, however, between families of hooks.

Hooks are found larger and smaller than these. It is important not to use too large a hook. Big fish can be landed on small hooks, but small fish will be spooked by hooks that are too large.

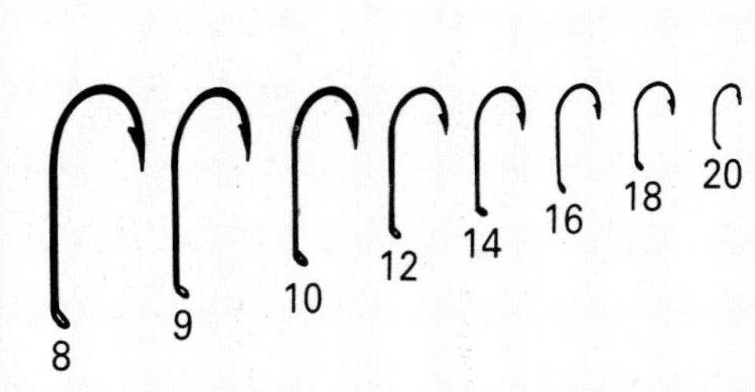

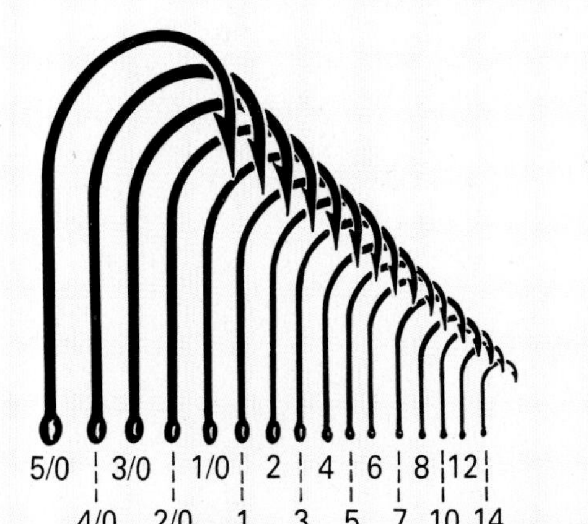

Styles of hooks It takes some study to discern the various discrepancies between hook patterns. Differences include the shape and angle of the point, curvature of the bend, length of the shank, and depth of the bite. Popular styles include:

Sproat
straight point; popular with flies and lures

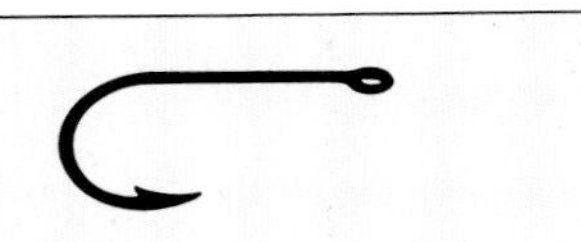

Kirby
point offset to the right helps prevent hook from slipping out; good for bait fishing

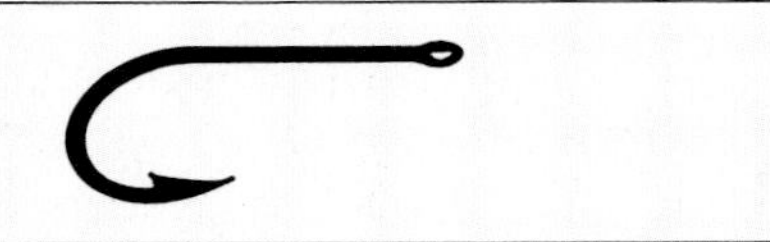

O'Shaughnessey
outward bend to point; heavy wire; many applications

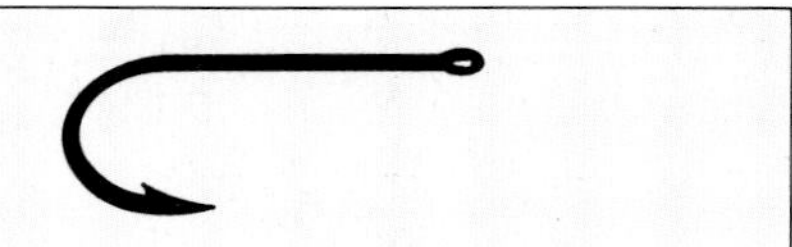

Aberdeen
light wire, round bend good for use with minnows; will bend before breaking

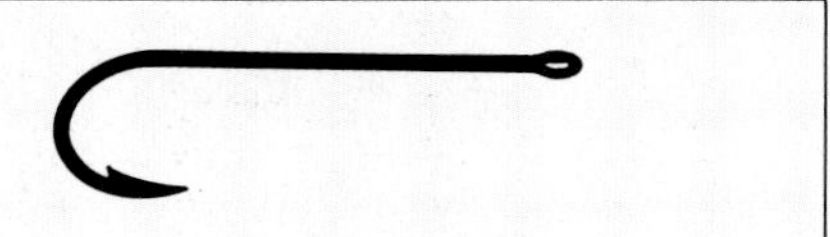

Carlisle
stronger than Aberdeen; used with bait; long shank prevents fish from swallowing the hook

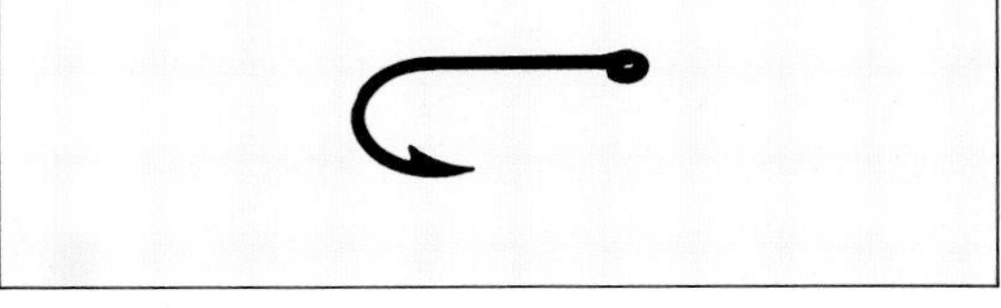

Siwash
heavy wire; extra long point offers good retention; used for big, active fish

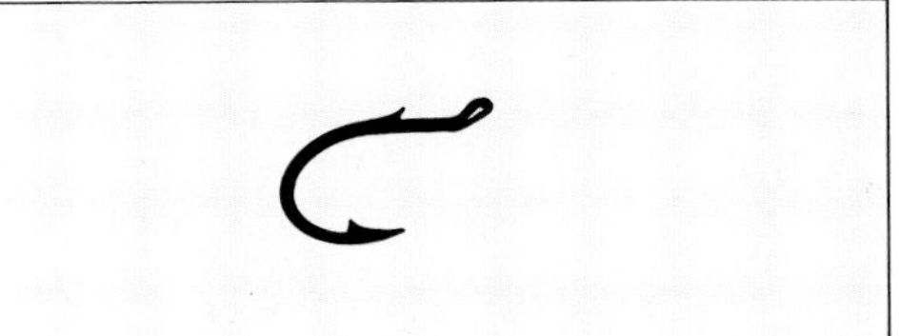

Salmon Egg
short shank; concealed by small bait

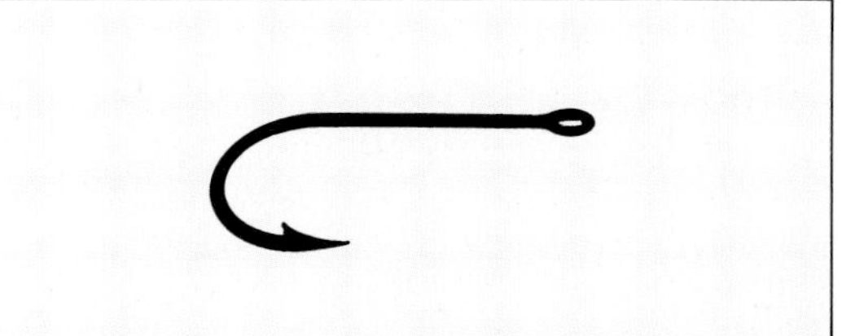

Eagle Claw
point is offset and curved inward to aid penetration; used often with bait

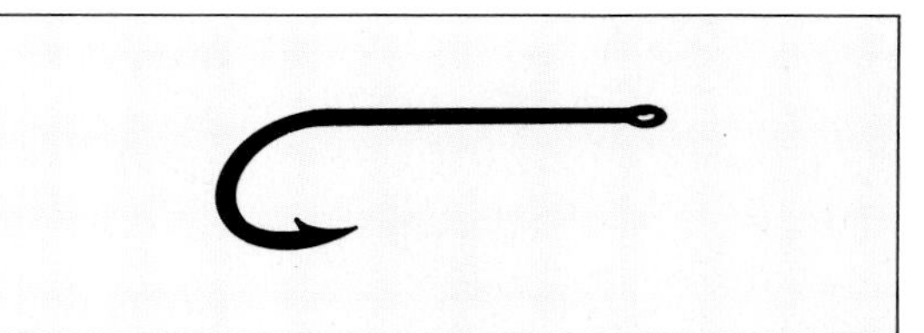

Limerick
long shank, wide bend provide extra hooking space

Beak
similar to Eagle Claw

Stainless steel hooks are used in saltwater, and where large pieces of bait are fished in deep water for big fish, the size of the hook must be correspondingly large.

A basic aspect of good hooks is strength, which is resistance to bending up to a stage where the hook almost would break, preferably bending instead of breaking. Resistance to pressure is influenced by hook style and size and is aided by forging.

The ability of hooks to withstand corrosion varies, particularly in saltwater, and is an important aspect of selection. No finish or design of hook is completely rustproof. Carbon-steel hooks are significantly less resistant to corrosion than stainless steel or cadmium/tin, and saltwater fishermen generally use the latter.

Looking after hooks Angling is such a broad endeavor that there are many styles and patterns of hooks to suit specific needs. Nonetheless, every good hook should have a sharp point, which can be made sharper by honing and which may be short for quick penetration or long for greater retention. Hooks are not necessarily as sharp as they can be when new. Once used, hooks become dull quite fast. The sharper the hook, the better the chance of hooking and landing fish. You can tell when your hook is sharp enough if it digs in as you scrape it over your fingernail.

The ideal is to sharpen all new and used hooks before fishing with them. Barbs should be sharpened as well as points, and points should be triangulated. The object is not to get a point that is long and thin (which will lack strength), but to keep it short and sharp without having a rounded tip. The cutting edges of the hook should taper to a true point, and the barb should be touched up to help hook penetration.

It is better to sharpen from the point back toward the barb than to sharpen in the other direction, which may cause the point of the hook to bend and thereby be less of a penetrating factor. Hold the hook so that the point faces you and file the point and barb in a motion that extends back toward the bend of the hook. Make it a practice to triangulate the point so that there are three cutting edges, rather than to simply file one side or just the top and bottom. Work back to the sides of the barb as well.

Hook-sharpening stones are most commonly used for this work, and these are adequate for most small hooks, although care should be taken to make sure that the point is not rounded. Fine-toothed files are also used by some fishermen, and there are

A sharp point is essential for hooks; used hooks need to be sharpened occasionally and even new hooks can be made sharper.

battery-operated sharpeners sporting swiftly turning cones.

Most hooks have barbs but some don't and a few anglers file the barbs down on their hooks to render them useless. This may afford better hook penetration but has the primary benefit of making it easier and less damaging to remove a hook from a fish that is to be released. An increasing number of remote fishing lodges mandate the use of barbless (and sometimes single) hooks on all lures used in their waters.

There are barbless hooks on the market, but you often can't find them in your local tackle shop in the wide range of styles and sizes that you may want. Some fly fishermen use barbless hooks, and places that cater to this branch of sport fishing may have a selection of barbless fly hooks or dressed barbless flies.

You can make your own hooks barbless simply by filing the barb off or by pinching it down. Filing works best with small light-diameter wire hooks. To pinch the barb down, use a pair of pliers, place the blunt end over the barb, and squeeze tightly to flatten the barb. Sharpen the point well afterward.

Sinkers

If you have any doubt about what can be cast out of molten lead, just look at all the types of sinkers available.

Trolling sinkers include the torpedo sinker, which has minimal drag or water resistance because of shape; a torpedo-style bead-chain sinker, which swivels and prevents line twist; a keel style, which tracks well with little swaying motion; a planing sinker, which dives and helps achieve depth; a clinch sinker, which is simple to add to or remove from fishing line; and a rubber-core sinker, which is simple to use and has no abrasion. Many sizes and weights are available. These are all fastened in-line, either being affixed on the main fishing line, or tied to a leader. The bead chain styles prevent line twist and, with a snap, aid leader and lure changing.

Sliding or slip sinkers include ball, egg or barrel, cone or bullet, and walking. Egg and ball sinkers slide freely on the line, are often stopped by a small split shot or a barrel swivel, and are preferred for open water. Cone-shaped sinkers provide minimal drag, are relatively weedless and are used with plastic worms, but may be pegged

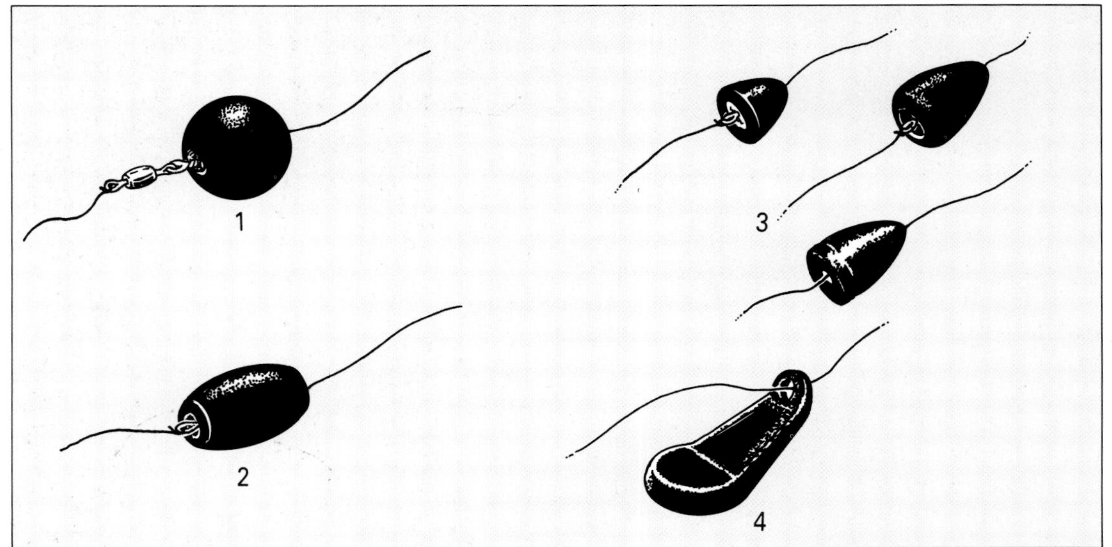

Sliding sinkers: ball (1); barrel (2); cone (3); and walking.

Below: Trolling sinkers: torpedo (1); torpedo bead chain (2); keel bead chain (3); planning (4); clinch (5); and rubber core.

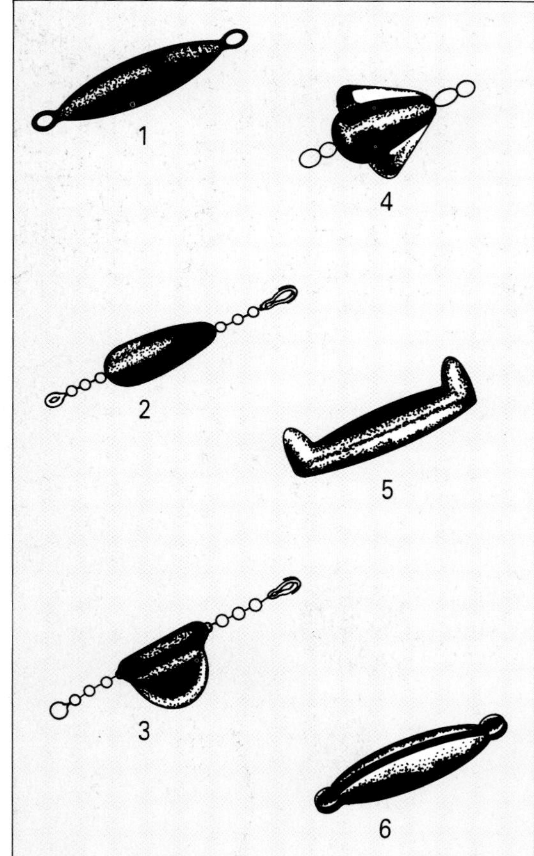

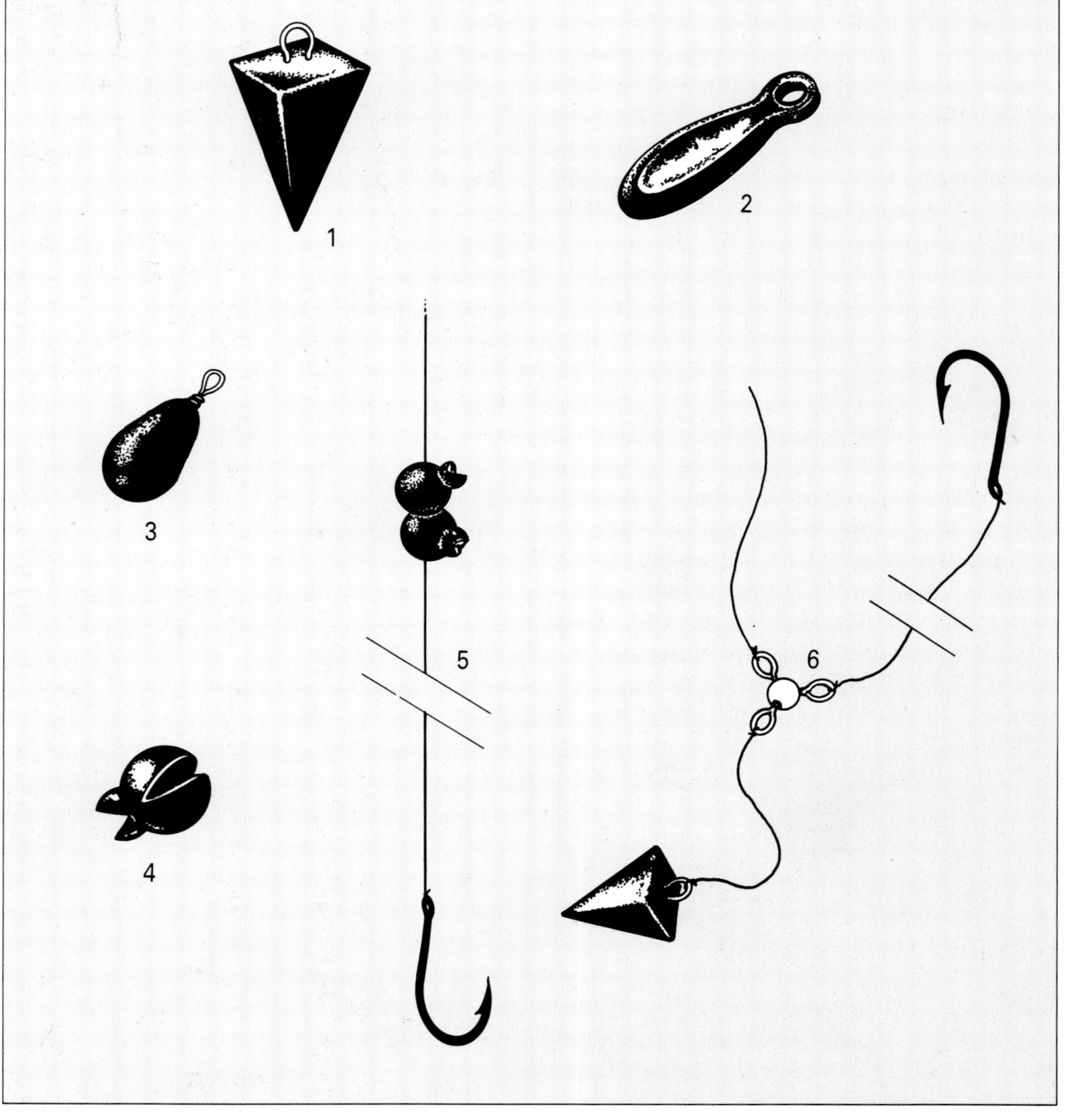

Right: Bottom sinkers: pyramid (1); bank (2); bell (3); and split shot. Sinkers can be affixed on the main line (5) or attached to a dropper line (6) via a three-way swivel.

With pyramid sinker in left hand, an angler rigs for drift fishing in saltwater.

with a toothpick to keep from sliding in heavy cover. Walking sinkers are used with a stopper when casting or trolling with bait along the bottom; they remain upright when a fish runs with the bait.

Bottom-fishing sinkers include pyramid, bank, dipsey, and split shot. Choice depends on fishing conditions, including the species you seek, the depth to be fished, and such factors as current and wave action. Pyramid sinkers hold bottom especially well where there is much current or wave action and are especially useful in surf fishing. Bank sinkers are good in deep water and cast well. Split shot are preferred for light tackle. Dipsey sinkers are also used with light to medium tackle and where bait is suspended off the bottom above the sinker.

Using sinkers Sinkers can be fixed on the main line or on a dropper line. Split shot is usually clamped firmly ahead of a hook and is primarily used for suspended bait and light line. A rubber core sinker is fastened by turning the rubber core around the line ahead of the hook or lure. Clinch sinkers are affixed like split shot. Split shot, egg, and pencil sinkers can be fixed to a dropper leader via a three-way swivel, which lessens hangups when fishing bait in fast water.

Bait rigs

Speaking of rigs, there are also a number of pre-formed bait rigs that are used where bait must be weighted to fish. A spinner rig, for example, is a popular freshwater bait-fishing rig used with worm or minnow. A fixed sinker or sliding sinker stopped by a barrel swivel will be used with it. Derivatives of this are the spinner and worm harness rig, with two or three hooks, and a spinner rig on a leader attached to a bead-chain sinker. A walking sinker rig uses a snap swivel to stop the sinker and hold the leader. A spreader rig is especially useful for bottom fishing and is very popular in saltwater; a springy wire is used for the horizontal section, with a nylon leader to the hooks, and fishing line extending from above. Another multi-bait bottom rig is one with two or three three-way swivels spaced well apart. A popular bottom fishing rig features a three-way swivel attached to a bell sinker and a leadered hook. The Baitwalker rig can be used in appropriate sizes for trolling and casting, and is relatively snagless.

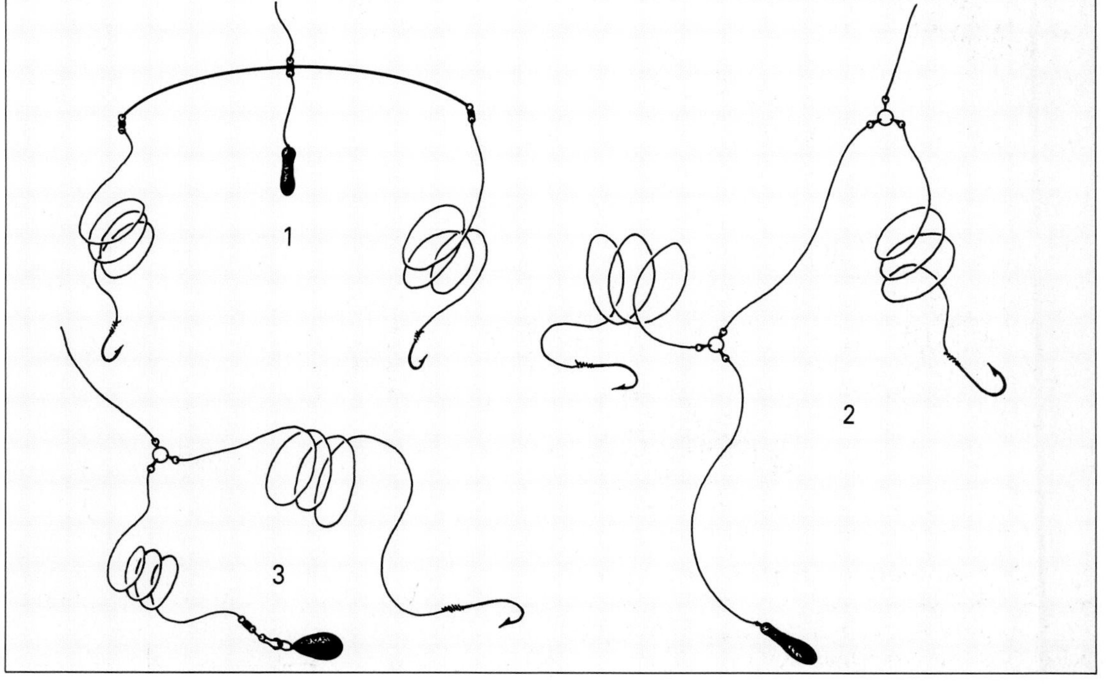

Popular bottom-fishing bait rigs in saltwater include a spreader rig (1) with bank sinker; a two-hook multi-swivel rig (2); and a standard three-way swivel rig (3).

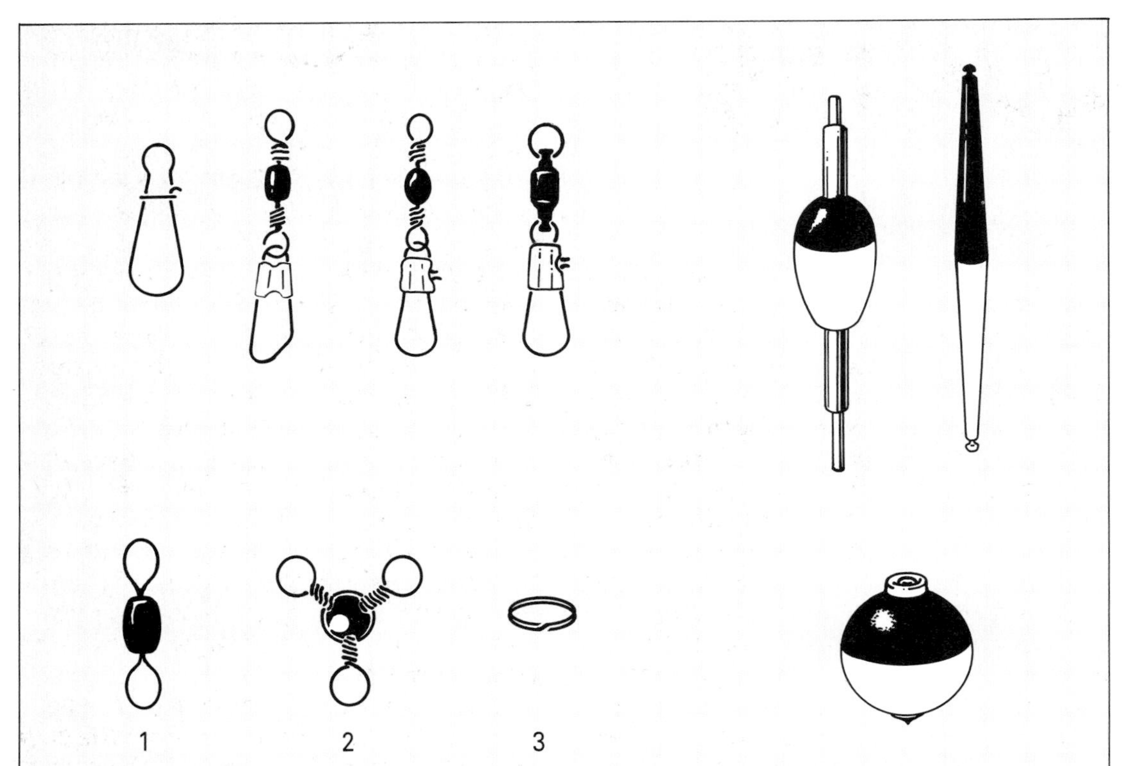

Assorted terminal tackle items include snap and snap swivels (top); bobbers (middle); and barrel swivel, three-way swivel, and split ring.

Snaps and snap swivels

Have you ever heard an angler say that he fought and lost a fish that broke his snap or snap swivel? That shouldn't happen. If it does, it's due to a weakened or defective snap that should no longer have been used, or to using a snap that was too light for the strength of line being employed. Snaps and snap swivels lead to more tackle problems than all other terminal gear together.

It would be worth while to take a few different snaps, clip them around a firm object, attach a reliable scale to the clips, and then pull on them until the clip breaks, noting how much pressure it takes to do so. The amount of force that it takes to break or separate a snap is a key to its usage. If it takes, for example, 15 pounds of force to do that, and you use the snap with 20-pound line, then it's easy to see how the snap would yield before the line if you hooked a fish large enough to require the utmost fishing pressure.

There is a difference between a snap and a snap swivel. In addition to being a snap, the latter has a rotating swivel. The principal reason to use a snap is because it facilitates lure changing. A snap also makes some lures work better (rounded snaps are preferred over vee-notched snaps). Snap swivels are used for the same reason, but also to avoid line twist when using certain lures. When you use a lure that doesn't invite line twist, and that runs well by itself, you don't need either of these devices. It's best to tie your line directly to a lure if you can, and to change knots when putting new lures on. However, use a snap swivel when trolling with spoons or spinners, and when fishing with these lures in current.

Types of swivels Ball-bearing swivels, incidentally, are far superior to brass swivels, albeit far more expensive, too. These swivels rotate freely, while brass swivels, especially cheap versions, frequently do not perform properly, thereby negating their effectiveness. The manner of locking is also important. Cross-locking, which is found in the newer breed of many snaps, has more holding power than the clipping version.

Other swivels include barrel versions, which have rings at both ends that rotate freely to reduce line twist, and are used to connect two lines; and three-way swivels, which have three connectors that rotate, and are used to separate bait or lure from sinker via separate leaders.

A general rule with snaps and swivels is to use only the smallest size that is compatible with the size of lure, strength of lure, and type of fishing to be done. Too large a snap is as much an impediment to successful fishing as one that is too small and weak. As for color, some anglers prefer flat black, but many anglers think the silver and gold colors help attract fish.

Bobbers

There are a number of bobbers used by bait anglers. Also known as 'floats' or 'corks', bobbers are usually brightly colored for visibility in water, although clear bobbers are used in some situations. When used with light baits and weights, bobbers help achieve greater casting distance. Different sizes are needed for use with different sizes of bait. Bobbers can be categorized as either fixed or sliding (sliders are also referred to as 'slip bobbers'). Fixed bobbers set the depth of bait at a predetermined level, which is usually no deeper than the length of the rod used. Clip-on plastic bobbers (red/white or red/yellow) are most popular. Sliding bobbers are usually fished close to the angler and in deeper water, and line slides freely through the bobber for deeper presentation.

Shown are snap swivels, used in some types of fishing to prevent line twist and facilitate lure changing.

ACCESSORIES

Fishermen really only need a rod, reel, hook or lure, and line to catch fish, but they somehow seem to possess far more than the basics. There are all kinds of accessories available, ranging widely in cost and utility. For some forms of fishing, what is labeled as an 'accessory' is in fact virtually a necessity in order to be productive and to have an enjoyable experience. Some of the most prominent such items are reviewed here and will be discussed further in Section II.

Electric motors Those who strictly troll out of large boats, fish from shore, do no casting, or who don't fish on lakes where outboard engines are prohibited, probably have no need for an electric motor. As for the rest of the angling fraternity, an electric motor is one of the best products to come along for fishing in this millennium. Commonly referred to as 'trolling motors' (although only a few people actually troll with them), these products shine for their ability to quietly maneuver a fisherman into places to make proper fishing presentations. Many small-lake fishermen, and those with small boats used for a variety of fishing applications, possess electric motors. They essentially take the place of oars and sculling paddles, but are quieter and interfere less with fishing activities.

All electric motors are battery-powered. Some are powered by just a single 12-volt battery; others use 24 volts, requiring two 12-volt batteries; and some have the capability of running off either one or two 12-volt batteries. Some produce considerably more thrust than others, which means they are basically more powerful. However, there are such things as sustained thrust and initial thrust, the former being the power generated while under way and the latter being the initial startup power. Initial thrust is greater than sustained thrust. The amount of energy (designated as amperes, or amp) consumed per hour by electric motors varies, and this figure, when known, will tell you how many hours of continuous use you can get out of a battery at varied motor speeds.

Check the specifications of these products and determine how much power you need and for how long you need that power in normal fishing circumstances. Generally, the heavier your boat and load, the more thrust needed. Another factor is how much fishing you do in areas of substantial current, or wind, which drains the reserves of a battery quicker than calm-condition operation. An electric motor does not automatically recharge the power source, and in the course of a full day's fishing you will likely drain the energy of a battery down considerably, so you need a charger to re-energize the battery.

One of the features you ought to look for in an electric motor is a breakaway bracket, where the shaft of the motor

An electric motor is one of the foremost accessories for anglers who fish from small to intermediate sized boats, and offers quiet maneuvering for making optimum casting presentations. This bow-mounted motor is operated by remote foot control.

Transom-mounted manual control electric motors are preferred by some fishermen, especially those with tiller-steered outboard motors.

can slip back if it collides with an immovable object. This will save you from having bent shafts, damaged lower units, and extraordinary stress on the mounting bracket when you get into tricky shallow spots. Another important feature is silence. Shallow-water anglers who use electric motors can conceivably get much closer to fish than boaters with far noisier gas outboard engines. Not spooking fish is obviously advantageous. Some electrics are considerably noisier than others, however.

On most fiberglass and many aluminum bass boats an electric motor is mounted permanently on the bow, with the bracket support installed on the starboard to help put a little weight on that side and counterbalance the console and driver weight on the port side. On many small boats, electric motors can be mounted on the front or back, but for convenience and best boat control, transom mounting is preferable, as is manual operation.

Permanent-mount electrics are used on conventional bass boats and large craft and can be operated manually or in remote fashion, depending upon the unit. Remote units are primarily operated via a foot-control pedal that is on the bow deck; some newer units have no wire foot control cable but an electronic cable that sends signals from anywhere in the boat. Manual models do not have a foot control pedal or cable running to the motor, and are steered by using your foot or hand at the head of the motor to direct it.

Sonar Most fishermen simply use the term 'depthfinder' when referring to what is actually sonar equipment. Certainly, transmitting depth is the foremost function of sportfishing sonar, but defining bottom types and contours and locating fish are also important functions. The first sportfishing sonar in use, in fact, was dubbed a Fish-Lo-K-Tor.

An outgrowth of sonar (short for 'sound navigation and ranging') applied by the military in World Wars I and II, today's electronic depth-finding and fish-locating equipment is helping anglers enjoy their sport and become more learned and proficient. In some circumstances it is viewed as being virtually indispensable. This is because sportfishing sonar is the boat angler's underwater eyes. With it he can find concentrations of migratory, suspended, schooling, and nomadic fish, plus he can locate unseen habitat that may be attractive to fish. With sportfishing sonar devices he can become accurately acquainted with the beneath-the-surface environment of a body of water in significantly less time than without it. Additionally, the use of sportfishing sonar allows an angler to navigate better, more safely, and quicker than he might otherwise. Locating fish with sonar, however, is no guarantee that they are the kind of fish

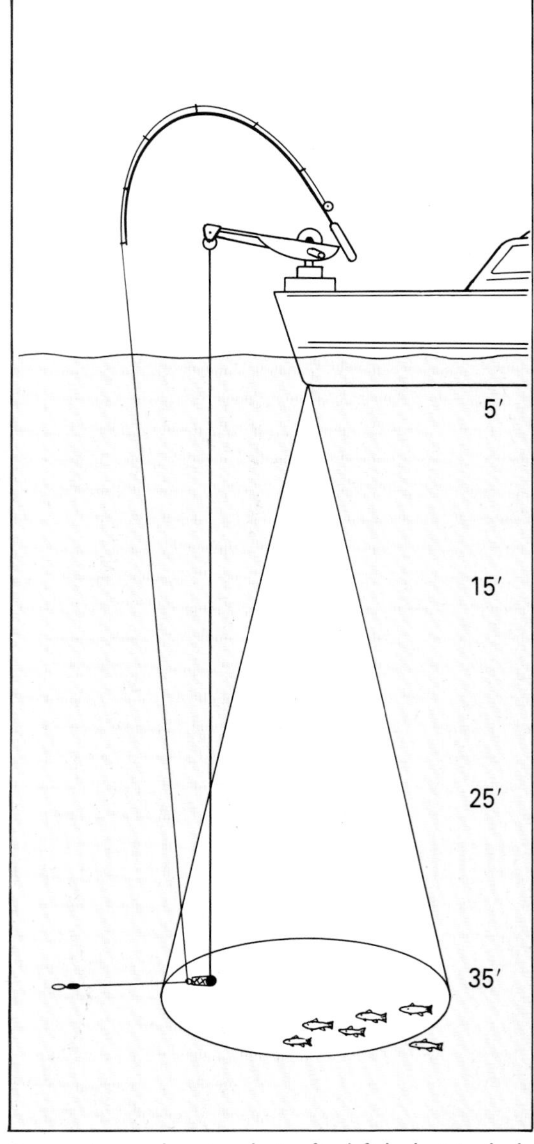

Sonar is used not only to find fish, but to help keep lures in the range of fish, especially when trolling.

you seek, or that you'll be able to catch them.

Sonar instruments employ transducers that swiftly send out pulses in a three-dimensional cone-shaped wave. Cone angles range from 8 (most narrow) to 50 degrees (extremely wide), and this in turn influences how much underwater detail will be viewed. Trollers usually prefer the widest cone and extremely deep water anglers the narrowest cone.

Categories of Sonar Sportfishing sonar falls into several categories: graph recorders, flashers, video recorders, and liquid crystal recorders (LCRs). Graph recorders make a chart paper printout of readings. The best graph recorders exceed all of the other types of sonar in the quality of detail that they provide; the cost of paper, and the need for frequent changing, are prominent drawbacks.

Flashers were once the mainstay of the sonar field, but have fallen out of general favor in recent years due to the emergence of LCRs; flashers have excellent detail but require some practice to learn to properly interpret their signals. Video recorders are the most expensive sonar and least preferred by most of the serious fishermen, although their multi-color TV-like appearance is entertaining.

LCRs have become the dominant force in sportfishing sonar, partly because of their simplicity and relatively economical cost. LCRs are getting better but are sometimes difficult to read because of the nature of the window and the number of pixels on their screen; most anglers leave them in the automatic mode, which is often inadequate.

With LCRs, signals appear at one side of the screen as you go over them, cross the screen and disappear at the other end. Some of the better models have a screen update to recall a full screen's worth of information; a zoom feature that narrows down the area being observed; an automatic depth-determining mode; forward and reverse displays; positive fish identification modes; fish and bottom depth alarms; split screens; target-separating gray-line; and other microprocessor-controlled features.

With sonar device on a board in front of him, a trolling angler is able to refer to it often in the process of navigating and looking for fish.

Getting the best from Sonar Sportfishing sonar is very important to many avid and successful North American anglers, yet a lot of fishermen have trouble learning to use their sonar well. Difficulties often center around the control functions, particularly sensitivity.

The sensitivity control (also called gain) is akin to volume. Many inexperienced sonar users keep this turned down too low. When the sensitivity is too low, sonar may fail to register key bait, fish, or bottom readings. When extremely low, only an indistinct bottom may be registered. On some units, a high sensitivity setting prompts a lot of false signals and distorted images.

On a flasher-style depthfinder, the sensitivity should first be turned up just enough to indicate bottom depth. Then it should be increased till a second reading, double the depth of the bottom, is recorded. Adjust the sensitivity control so the echo signal is faintly distinguishable. As you move into deeper or shallower water you will have to respectively increase or decrease sensitivity.

Liquid crystal recorders, such as the portable model in this boat, are the most popularly used sonar, particularly in freshwater.

With a graph recorder it is best to turn the sensitivity up high, usually at a two-thirds to three-quarter setting. Increase it till you have a strong, well-defined bottom marking. If you turn it too high you may get black marks all over the paper or interference signals; turn the sensitivity down slightly to avoid this. If you are getting no marks (good machines can detect algae, debris, tiny baitfish, and severe water temperature changes) between the bottom and the surface, or the bottom is indistinct, the sensitivity setting is too low. As you increase or decrease depth, or if water conditions change markedly, you may have to alter the sensitivity slightly. Sensitivity is adjusted automatically on LCRs, but it is sometimes necessary to switch to the manual mode and adjust the sensitivity setting to get finer details on the screen; you usually sacrifice some other functions, however, when you do this.

Flashers are harder to read than graph or liquid crystal recorders because signals disappear quickly, and at times flashers produce so many signals that you cannot digest the information quickly enough to interpret it. A flasher can reveal almost as much as a graph recorder, but you have to watch it virtually all the time and need practice to confidently determine what every signal is. Depth is gauged by watching the innermost part of the signal band. A hard bottom typically gives off a wide signal. A soft bottom produces a weaker signal and a narrow band. A dropoff will appear as a wide series of signals, which is actually the transducer receiving several signals of varying depths at one time. A rocky bottom appears choppy and broken up, while a sandy bottom is solid. Even a sandy bottom can appear choppy if the boat is moving through substantial

Paper graph recorders show the finest detail; this simulation of an actual scene depicts fish (inverted V marks) on the bottom as well as suspended.

waves, which cause the boat to bob up and down. Weeds return a thin, pale signal; fish in weeds show up as brighter signals. A school of baitfish produces a flurry of short-duration signals.

On recorders the bottom is easily distinguished. Trees, stumps, boulders, dropoffs, and the like, are all readily observed, without having to watch the monitor continuously. A grayline feature, which issues a light band below the bottom that helps distinguish bottom terrain features is helpful in identifying targets.

While you seldom can be sure of size or species of fish, you can tell if fish are active or not, and thus potentially susceptible to angling. With some species, suspended fish are likely to be inactive, while others, situated on top of a stump or edge of a drop, may be waiting in ambush. At times you can watch fish hit a jig worked vertically below the boat, or see fish follow a lure. It is possible to watch fish come off the bottom, follow a trolled lure, strike it, then be played out of the cone angle up to the surface.

Paper graph recorders make a permanent record of underwater structure and fish, and are easy to interpret. The graph at right clearly shows a hump with trees and fish on it and helped lead this angler to success.

Downriggers allow trollers to control the depth at which they fish, and to use lighter tackle in the process.

Downriggers Downriggers are the best thing to hit the trolling scene since outboard motors were invented. They have not only revolutionized trolling techniques, but they have made trolling a more sporting, fruitful, and fun endeavor. They won't help the stream trout fly caster, the heavy-cover bass angler, the flats fisherman, the snook caster, and certain others, but they will benefit just about anyone who rolls, and are becoming almost as common on fishing boats as sonar and electric motors.

The reason why downriggers are proving useful in angling for so many species of fish is rather elementary: they leave less to chance. Downriggers put your offering in the right place, time after time. It's a snap to raise or lower a lure; you don't have to fight a fish encumbered by burdensome tackle; you can change offerings quickly; you can easily run more than one fishing line on the same downrigger; you can maneuver in tight quarters if your lures aren't set too far back; you can fish just about any kind of lure or bait; and it's simple to use.

In the pre-downrigger age, trolling basically consisted of running an object on a weighted or unweighted nylon monofilament, braided Dacron, or fly line; behind a lead-core or wire line; or behind a diving planer or releaseable weight. Each of these systems can suffer from imprecise depth control because you often don't know exactly how deep you're fishing. When you do know, you may have an extreme amount of line out, or you're using tackle that could subdue a submarine. Downriggers overcome all of these problems because they take the burden of getting a lure to a specific depth away from your fishing line and put it on an accessory product. In brief, downriggers offer controlled depth presentation, and can be used with light as well as heavy tackle.

Components The equipment components of downrigging include a reel, cranking handle, boom, wire cable, and pulley that are part of the basic product referred to as a downrigger; a heavy lead weight (8 to 12 pounds) that attaches to the end of the downrigger cable; and a line release mechanism that may be located on or near the weight or at any location on the cable.

In use, a lure that is attached to your fishing line is placed in the water and set at whatever distance you want it to run behind your boat. Then the fishing line attached to that lure is placed in the release. Fishing line and downrigger weight are lowered simultaneously to the depth you want to fish. When a fish strikes your lure, the fishing line pops out of the release and you play the fish on your fishing line, unencumbered by a heavy weight or strong cable. In sum, you piggyback your fishing line to a heavily weighted nonfishing line, and the two separate when a fish strikes.

Models Downriggers come in manual or electric models. Many small boaters have manual downriggers or started with manual models and worked up to electrics. Manuals come in small versions that clamp onto the transom or gunwales of boats or even into the oarlock receptacle, and some are available in either right- or left-hand-crank versions; electrics are generally made for permanent and sturdy mounting locations and some manuals are similarly mounted.

Electrics are more expensive than manual downriggers, require a power source, and are more prone to malfunction, but are preferred because of their ease of use. Electric downriggers are raised and lowered by flicking a switch, while manuals are always hand-cranked up and in some models are also cranked down (on some you can release clutch tension to lower a downrigger weight instead of handle-cranking versions) electrics are generally made for permanent and sturdy mounting locations and some manuals are suitably mounted.

To begin downrigger trolling, open the bail or push the freespool button

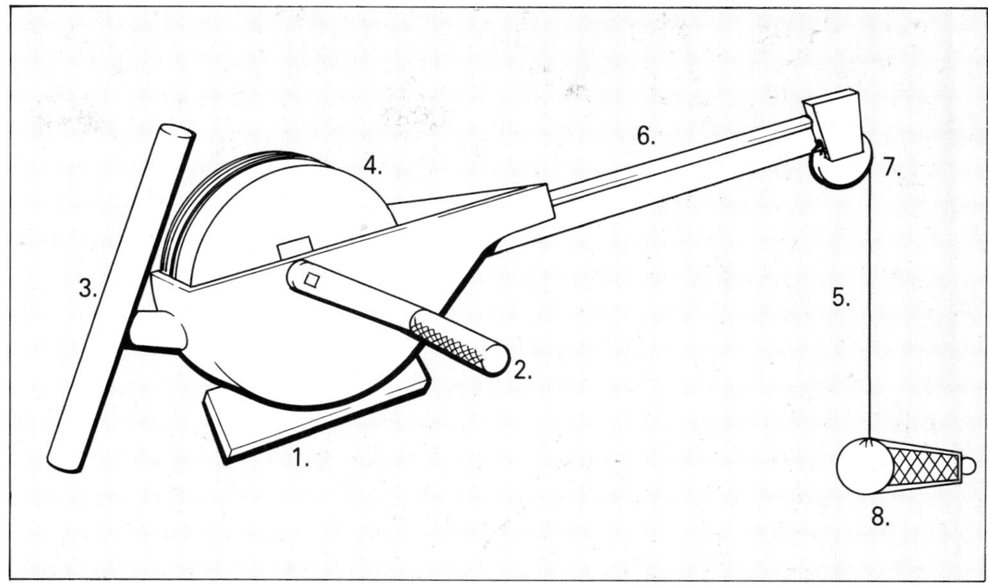

The components of a manual downrigger are: 1. base; 2. cranking handle; 3. rod holder; 4. line counter; 5. cable; 6. boom or arm; 7. pulley; 8. weight. Most models also have a clutch, which is not illustrated.

on your reel and let your lure out to whatever distance you think it should be swimming behind the downrigger weight. Keep the reel in freespool with the clicker on if it's a levelwind reel and either loosen the drag or keep the bail open with a spinning rod. Bring the downrigger weight and line release close to the boat where you can reach them without stretching far overboard. Grab the line at the top of the rod and place it in the release, twisting the line first if necessary. Set the weight back overboard if you brought it onto the gunwale of the boat or swing the boom back to proper position so the weight can be lowered.

Take the rod in one hand and make sure that the line is not fouled at the tip and that line will freely depart the reel spool. Use your other hand to lower the weight, either by depressing the down switch on electric downriggers or lightly releasing clutch tension or back-reeling manual downriggers. Stop the weight at whatever depth you want, as indicated on the line counter. Set the rod in a holder and reel up slack so that the tip is bowed over sharply.

Side planers Side-planer boards are plastic or wooden surface-running planers that evolved on the Great Lakes for trout and salmon trolling a few years ago, and which have caught on wildly in fresh- and saltwater environs where trolling – especially in shallow water – is a necessity. These devices solve many of the difficulties of shallow trolling, and make presentations much more versatile than merely running a flat line out behind the boat.

Side-planer boards work something like a downrigger on the surface. A non-fishing line or cable tethers the planer to the boat, and allows it to run at varied distances off to the side. One or more fishing lines are attached to the planer or tow line via release clips; you are free to fight a fish unencumbered when it strikes your lure and releases the fishing line from the clip. (Another type of planer, which is smaller, attaches directly to your fishing line, and pops free when a fish strikes. This side planer has a calm water fishing advantage, but must be retrieved after a fish is caught, and makes hooking fish a little difficult.

Side planers can be used in trolling for many kinds of fish. They vastly increase your presentation capabilities

An electric downrigger, shown here, is preferred by large boaters, those who fish deep often, and those who do a lot of trolling.

because they allow your lures to pass near fish that may have been spooked by the passage of your boat (or would be spooked if you ran your boat near them) or are in areas where you can't or don't want to take your boat.

How far you set the side planers out depends on how close you want your boat to shore, how far apart you want to spread your lures, how much room you have to fish, and how much boat traffic there is in the area, among other factors.

To use side planers you must have a method of tethering them to your boat and retrieving them. You can use manual downriggers for that, though this limits your range. A few companies are making side-planer reels, but you can fashion your own retrieval system with an old high-capacity level-wind reel or other reel-like storage mechanism, spooled with 150- to 200-pound-test monofilament or Dacron, and attached to a stand pole with a swiveling pulley at the top.

You can run lures any length behind a side planer that seems feasible. Because the lures are trolled well off to the side of the boat, and behind a relatively unobtrusive planer, they often don't have to be run as far back as when using a flat line. Obviously, a host of fishing combinations are possible.

The drawbacks to using side planers are that they require a little more equipment and cash outlay, it takes some practice to get used to them, it can be tough to work everything if you're alone in the boat, and they pose logistical problems at times. However they'll put you over a lot of fish that you couldn't otherwise reach.

Shown are several different side planers and a dual retrieval reel.

Boats It is no coincidence that each year a high percentage of people who purchase boats and motors list fishing as the primary intended use for that equipment. So a boat, especially one set up for fishing, is in a sense a vital accessory for anglers who want to be highly mobile and find fish that aren't accessible from the bank or surf or pier, or by wading.

Water conditions, distance to be traveled, type of fishing to be done, equipment needed, and myriad other factors heavily influence the choice of boat. Boats tend to run larger in saltwater fishing because of the influence of ocean tides, current, waves, weather, and size of fish. Long, broad-beamed fiberglass 'sportfishermen' are the pride of the fishing fleet, used for offshore big-game forays. Eighteen to 25-foot fiberglass vee-hulled boats fill the bill for most inshore saltwater anglers, with center console models being preferred in warm-weather climes and where a variety of casting, jigging, and drift fishing by several anglers is done. For shallow-water flats fishing, aluminum or fiberglass shallow-draft boats, many with bow casting and aft poling platforms, get the nod.

In freshwater, a vee-hulled fiberglass boat is especially suitable for large lakes, ponds, and rivers, where rough water dictates sturdy craft and where a big boat with a lot of engine muscle can help cover a lot of distance quickly. Aluminum boats can also be used under these conditions, although flat-bottomed models (johnboats) simply do not handle rough water well. The vee-hulled aluminum boats take rough water a little better, but still not as well as fiberglass boats; they sit up higher in the water and, because they are lighter, are more susceptible to being blown around in the wind. Sixteen- to 25-foot boats, aluminum and fiberglass, fill the bill for a wide range of freshwater fishing.

A smaller aluminum or flat-bottom boat is very functional for fishing on small lakes, rivers, and ponds, where it is not necessary to cover a lot of territory and where adverse conditions are seldom present. Small aluminum vee-bottomed boats can be used in the same manner, except that they are less suitable for small river fishing and more suitable to moderate-size lakes owing to their deeper-draft design. Canoes are popular in small lakes, ponds

Almost any kind of craft can be used for fishing, and sometimes it doesn't matter which type of vessel is used, but usually water conditions and type of fishing narrow the practical alternatives down.

and in flowing water, although they are an unsteady craft and are highly susceptible to positioning problems.

This overview is necessarily generalized. But whatever boat you have, or find interesting, should be thought of as a fishing tool. It has to get you where the fish are. It must weather the best and the worst water conditions. It must be reasonably comfortable to allow you to put in long hours. It must be versatile to handle a variety of angling pursuits. It must be designed and/or modified to allow you to fight and land fish (especially big fish). And it should have readily available accessories.

Rod holders An essential tool for boat fishermen, rod holders come in many forms and are made by many manufacturers. Open boats, centre-consoles, and cabin craft often sport through-the-gunwale or flush-mounted holders that keep the rods upright for storage. This isn't practical for many small boats; for those, horizontal mounting is preferable. The decks of many boats are often cluttered with rods, and some anglers leave these to bounce freely when the boat is moving at high speeds. A flush-mounted holder placed on the deck securely retains them. Holders such as these can also be used on the seats or sides of aluminum boats.

A deluxe arrangement of rod holders and other fishing paraphernalia is typical on many boats where trolling is a way of life, and where many boaters erect a board that goes across the transom. Two downriggers are usually mounted on the boards, with another two on the gunwales. Ample rod holders are placed on the board to allow rods in use to be within a narrow scope of vision and also to keep the lines clear of the motor to avoid cutoffs when turning sharply.

Waders Anglers who fish from the bank, wade, or get in and out of boats during the course of fishing (such as river drifters), need waders or hip boots to keep them dry and to help provide good footing. There are several types of waders. Boot foots are probably most

The larger the boat, the more you need to have rod holders, especially for trolling but also for storage.

popular, and feature one-piece construction with a boot that is permanently attached to a chest-high upper section and is firm enough to walk on. Stocking foot waders are also chest-high, but have a soft foot section that is worn inside a pair of wading shoes (or sneakers in warm water). Boot foot and stocking foot waders are worn with suspenders and should be used with a waist-level outer belt to help keep water out and trap air inside in the event of a spill.

Hippers are short waders that are very similar to the lower section of boot foot waders in construction, but they have separated legs which reach only to the hip and are held up by a strap that loops onto the wearer's belt. Though they are often referred to by fishermen as 'hip boots,' they are slightly different; hip boots cover the same area, but they are made from heavier material from top to bottom.

Hippers or hip boots are meant for wading in relatively shallow water. It is easier to get in and out of a boat or car in hip-length products, and they are easiest to take off or put on. They are also cooler to wear in warm weather, and good for long-distance walking on land.

The biggest advantage of chest-high waders is that they get you to deeper fishing holes, either by allowing you to wade deeper to cast or to ford deep places to get to locales you can't access otherwise. They are a bit heavy and bulky, however, which provides more warmth but makes for more difficult distance walking or climbing. Boot foots are easier to take off or put on because of their one-piece construction, but generally are not as comfortable and are heavier than stocking foot waders with wading shoes. Stocking foot waders fit the body closer, which can mean less drag in the water and easier climbing, and the wading shoes worn with them often provide better foot support and traction.

The materials used in the construction of waders and hip boots have come a long way. Stocking foot waders have undergone the greatest transformation, with many ultra-lightweight products available. Closed-cell neoprene, a material akin to that of wetsuits for skindiving, has become very popular for both stocking foot and boot foot waders. Products made from neoprene are light, very flexible, and more form-fitting than waders of old. This synthetic rubber material is very stretchy, meaning that neoprene waders do not impair mobility or climbing. They are time-consuming to put on, however, and they are warm – too warm for long-distance walking and for warm-water or warm-weather use – though very good for cold weather and cold water.

Float tubes Float tubes for fishing purposes are becoming more popular. Fishing from a float tube is not as effective as fishing from a boat, but it is a good way for anglers who don't have a boat and other boating-related accessories to reach spots they might not be able to get to otherwise, and it is simply a different and very pleasurable experience. Float tubes are conducive to a slower, more thorough pace of fishing, and, though used on large and small waters alike, are particularly favored for ponds and small lakes, including hard-to-access remote bodies of water.

Most float tube users wear chest-high waders when fishing. Neoprene waders or insulated rubber waders are used where the water is cold, and lightweight models in warmer water. Footwear is the key, because you need some method of propelling yourself around. This is done either by the use of swim fins or paddle pushers. The latter are a device that strap around the boot heel and have a paddle that allows you to go forward by moving your legs as if you were walking. Swim fins are preferred by many because they provide quicker movement from point to point if your leg muscles are in good shape. However, you must move backward in them virtually all the time to get anywhere, and they are tough to walk in on land or a murky lake bottom.

The better float tubes are lightweight and don't actually use a truck tire inner tube (earlier models did), but are self-contained products made of sturdy material that is blown up via some type of pump. Some have two or three inflatable compartments, and some have accessible storage compartments. All have an apron that sits over the front of the tube, to be used as a place to

Wearing a chest-high stocking foot wader that requires a separate boot, this angler is prepared to wade fairly deep if necessary.

A float tube fly fisherman uses his own power to fish a small pond.

rest tackle or to drape fly line while casting.

Tackle selection has to be a little conservative. You generally only have one rod with you, and can't take a full tackle box full of equipment, though with a fishing vest or suitable storage compartments on the float tube, you can still bring a fair amount along.

Tackle storage methods The traditional tackle box was a metal container, but the realm of items in which to hold tackle has vastly expanded to a potpourri of systems, many suited to specialized applications. Plastic boxes are by far the most popular these days, for ease of care and also because plastic can be molded into a great range of designs, yet there are still a few metal boxes, particularly small aluminum models used by fly fishermen, and even some wooden ones, to be found. Leather and cloth tackle satchels ar also in use, as well as flexible, foldable tackle systems made of dense sailcloth, with compartments covered by vinyl.

The traditional style of tackle box comes in trunk, hip roof, and drawer configurations. A trunk box has one or more trays that pivot up together to reveal a large open compartment at the bottom of the box. Hip roof boxes are similar, though they have two sets of trays facing each other. The drawer box has trays that slide out, and usually has the most compartments for storage.

The type of box to use largely depends on the amount and size of objects that you need to store. Typically most fishermen outgrow their boxes and purchase more or larger ones as they accumulate tackle and/or their fishing interests expand. Tackle boxes with movable dividers allow you to fashion the number and size of storage compartments to suit your needs.

Many fishermen who do a lot of angling and/or who fish for various species keep several boxes, often organized by lure types or tackle-by-species. Single- and double-sided plastic tackle boxes with see-through lids are particularly favored by avid anglers. They have movable compartments, hold a surprising amount of gear, and can be readily stowed or stacked on top of one another.

A fishing vest is a multi-pocketed and compartmented tackle storage system that is worn over shirt or jacket and predominantly used by fly casters and river and stream fishermen. Full-length versions are standard, but shorter models are used by deep-water waders and float tube anglers. Both have many pockets, some designed especially to hold specific items (reel spool or sunglasses).

Maps Maps, especially if they detail

underwater, contours and hydrographic features, help in navigation and in finding locales that may provide good fishing. Most preferred are underwater contour (hydrographic) maps and navigational charts, which are distinguished from topographic maps. Topographic maps seldom denote water depth or the location of reefs, rocks, shallows, and such, while the other two do. Underwater contour maps are available for many natural and manmade lakes, and these can be particularly useful because their high level of detail pinpoints important hydrographic features that may be attractive to various gamefish. When used in conjunction with a compass, they help you maintain course, especially in fog or low-light conditions, or at night. The same is true for navigational charts, which are available for all marine waters, navigable waterways, the Great Lakes, etc., and which also plot latitudinal and longitudinal coordinates for Loran navigation.

Navigational charts are produced by American and Canadian federal agencies and are available at some sporting goods stores, tackle shops, marinas, and major-city map stores, and cost a few dollars apiece. Dealers usually stock local area maps and can order others. Remember that the larger the scale, the more detail is provided.

Other maps of big freshwater lakes may be available from jurisdictional agencies such as the Corps of Engineers or TVA, (Tennessee Valley Authority), although their maps are rarely detailed enough to provide more than general information. Maps for freshwater lakes supplied by private firms, however, are often geared to fishermen's interests and provide a great deal of underwater contour information. Their size and scale level will determine how helpful they are as boating and fishing aids.

Two popular modern storage systems are the double-sided see-through box, shown here containing plugs, and a soft vinyl satchel, shown here containing soft-plastic lures.

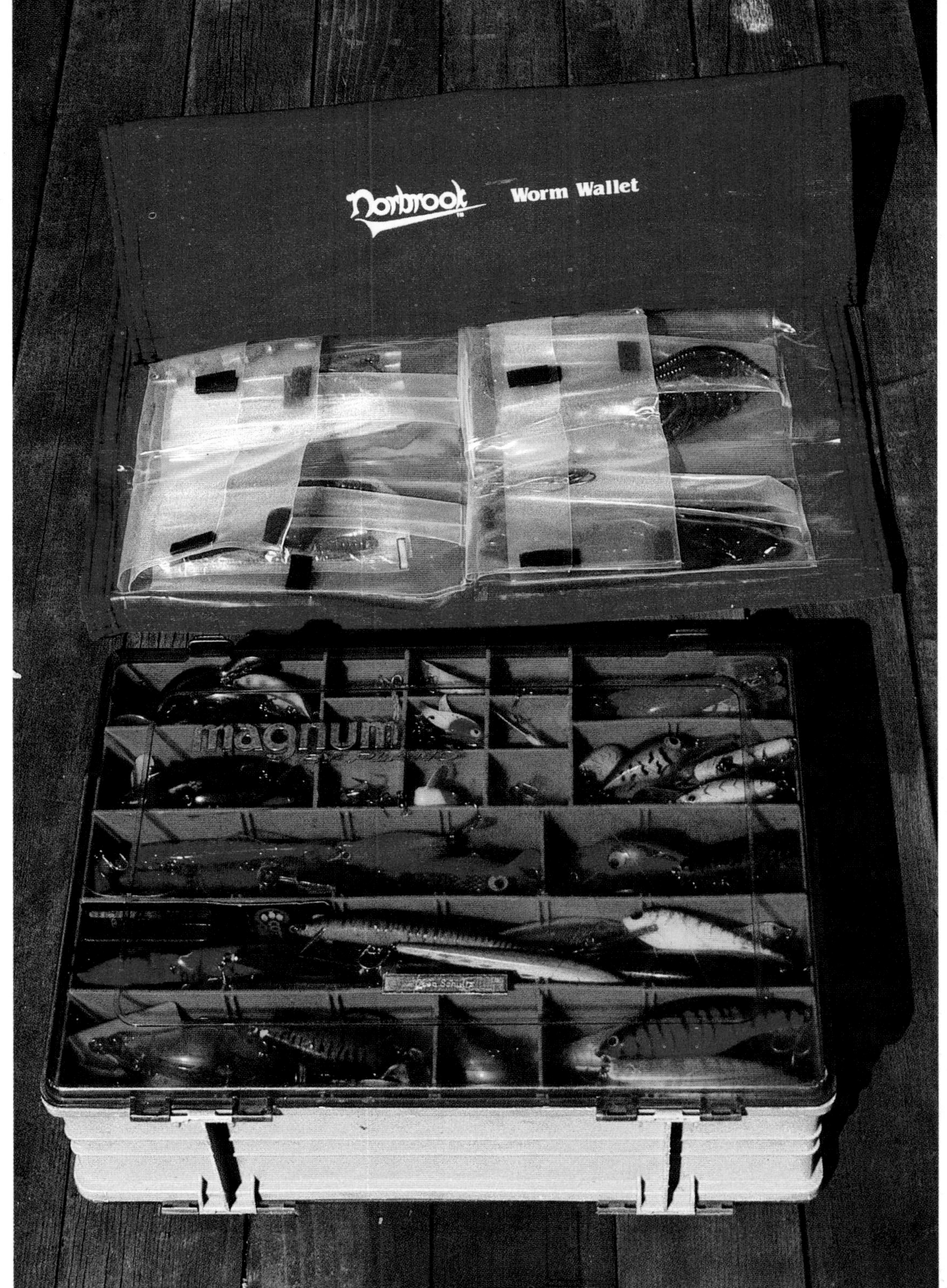

Nets Landing nets are an accessory in high demand, although more netting is done in freshwater than in saltwater. Naturally, nets should be suited to the kind of angling being done and the fish anticipated. Stream nets have a short handle and small hoop diameter (12 to 14 inches) for small fish while boat nets have longer handles (perhaps collapsible) and larger hoops. The further one has to reach (from boat or pier), the longer the handle needed. Pier and bridge fishermen use a large, handleless net that is lowered and raised on a rope. With all nets, the larger the fish, the bigger the hoop and the deeper the bag. While it seems foolish to net small fish with big nets, it's worse to be caught with a net that can't fit the fish. For small-boat fishing a net that is at least 4 feet long from net rim to handle butt, with a wide rim and a deep net bag, is a popular choice. Most nets feature aluminum handles and frames. Mesh bags are rubber, nylon, plastic, or cotton, although cotton tends to rot, especially in saltwater environs. All nets should be rinsed after use to increase their longevity.

Gaffs A sharp hook attached to a handle, a gaff is used in lieu of a net to land certain fish, mostly in saltwater. With a short-handled gaff, a fish can be hooked in the lip and released without harm. Most gaffs are longer, with the average being 3 or 4 feet, and those up to 6 or 8 feet are used on large boats for big game fish and sharks. With shorter gaffs the normal hook measures 2 inches from tip across to shaft. Flying gaffs, which separate from the handle and are attached to a strong rope, are used for big game also.

Fish storage Something to put fish in is still another highly useful accessory. That item might be a stringer, creel, cooler, livewell, or wire mesh bag. Small-boat fishermen who don't have a livewell or a cooler with ice to keep fish in will employ a stringer, which is attached to the boat and holds fish in the water. Rope stringers are the simplest and cheapest, but fish get bunched together on these. Metal or plastic clip-on stringers, with individual clips for securing fish, are a better alternative as long as they are sturdy enough to withstand the weight of fish being contained.

Canvas or basket creels are used by some mobile stream fishermen. Metal mesh bags, with a foam collar to keep them afloat, are favored by some boat

A good-sized net with deep bag is needed for large fish. The boat net used here is fairly standard in terms of handle length and bag size.

and dock panfishermen, who find it easy to slip a fish through the top door and keep the catch alive. Livewells in many boats have eliminated the need for these devices, especially stringers, and have allowed anglers to keep their catch alive and fresh for long periods of time. Livewells are nice to have if you want, or need, to keep fish alive during the fishing day, or to keep large bait alive. They are not practical in many small boats, however, because they take up a lot of room and, when full of water and fish, add a lot of weight. You can utilize a 48-quart cooler with an aeration pump as a livewell if you'd prefer, as long as you have a battery to power the pump. In panfishing, it's popular to use wire mesh bags that float in the water to contain the day's catch of relatively small fish.

Bait containers Bait containers rank high on the accessory charts, too. For baitfish, steel or plastic buckets, including some with a perforated insert pail, which contains the bait and which can be easily removed to facilitate water changing, or floating plastic buckets with springloaded door, are the primary models. The latter can be kept in the water and is especially useful for slow trolling. Both can be used for other bait, such as leeches, crayfish, or salamanders. Worms, however, are usually kept in small plastic or fiber containers, or simply in the styrofoam container that small quantities are sold in. Larger bait, especially that used in saltwater, are kept in boat baitwells or large storage containers. For some species, particularly herring, the containers must be round.

Above: A stringer is the most common device for containing freshwater fish that are to be kept for consumption.

Incidentals Among the other practical and oft-used simple accessories for anglers are pliers, either needle-nosed for hook removal or blunt-nosed with wire cutting edges; nail clippers, to cut line and knots; a spring scale, including those with a tape measure (useful where length limits are employed); a fillet knife, preferably with a thin and somewhat flexible blade ranging from 6 to 10 inches long; a surface temperature gauge, which is especially useful in spring and early summer; a trolling speed indicator, which is predominantly used on the Great Lakes to define slow boat speeds; marker buoys, for use with sonar to identify open-water angling locations; rod belts and harnesses, with or without gimbal socket, for holding a rod and providing lower back support while fighting a large fish for a long time; polarized sunglasses, for eye protection and enhanced visibility; and sunscreen lotion, which, though it plays no part in fishing *per se*, does protect the skin from possibly harmful exposure to the sun.

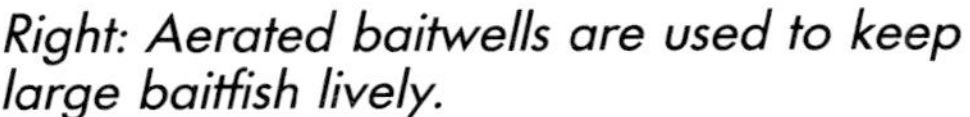

Right: Aerated baitwells are used to keep large baitfish lively.

TECHNIQUES

FINDING FISH

Successful fishing is the result of many activities. In the matter of actually finding fish, the key aspects involve a combination of visual observation, understanding the habits of fish and the habitat in which they are found (this varies from freshwater to saltwater and from species to species), and using savvy to realize how these elements relate to one another and then be able to take advantage of that.

Visual observation is one factor in selecting places to fish and in looking for signs of feeding actions that in turn indicate the presence of fish. Examples of the latter include fish feeding on insects or schools of baitfish. Sight-fishing is used in saltwater on the flats, for example, when looking for schools of such fish as bonefish or tarpon, or when looking for individual feeding fish, such as permit and bonefish. It is used when looking for birds, primarily seagulls, that are frenziedly working an area where game fish (bluefish, tuna, etc.) have corralled bait and are tearing into them, with the birds diving to pick up remnants. This schooling action occurs in freshwater, too, primarily involving striped bass, but also white bass and largemouth bass. In stream trout fishing, and occasionally in other forms of freshwater angling, fish will be seen rising to inhale natural insects.

Most often, however, anglers don't observe fish but search for them, which frequently means that they need to watch water conditions to determine where fish may lie and how to present lures to them. This is referred to as 'reading water.'

Reading flowing water

The reading of water is most obviously practised by anglers who fish in flowages. Current in rivers and creeks is a premier influence on where and how fish are situated, both for resting and feeding purposes. Fish face flowing water, so lures must generally come downcurrent toward them in a natural manner.

In flowing water it is the deeper places that often hold fish and which are sought by anglers. Slow-moving water is a sign of depth. Water is deepest where the current comes against the bank; years of this have gouged the bank and bottom, resulting in deeper water. Shallow water is found on the inside of a bend. In many places the bank is much steeper on the outside of a bend than on the inside, and this is another clue to the location of the deeper and shallower portions. This is not only important from a standpoint of angling, but also for the purposes of navigating a boat or wading safely.

When current strikes an object it may cause less turbulence in front of, or behind, that object. This may be a place where fish locate because they don't have to work as hard to resist the flow, and also because it may be a good place to find food. Boulders are the most common object in currents, but

Rivers and other flowages require that an angler determine which places are most likely to hold fish in order to make a proper presentation. Pools, deep runs, undercut banks, and around large rocks are some of the most common holding spots.

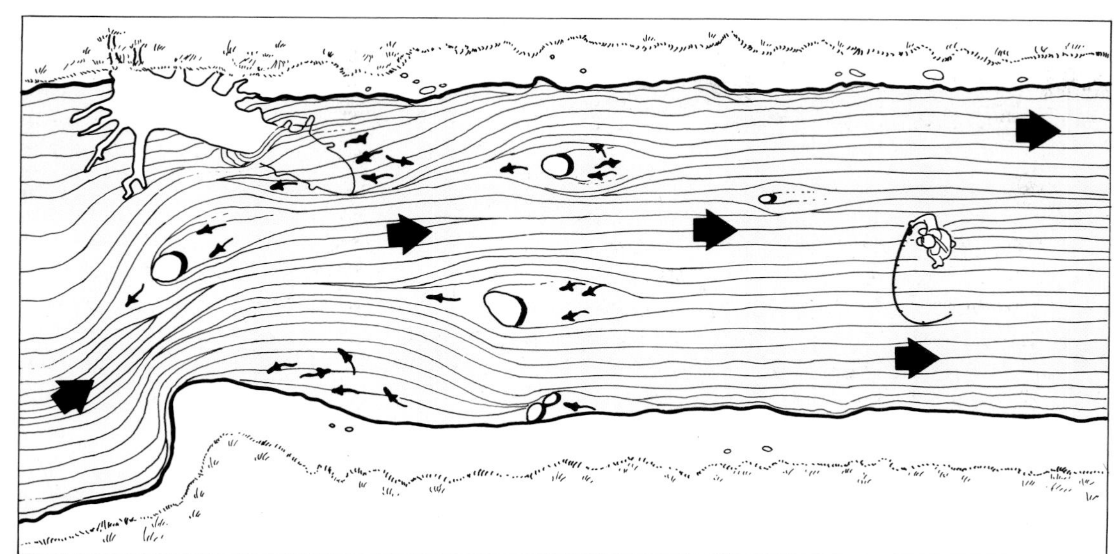

Stream trout fishermen do a considerable amount of reading water, watching for, and fishing, those places that provide food and where these fish are most likely to hold.

small islands or shoals also exist, and in high water, stumps and fallen trees are also objects that can attract fish.

Reading still waters

Still-water environments, such as lakes, reservoirs, and ponds, are different, of course, and much of their characteristics are hidden below the surface. That is one of the reasons why fish- or depth-finding sonar equipment has become such a valued tool of anglers who fish still waters from a boat. However, with or without sonar, there is much that can be learned in these environments simply by observing the shoreline and surrounding topographical features.

If the shore is sandy or rocky, it's likely that the bottom of the body of water nearby will have a similar characteristic. When the land declines steeply down to the water level, the lake there will drop off sharply into deep water, but where the shore is of a gradual slope, the lake near shore will be likewise. This is particularly true in manmade bodies of water and in times of high water.

Points are an important landform for anglers to be aware of. Many points extend underwater well out into a lake before dropping off abruptly into deep water. This can attract both migratory and nonmigratory species of fish and can be worth exploring, although by looking strictly at the water's surface you seldom have a clue that there is something unusual below and near the point. Perhaps a little more obvious are such features as rock walls, fence posts, and roadbeds, which are typically found in manmade or man-enlarged bodies of water, and which extend from shore into the water and provide cover for some species of fish.

Even more obvious, of course, is vegetation, stumps, timber, docks, and the like, which provide cover and

In freshwater, obvious cover, such as this timbered flat, can provide ambush spots for some species of game fish.

Searching for fish using sonar is done in saltwater and freshwater environments. Paying attention to depth, bottom terrain, and temperature is sometimes necessary to achieve success.

attract bait and smaller prey fish. Some species of fish are especially attracted to various forms of cover and fishermen want to look for emerged and submerged cover, especially if it is near deep water, because it may hold the fish they seek. By judiciously casting to these objects, and in the case of vegetation, seeking the pockets and edges within, they can enhance their opportunities for catching fish.

Reading big waters

For many anglers it is comforting to fish in streams, ponds, rivers, inlets, marshes, and small lakes because of the relative small size of those waters, not only from an accessibility or boating standpoint, but because the options are narrower. But when one leaves the estuary or the launch ramp and heads out to face an ocean of saltwater or a lake with miles and miles of shoreline or a maze of islands, the big water can be inhibiting.

Big waters have abundant populations of major game fish, in many cases species and sizes of fish unknown to, or infrequently found in, small waters. To enjoy these bounties you have to solve the problems posed by fishing big water, and not be overwhelmed by them.

How the water stratifies in a lake or reservoir can be a key to finding fish. The area around the thermocline is particularly attractive to some species.

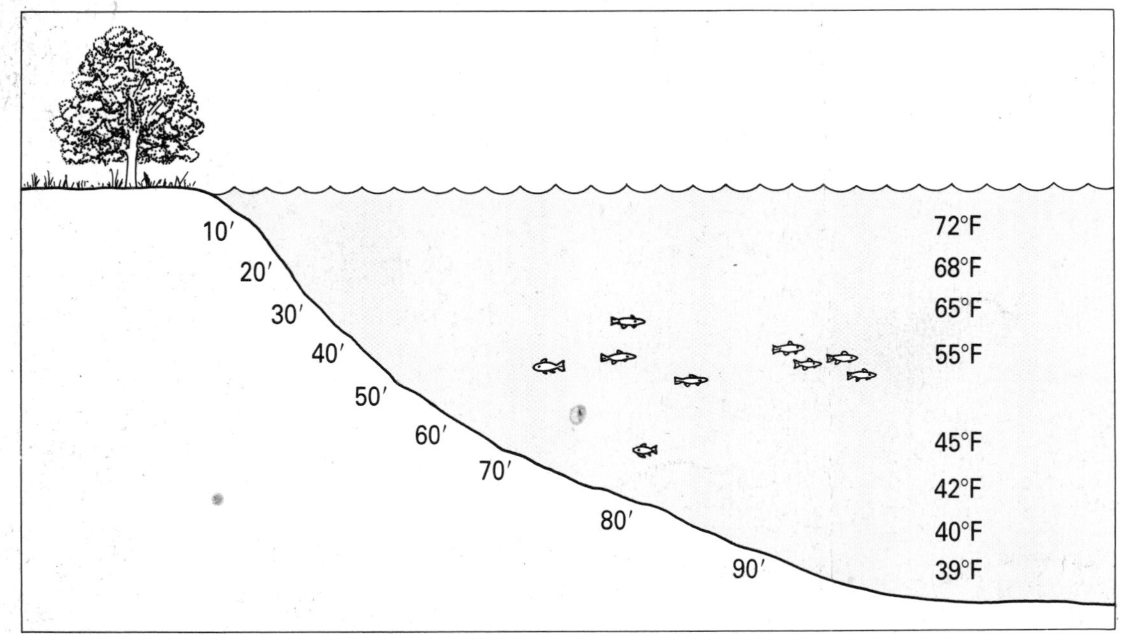

There's little doubt that in big lakes and river systems, tributaries play a critical role in game fish behavior and therefore fishing success. This is especially true in the spring, when many predator and prey species enter tributaries to spawn, or come into the nearshore areas influenced by tributaries because of the presence of food and more comfortable conditions.

Temperature changes in big waters Tributaries, whether they are major rivers, small streams, the outlet of upstream dams, etc., are the lifeblood of big water. In the spring they bear the rain and snow-melt runoff that helps open up the lake, then the warm water that ultimately raises the temperature of the cold main lake. A warm rain is a blessing for a big body of water that is influenced by a major tributary, because it will stimulate activity, feeding, and possibly spawning, though it sometimes takes two or three days for a heavy warm rain to have an impact on a big lake system. This phenomenon is most evident in large mid-South impoundments hosting stripers, white bass, black bass, and walleyes, and to an extent it applies to inshore saltwater areas as well.

However, the area where a tributary intersects a lake is an edge that attracts bait and major game fish. Water that is a few degrees warmer than the main lake temperature flows into the lake and mixes with it, encouraging fish activity. There is often a distinct mudline created around tributary mouths, which

Right: Places that are protected and warm up quickly in the spring, such as a bay, cove, or slough, are good to try.

Largemouth bass are one freshwater fish that usually move into the north coves, or the shallows along north coves or shorelines in the spring, prior to spawning. Sunlight and wind from the south warm these areas up first.

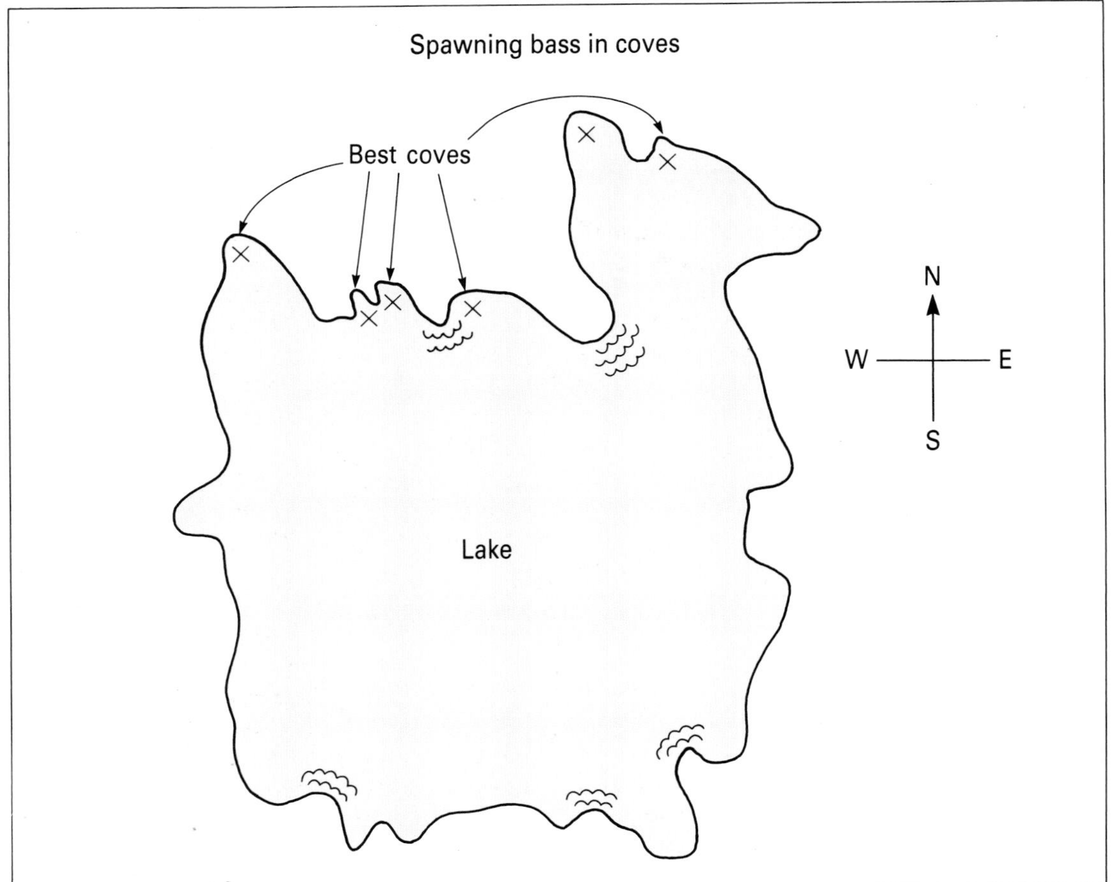

results from stained or muddy spring runoff. On some waters, this attracts game fish because there is usually a thermal break here as well, with the inner edge being warmer and the mudline itself being attractive to bait and prey species.

Water temperature is certainly a key to game fish behavior. In the Great Lakes, for example, early-season fishing primarily occurs in fairly shallow water close to shore. Trout and salmon seek warm water there, as do the alewife and smelt that they feed on. Sometimes the way to get action is to find the warmest water along the shore (use a pool thermometer or surface temperature gauge).

Elsewhere, however, the upper layer of water may be warmed up a bit on a mild sunny spring day, and act as an attracting edge. This might cause fish to be caught very shallow. This is especially so for bass, for example, which will eventually make nests in warm shallow water, or for trout or salmon, which will be attracted to pockets of warm water or vertical separations of different temperature water away from immediate tributary areas. This may be in the vicinity of a warmwater discharge, or it may simply be the phenomenon of water movement and mixing. Nonetheless, surface temperature variants can be edges.

Perhaps the most extraordinary example of this phenomenon is that of the so-called thermal bar that exists in mid to late spring on the Great Lakes, where there is a sharp surface distinction between temperatures offshore at a time when near-shore environs are relatively warm and theoretically in a temperature range that should attract trout and salmon. Nevertheless, colder offshore water on a distinct surface thermal break is the better place to be looking for fish, particularly salmon and steelhead.

Temperature remains a factor after spring for many fish species. Water stratification sends cold- and coolwater fish to deeper freshwater locales in the summer, meaning that when you fish open-water areas you have to know the preferred temperature of the species you seek, attempt to find out the depth that this temperature is found, and try to relate this to prominent areas that would attract your quarry (such as long sloping underwater points, submerged creek channels, sharp dropoffs, and so forth).

The thermocline is usually a fairly narrow band of water, but it is found where temperature drops off sharply, often averaging a drop of one-half to one degree every foot. Sometimes it is only 10 feet wide and 15 to 20 feet below the surface; usually it is a bit wider and begins deeper. To locate the thermocline you should lower a thermometer down on a rope or fishing line, checking it every 5 feet or so. Give the thermometer enough time at checked depths to register the proper reading.

Most lakes that stratify like this have a good deal of deep water. Shallow lakes don't stratify, as they become uniformly warm with too little variation from top to bottom. Fewer southern lakes stratify than northern ones, but in many generally the same patterns hold from year to year.

In lakes with clearly defined thermoclines it is possible to identify the thermocline on a good sonar instrument, primarily with paper graph recorders and LCRs. With LCRs you will seldom observe the thermocline when the unit is in the automatic operating mode, so it's usually necessary to use the manual mode and increase the sensitivity function.

Where there is a thermocline it's important to fish in and around it because that is where there is the best combination of food, oxygen, and temperature. But keep in mind the temperature preferences of the fish you seek, because the actual temperature of the thermocline will vary by locale and fish may be just above or below it.

A thermocline usually lasts until the fall, or when there is a trend toward cool air temperatures. When the surface water cools off enough, a body of water mixes and the thermocline dissipates. This is often referred to as the 'fall turnover.'

Big waters are slow to warm up in the spring, and slow to cool off in the fall. This can mean that small bodies of water may be better to fish in the earliest part of the season, till the larger waters warm up, and that big waters may sustain good fishing for a longer period of time in the fall.

Other places offering warmth are bays and coves, especially if they are shallow and contain the type of cover preferred by the species you seek. Bays are especially good places to fish in the spring on natural lakes that are not fed by major tributaries, and may also be productive in sprawling manmade lakes that do have tributaries. Bays with a north and northwest exposure (or sections of a bay with such an exposure) get the most sun in the day. They also benefit from southerly winds, which stack warm surface water up on their shores. Thus, they tend to warm up fast and may attract certain species if the habitat is right.

Other features that attract game fish Grass, weed beds, and other forms of vegetation may also be important fishing areas of big lakes, but this habitat may not be readily observable, or may not be found in all sectors of a lake. Bays, coves, islands, and shoals are usually good places to start the search for vegetation, which is as likely to be submerged in moderate depth water as it is visible and close to shore.

A good tactic for anglers apprehensive about where to begin fishing is to approach big water as if it were several smaller bodies of water, and focus on one section at a time. Some anglers become familiar with big lakes by zeroing in on prominent points. Some fish use points as fulltime domiciles, because they offer frequent opportunities to ambush prey. Others migrate by them often, or leave deep-water haunts to visit points temporarily to feed.

There's no doubt that knowledge of fish habits and habitat requirements through the seasons is one of your greatest allies when solving the mysteries of where to fish and what to look for in a big body of water. In freshwater, for instance, if lake trout are your quarry you should be looking for rocky shoals, reefs, and islands near deep water, as lakers are prone to come in from deeper water to such areas, feed, then leave. Open-water salmon don't orient much to underwater features, so when they aren't close to shore in spring or fall, you have to fish specific temperature zones (mostly in deep water), and aggressively search for them and for baitfish. Stripers, too, are often nomadic and follow schools of bait, but in many impoundments where they are found, the tops of submerged timber, old river channels, and other identifiable underwater terrain give them a place to find food. Largemouth bass and pike orient strongly toward various forms of cover, usually near shore, so they present different demands upon the angler. Draw upon your knowledge of a species when deciding where to go and what to do.

Also, think in terms of edges. Fish, like most animals, are attracted to some type of edge, be it structure or temperature, and anglers may find it helpful to be thinking of what type of edge –such as a long sloping underwater point, a reef or shoal, or even a rocky versus sandy bottom – may appeal to the fish they seek because of comfort, security, or feeding reasons.

A prominent edge lair might be a shoal or reef; an underwater mound or island, sand bars, and gravel bars, are similar. These locations may be rocky or boulder-strewn, or they may be sandy with moderate weed growth, but they attract small baitfish, which in turn attracts predators. Often, there is deep water on one side.

How you fish such places is almost as important as the fact that you do fish them. When trolling the perimeter of weeds, sand bars, shoals, and so forth, for example, you might have a shallower running lure on the side of the boat nearest the edge, and your deepest running lure on the opposite side. If fishing two lures off the same gunwale, put a deep runner on the inside rod on a short- to medium-length line and a shallow runner on the outside position but on a longer length of line (it might get as deep as the other lure but be further back to avoid tangling and also aid fish playing and hook setting). Or, use a lure on a short line behind a downrigger and a diving lure on a longer flatline.

The deep-water/shallow-water interface near islands can be similarly thought of as an edge, incidentally, as can a sharply sloping shoreline. These are places where bait migrate naturally by, and logically present feeding opportunities.

Current is also a factor in this business of edges. A locale where strong current can bring bait washing by, or which retards the movement of weak, crippled, or wounded fish, is another. Back eddies, slicks, tidal rips, and current edges are more good spots. In rivers where a secondary tributary meets a major flow is also a promising intersection, especially in summer when the secondary tributary may be dumping cooler and more oxygenated water into the main flow.

Knowing what types of edges appeal to which species of fish makes a difference in fishing in current. For example, the inside bend of major tributaries is often a hotspot to troll or cast for stripers in the spring. Stripers like a point where water rushes by, so they hold

Many freshwater fishermen cast along the shorelines; points are often places to locate fish, either shallow in cool weather or deeper when the water is warm.

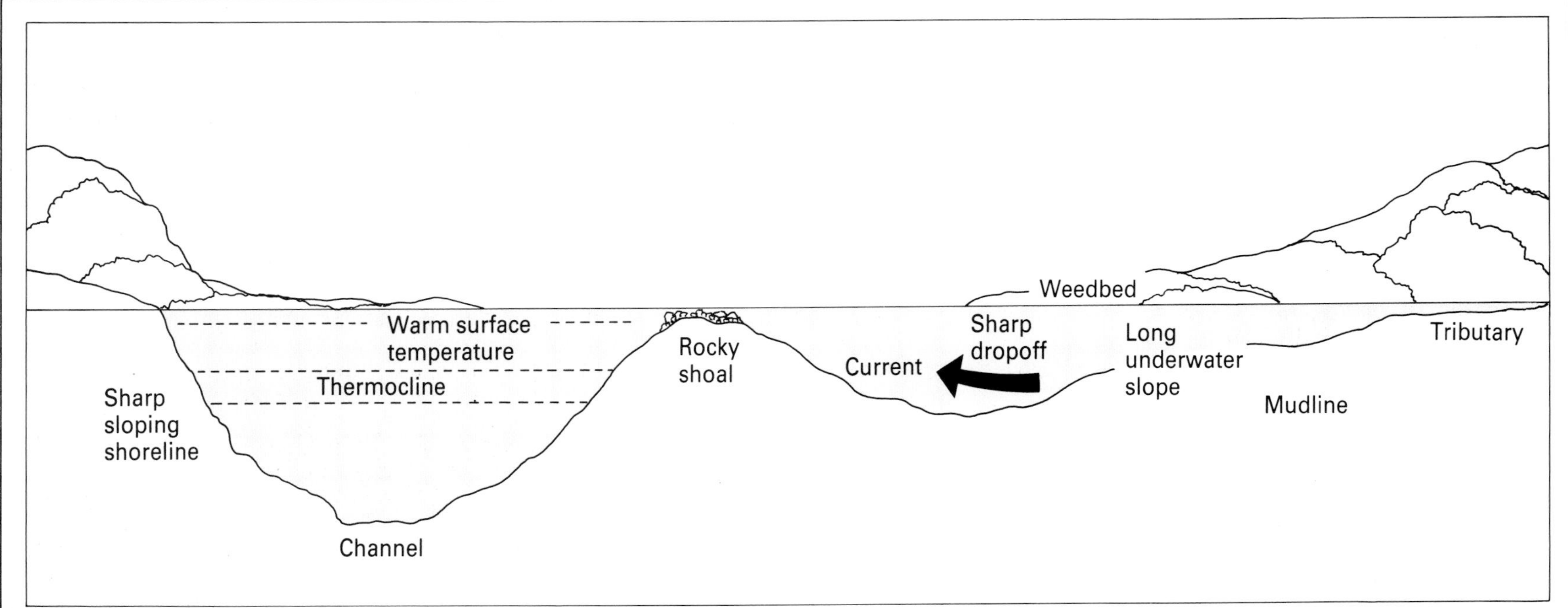

There are a number of different edge-like areas in a lake that can be attractive to fish.

on the inside bend of a channel and use this spot to ambush whatever comes around. Walleyes are a fish that are particularly known for locating along an edge, particularly along a deep-water breakline. It is common, for instance, for walleyes to move shallower in the evening to the fringes of a bar or a rock or gravel point that breaks sharply to deep water. One successful fishing tactic is to use plugs that dive to 8 or 10 feet deep and troll from deep water to the point, then go along one side and work along the edge.

Some fish are particularly known for congregating in or along the edges of vegetation. Weeds attract small baitfish and larger fish in the food chain, and they also offer protective cover. Working submerged weed lines, where the weeds end and the bottom begins to drop off to deeper water, is not only possible, but an especially effective fishing method, as well as a prime example of the edge effect. A surface example of this in saltwater is the proclivity of dolphinfish to hold around a floating weedline far offshore in the ocean; savvy anglers troll or cast around these objects with success.

Many fish use the edges of vegetative cover or other structures to hide and to ambush prey. They lurk in or by places where food is abundant and where they can lie relatively concealed to pounce on appropriate-sized forage. Some anglers refer to such feeding stations as ambush points, and, often, the closer they are to deep water, dropoffs, shelves, ledges, creek beds, channels, and the like, the better. Whether you

In a large lake or reservoir, many good places to fish, such as an old creek bed or sand bar, are flooded and not readily found without some searching.

angle for fish that prefer the confines of cover or the vastness of open water, be aware of the subtle borders and margins of these habitats and seek and fish those places.

Remember that sonar devices are a particularly valuable aid to locating fish or potential fish-holding habitat in nearly all waters. If nothing else, they tell you how much water is below your boat and help keep you out of navigational trouble. Underwater obstructions pose a problem to boaters unfamiliar with big waters. Many big waters sport shoals, sand bars, and shallow areas, even in unexpected places. But more importantly, sonar helps you locate fish or places that are likely to hold fish, and thus help ease the problem of where to find fish.

Get to know the waters you fish by studying navigation, hydrographic, or underwater contour maps, if available; by studying your sonar readings diligently; and through observant on-the-water fishing experience. It takes a combination of all three. Even the best maps often fail to pinpoint a certain underwater feature that attracts game fish. That might be a trough, for instance, near shore and created by wave action. Or it might be a slight pinnacle or mound or hump that rises off the lake or ocean floor enough to attract baitfish and thus predators, but not enough to be highlighted between charted depth-sounding information.

Whether fish roam or hide, stay deep or shallow, their habits and habitat have to be understood in order to have more than accidental or casual success.

CREATING and FISHING MANMADE STRUCTURES

Many fish are found close to structural objects of some kind, be they natural or manmade. Some of the manmade structures have resulted from accidents (sunken boats), or actions that were unintentionally beneficial for fishing (oil rigs), but many were deliberately placed (artificial reefs). The construction and planting of artificial habitat has become a very popular activity, by groups and individuals as well as by state agencies, specifically to attract fish for anglers. These structures, called 'attractors,' provide shade, shelter, and food. They concentrate small plant and animal life that attracts the intermediate-size fish that larger fish prey upon.

Above: Attractors made of brush or trees and old auto tires are commonly planted in large lakes to attract fish and enhance angling opportunities.

Right: Anglers who fish over planted structure use sonar and one or more marker buoys to return to the site.

Thus, they make good places to angle throughout the year, and especially in the summer.

In saltwater, the creation of artificial reefs is a large undertaking, and there is virtually no creation of fishing structures by individual anglers, although there is a lot of fishing done around manmade structures. In freshwater, through the planting of brushpiles in some lakes, ponds, and reservoirs that are largely devoid of cover, individual fishermen have created a habitat that attracts fish and offers open-water angling opportunities. Channel catfish, bluegill, largemouth bass, and crappie are particularly concentrated by the existence of brush and tire attractors.

In some freshwater locales, large attractor structures planted by fisheries agencies or sportsmen's clubs are well-marked and known to the general public. But many individuals plant their own. Private and commercial dock owners, for example, often plant brushpiles to provide fish habitat at arm's length. Some guides and avid fishermen plant their own brushpiles to have 'secret' fishing holes that often are very productive places. These sites are usually unmarked.

If you have a notion to create your own hotspot, check first to make sure that it is legal to do so. Some states prohibit them, though many don't. In some bodies of water you must first check with the controlling agency (municipal water supply, Corps of Engineers, etc.); a permit may be required.

Shallow flat areas, large sandy bars, and ledges adjacent to dropoffs are popular sites for planting attractors. Small trees and an accumulation of brush and limbs are the most favored attractors for individual planting. Hardwood trees last longest, though discarded Christmas trees (which are softwoods), because of their abundance, are widely used, especially for crappie shelters. Trees can be planted singly or in clusters; they must be weighted and tied down. Cinder blocks work well for weights. Tying should be done with nylon rope or nylon coated wire. In northern areas, brushpiles can be constructed on the ice and left to sink when the ice melts. Elsewhere, you must put the brush or trees on a boat (pontoon boats can be good for this), bring them to the site and then plant them. On lakes where the water level is lowered in the winter, you may be able to affix an attractor to a stump or rock which is exposed and which will be well-covered by spring. Don't plant in places where navigation may be impeded or where motors may strike the structure. Attractors are usually planted 3 to 20 feet deep.

On large bodies of water, you should use the sonar on your boat to precisely pinpoint the place to set the attractor, and use permanent landmarks as reference points to line you up when you want to return unerringly to the attractor without having to do a great deal of searching.

As for fishing the attractor sites, use minnows, jigs, and plastic worms in freshwater; light wire jigs are best because the hook can be bent to work free when it is hung. In saltwater, live and dead bait, usually fished on the bottom, are used, with or without chumming. Jigging is very common, and some trolling occurs around artificial structures in saltwater, but deep fishing, primarily when anchored ratter than while drifting, is generally preferred. Casting with plugs and flies, on or close to the surface, is possible if fish can be chummed up from deep water.

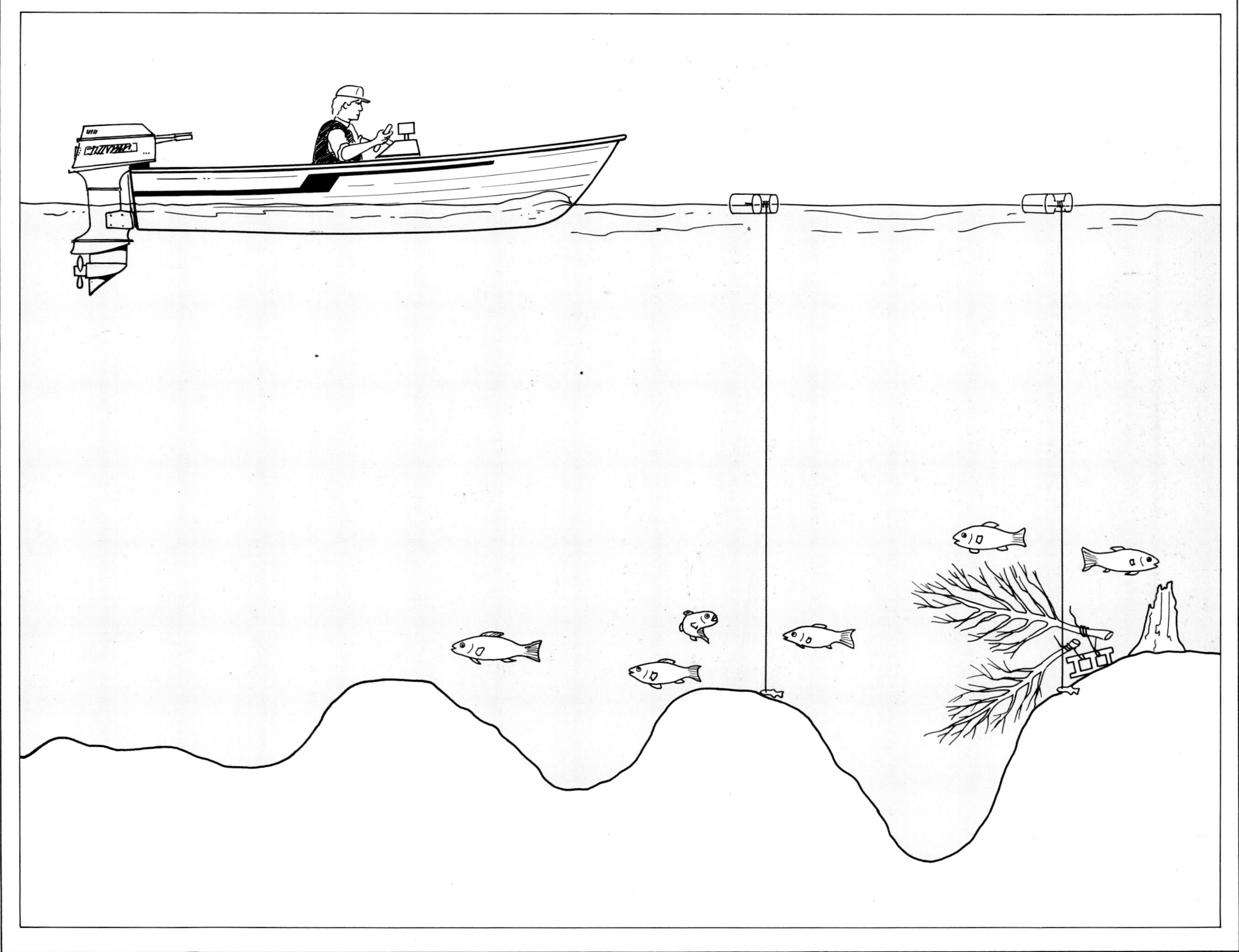

CASTING

Being able to cast precisely is a major component of angling success for nearly all situations in which launching and retrieving some object is an essential activity. Obviously, then, casting technique is something that all anglers should master fully. This isn't difficult, and most fishermen have basic casting procedures down adequately, though more practice wouldn't hurt. Often, however, the finer points of casting need sharpening.

The actual casts made with spinning, spin-casting, and bait-casting tackle are very similar, but fly casting is not because the principle is different. In the former, a weighted object propels a light line (usually nylon monofilament). In fly casting, a weighted line propels a virtually weightless object (the fly).

With spinning, spin-casting, and bait-casting tackle, the basic casts used are the overhead, sidearm, and underhand casts. In most types of fishing the overhead cast sees perhaps 75 percent usage, while the other casts are infrequently employed. In some situations, however, either because of the nature of the cover in which some species are found or because of the necessity of accurate lure placement, there is a regular need to utilize all three of these casts and perhaps some others.

Although principles differ between casting a fly, shown here, and casting other lures, the need for good technique and accuracy is common to all efforts.

Overhead cast

The wrist and forearm do all the work in this cast, using the top section of the rod for thrust. The cast begins with the rod low and pointed at the target. Bring the rod up crisply to a point slightly beyond vertical position, where flex in the rod tip will carry it back; then, without hesitating, start the forward motion sharply, releasing the lure halfway between the rod's vertical and horizontal positions. The entire casting action should be a smooth, flowing motion; you are doing more than just hauling back and heaving.

Sidearm and underhand casts

The sidearm cast is essentially similar in motion to the overhead, except for horizontal, rather than vertical, movement. The sidearm cast can be dangerous if performed next to another angler in a small boat, so you must be mindful of the position of your companions at all times. To cast underhand, hold the rod waist-high, angled halfway between vertical and horizontal positions. The rod must be flexed up, then down, then up again to gain momentum for the lure through the flex of the rod. Many rods, incidentally, are too stiff to permit this kind of casting.

Short-distance casts

There are a few other casts used in special situations. One, employed in tight quarters or for short ranges, is a flip cast, which is something of a cross between the sidearm and underhand cast (different from flipping). It starts with the rod horizontal to your side, but you only bring it backward a short distance and then make a loop with the tip so that the tip springs around in a 270-degree arc and flips the lure straight out and low. This cast is used for short-distance (under 20 feet) work in areas where you can't bring your rod up or back for a conventional cast. It is also almost impossible to accomplish while sitting down in a boat.

Another is the bow-and-arrow cast, which is a short-distance cast used with a limber rod in tight quarters in which you hold a lure by its rear hook in one hand and simultaneously release the hook and line from a freespooled reel. This cast is rarely used currently in actual angling situations.

Flipping A popular casting technique, however, is flipping, which is done primarily with bait casting tackle, but also with spinning. This is essentially a controlled short-casting technique used by standing anglers in close quarters for presenting a moderately heavy jig or plastic worm in a quiet, accurate manner to cover that cannot be properly worked by a lure cast from a long distance away. A long stiff rod and fairly heavy line are customarily used in heavy cover, although the principle can be adapted to other situations. Steelhead anglers, for example, use

Left: The lure is still in midair as this angler completes a short sidearm cast to bring his offering close to near-shore brush.

long, light rods and light line to flip small lures or bait into midriver pools for drift fishing.

To flip, let out about 7 to 9 feet of line from rod tip to lure. Strip line off the reel until your free hand and rod hand are fully extended away from each other; this will give you 5 to 7 feet of line in your free hand. Raise the rod tip and swing the lure back toward you under the rod. The motion utilizes wrist action, not elbow or shoulder movement. The bait swings back toward you and when it reaches the top of its pendulum-like swing, flick your rod-holding wrist to direct the lure toward its target. Lower the rod tip, and

Below: Flipping is a specialized method of making a quiet, close-quarters presentation; it is principally used in bass fishing.

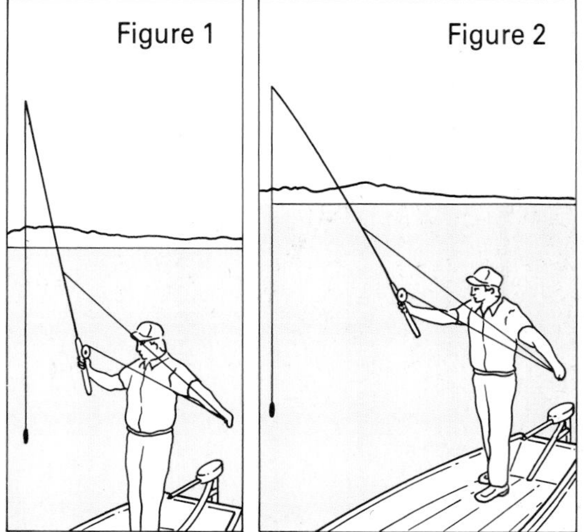

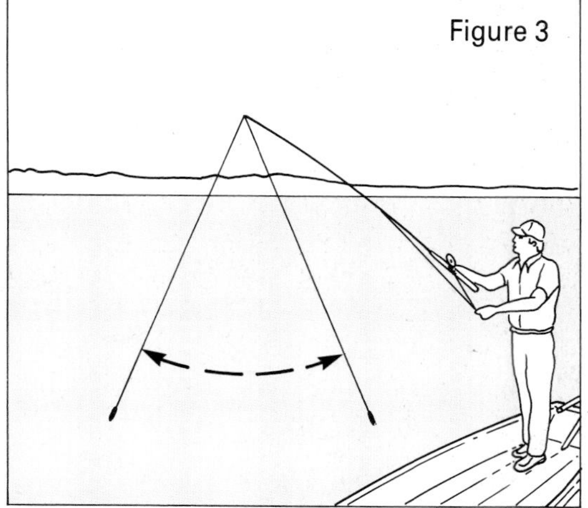

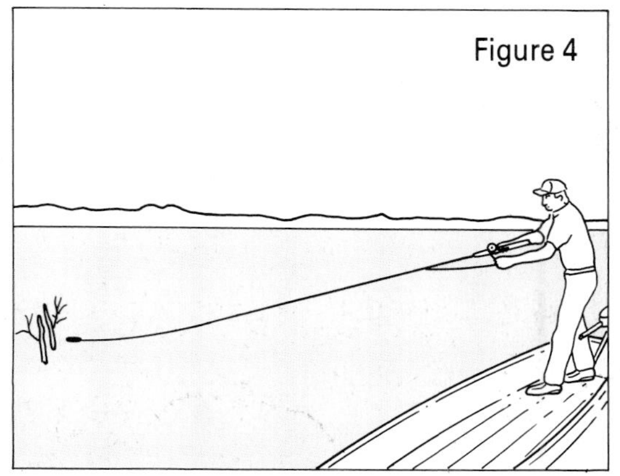

Casting in surf

Surf fishermen cast both in a conventional overhand manner for short distances, and use a sweeping sidearm cast or a pendulum cast for long tosses. The pendulum cast starts with the angler in a baseball player-at-bat body stance and the casting weight is hung several feet below the rod tip. Using primarily wrist movement, swing the weight in a pendulum motion backward and forward several times, raising the weight till the line is parallel with the ground. With the weight at the top of its backswing, come forward sharply with the rod, twisting your hip and shoulders.

Fly casting

This has the aura of being difficult but it needn't be. It does require an adroit combination of coordinated wrist and forearm movement, but brute strength isn't necessary, nor is a lot of wrist action or quick, whippy rod movements. There are two primary casts –the overhead and the roll, with the former predominant.

Opposite top: The overhead cast, fly fishing.

Opposite bottom: A river fly fisherman makes a backcast; just as the line unfurls behind him, he will bring the rod forward to send his fly on its mission.

Below: To execute a pendulum cast while surf fishing: Start by swinging the sinker in the opposite direction of the intended cast (1). The pendulum movement of the sinker brings it back in the direction of the cast (2). When the sinker reaches its highest point, the caster pivots in the direction of the cast (3) and whips the rod in a baseball-like swing, bringing the sinker around and behind him. As the sinker nears its highest point behind the caster (4), he leans forward as he brings the rod upward, ready to release the cast. With the rod pointing skyward at a 45-degree angle, the cast is released. The caster holds this position until the sinker reaches its destination.

The need to achieve great distance, and the use of long rods, separates surf casting from other forms of casting.

let line flow through your free hand. Extend your rod arm if necessary to reach the target, and keep the line in your hand until the lure enters the water. When you retrieve the lure to move it to another spot, lower the rod tip and point it toward the lure, grab the line between reel and first guide with your free hand and strip it back while lifting up on your rod (similar to the double hauling technique used by fly casters). Swing the lure out and back and send it forward again to the next object.

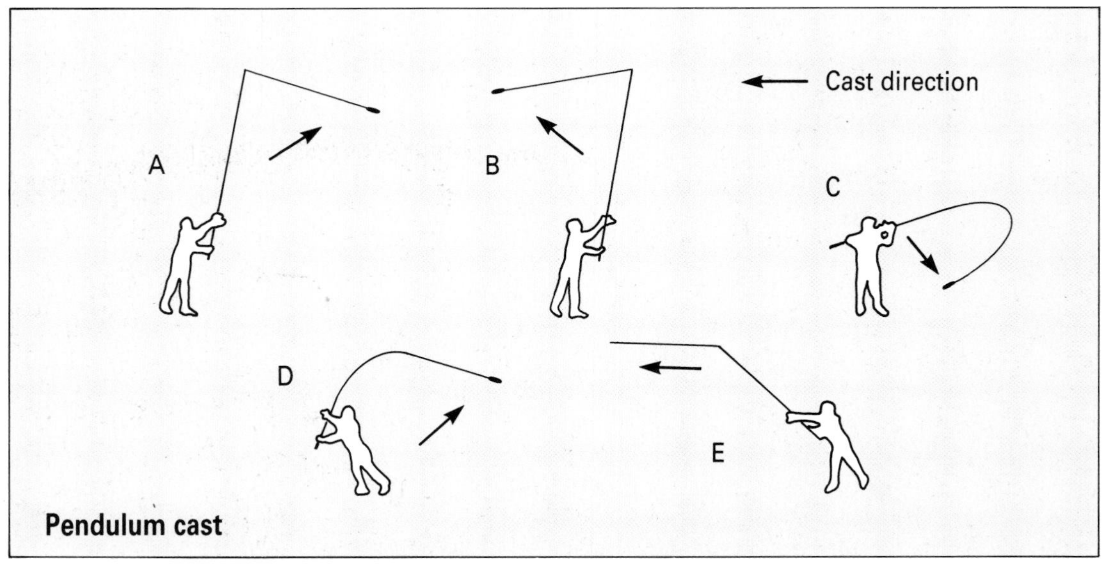

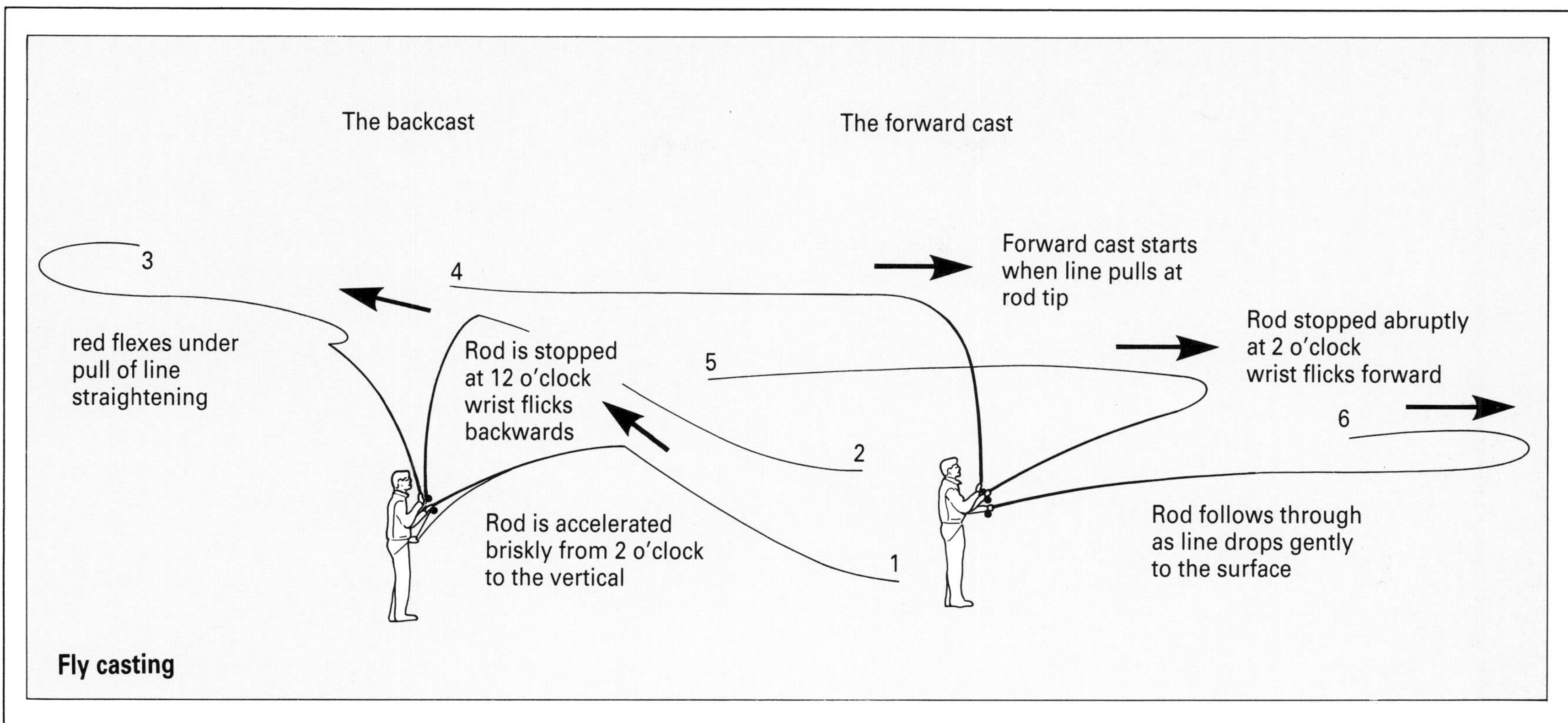

The backcast
The forward cast
3
4
red flexes under pull of line straightening
Rod is stopped at 12 o'clock wrist flicks backwards
5
2
Rod is accelerated briskly from 2 o'clock to the vertical
1
Forward cast starts when line pulls at rod tip
Rod stopped abruptly at 2 o'clock wrist flicks forward
6
Rod follows through as line drops gently to the surface

Fly casting

The overhead cast has both forward and backward movements and you can't present the fly ahead of you properly without having made an adequate back cast. Beginning with the fly line and leader extended straight out in front of you and the rod in an approximate 2 o'clock position, raise the rod decisively to the 12 o'clock position and flick your wrist sharply, allowing the rod to go no further than an 11 o'clock position. This action brings the fly line and leader off the water and sends it in the air behind you. Pause for an instant to let the line straighten out, and just as it does, bring the rod forward to the 2 o'clock position again. A tight loop should unfurl and, as the line straightens and the fly reaches its destination, follow-through by lowering the rod tip. The forward casting movement is akin to that of hammering a nail into the wall, and it is a matter of timing to know when the rod is loaded properly to provide the optimum forward impetus.

This overhead cast is used for short and long distances, although as distance to be cast increases, there is a tendency for many anglers to try to push at the end of the forward cast, or wait too long for line to unfurl in the back cast. Shooting tapers help achieve distance, as does employing coils of line in one hand for shooting or using the double-haul technique.

In the double haul, the angler uses his non-rod hand to give some speed to the pickup and forward momentum of the fly line. It is a technique that takes practice to master, as the motions have to be blended properly together. Assuming that you cast with the right hand and hold fly line in your left, you would accomplish this as follows: hold the line firmly in your left hand ahead of the reel, and a moment before bringing the rod up (in the overhead casting maneuver) to lift line off the water, pull sharply on the line, bringing it down to your hip in your left hand as the line flows backward; as the line straightens out, bring the left hand up to the reel and, at the same time as your right hand begins to power the rod forward, pull sharply on the line with your left hand; as the rod comes forward, release the line to shoot extra line forward through the guides.

The roll cast is a very practical cast for both making fly presentations at a distance of up to 40 to 50 feet and also as a means of laying out line to pick it up for a standard or double-haul cast. In a roll cast there is no back casting motion per se, and the line is not lifted off the water as in an overhead cast. To roll cast, lift the rod tip up steadily but not quickly until it is just past a vertical position and at a point where there is a curved bow of line extending from the rod tip behind you, and then bring the rod sharply forward and downward. The last motion brings the line rolling forward with leader and fly following.

Although not actually a casting function, the technique of mending fly line is used in flowing water to give the fly a natural drift, and is something not done with other lines. Mending is a method of lifting and flipping the belly of fly line upstream so that the fly does not drag in the current.

The roll cast is fairly simple to execute if you don't rush it. Starting with the fly line on the water (1), gradually lift the rod up until it is just past the vertical position (2), then punch the rod tip forward (3) and follow through.

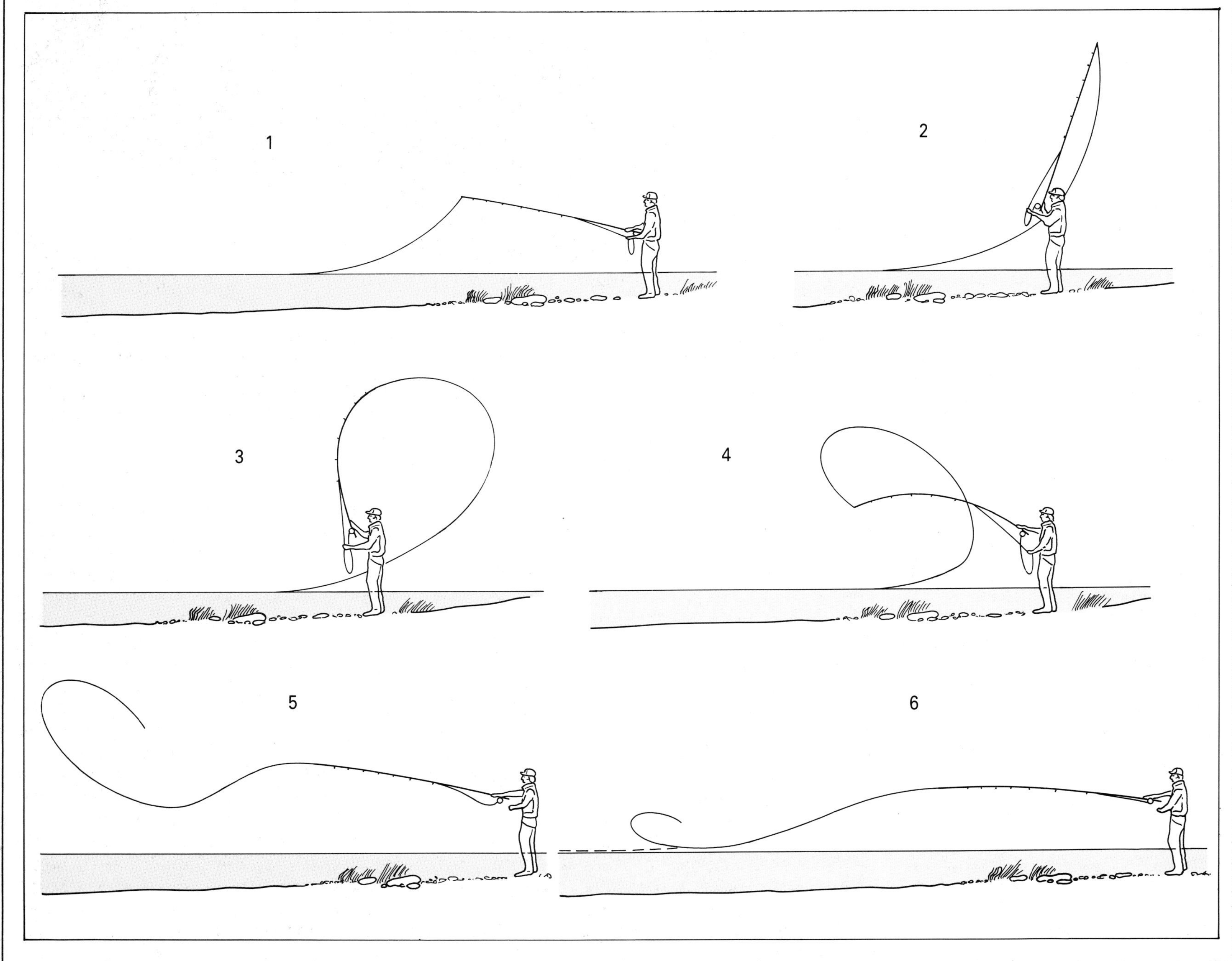

Being accurate is less critical in open-water environs than in places where there are many objects. If this angler doesn't have good casting control and accurate placement, he will be picking his lure out of the tree branches often.

Accuracy and distance

Knowing the mechanics is the most basic part of casting, but one has to also develop the skill of being accurate (even in adverse conditions, such as wind). Getting the right length of line out and placing it properly is the key with all tackle. With spinning tackle you should use your index finger to control the cast and water entry. With bait-casting gear you do the same via delicate thumb control on the reel spool. Raising your rod tip at the last moment helps soften lure impact, but is not reliable as a means of controlling accuracy. In many situations, especially in freshwater, the first cast to a prospective fish lair is often the most important one, so it pays to make each cast count.

A lot of people feel that casting with two hands, incidentally, is preferable to casting with one, and find that they are able to obtain greater accuracy and distance this way. Too many anglers strive for distance alone, however, especially in open-water situations, and this can be a mistake. A move to longer fishing rods has occurred recently, partly as a response to better reels and line, and many anglers have discovered that it is easier now to toss a lure further than they ordinarily used to. But distance is a two-edged phenomenon.

Long casts aren't always necessary but there are times and situations when they can be advantageous. One of those is when trying to make a presentation to spooky fish, as might occur in shallow, clear water. One might also need a long cast when it isn't possible to maneuver a boat close to a particular location, or when trying to make a presentation to schooling fish, which are characteristically feeding actively and moving quickly out of casting range. A long cast is also useful where deep diving lures are concerned, particularly when trying to reach a certain depth level and keep a lure at that depth for the majority of a retrieve, or when fishing parallel to a deep bank.

On the other hand, you also run a very real risk of losing a fish that strikes your lure at long-range distances because distance and line stretch. This is more of a factor with nylon monofilament than with cofilament line, and may keep you from setting the hook properly, which can result in the fish throwing the hook or pulling free from it, or from setting it as well as you would with a shorter line. Also, you can't control the fight as well since a good fish will be able to run for cover. Lastly, by unnecessarily casting long distances and covering a lot of water through most of the retrieve, you ultimately squander a lot of fishing time during the day. To compensate for these problems and to help minimize losing fish, make short but accurate casts where appropriate, and pay more attention to hook-setting efforts.

RETRIEVING

There's a lot more to productive fishing than just possessing a well-stocked tackle box. Recognizing the abilities of a lure, using it to its potential, and injecting a dose of angling savvy are all vital factors. When casting to any kind of fish, what you do after you get the lure in the water is critical. Proper retrieval and presentation often separate the casters from the catchers.

The keys to successful retrieval of most lures are depth control, action, and speed, all of which vary in importance depending on the situation and the lure. Achieving the proper depth is perhaps the most important factor, since you can't hope to catch fish without getting your offering to the fish's level. In the case of many lures, the ability to achieve a certain depth is a function of the design of the lure and the way in which it is used.

How to work your lure or fly to get it in front of fish and be appealing is one of the basic keys to fishing success.

Speed is often the most ignored factor. In cold water it's best to fish slowly; speed up the retrieve in warmer water. Fish bottom-crawling lures slowly at all times. Retrieval speed is influenced by the diameter of line, type of lure, current, and retrieve ratio of your reel. To some extent, speed is a factor in the retrieval of all lures. Moderate speed for plugs generally catches the least fish, with more succumbing to high-or low-speed retrieves. Some lures can be retrieved too fast, at which point they lose their tight action and run off to the side. Achieving the proper action, of course, is a necessity in order for the lure to have its maximum attractiveness.

As noted in the previous section, every lure is designed to do a certain function. But that function must be coordinated with the current fishing conditions, and achieved through proper lure retrieval. Let's review specific retrieval techniques then, as they apply to the major categories of lures.

Spinners

In moving water you generally don't fish a spinner downstream, but cast it upstream at a quartering angle (ten o'clock viewed from right, two o'clock viewed from left). The lure is tumbled by the swift water and also reeled forward at the same time. Fish spinners as slowly as you can under the circumstances; you should be able to feel the blade revolve with a sensitive rod. The depth of retrieve can be altered by raising or lowering the rod, or changing the speed of retrieval. Though spinners receive criticism for frequent hangups, this is often a matter of misuse. In streams it is important to get the lure working the moment it hits the water. Hesitation often means hung spinners, particularly when casting across-stream in a fast flow.

In lakes, spinners can be cast parallel to the bank and allowed to sink to the bottom, then retrieved just slowly enough to rotate the blade and keep the lure swimming over the bottom.

Some lures, like a spinnerbait, can be retrieved close to the surface and worked around, over, and through such cover as lily pads.

Spinnerbaits A spinnerbait is a good lure for fishing in and around cover, and its appearance evidently triggers a reflexive strike. Lily pads, grass, stumps, brush, treetops, boat docks, rock piles, logs, and similar fish-holding places can all be effectively worked with a spinnerbait, and shallow water is generally where they are most productive.

The most common technique of fishing a spinnerbait is to retrieve it close enough to the surface so that you can see the lure through the water on the retrieve. The depth of water fished below the surface ranges from a few inches to several feet, depending on the clarity of the water and the structure present. When working the shallows, begin retrieving a spinnerbait the moment it hits the water for maximum effectiveness.

Occasionally spinnerbaits are retrieved out of sight along the bottom, or fished very deep by fluttering them down sharply sloping shorelines, dropoffs, rocky ledges, and the like, using a short-armed spinnerbait, and working it in a series of short hops or in a jigging-like motion.

For fishing weed beds and weedlines it is sometimes effective to crawl a spinnerbait slowly over the tops of the grass, when it is submerged a few feet. For grass beds with definable weedlines, however, cast parallel to the edge or bring the lure over the top and let it flutter down the edge. For lily pads it is best to work the channel-like openings, but don't be afraid to throw

Cast a spinner up and across current and retrieve it slowly as the current carries it along.

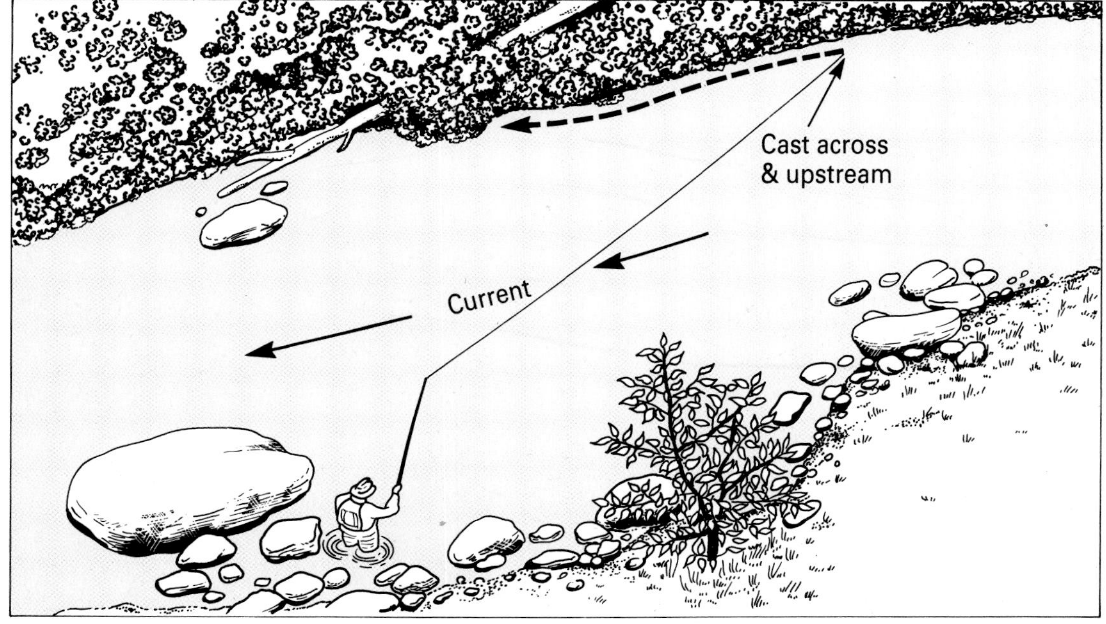

Though the common tactic is to work a spinnerbait quite shallow, it can be very effective when fluttered deep, perhaps along a rock ledge or bluff.

Keeping the rod at a low angle will help diving plugs achieve greater depth.

into thick clusters, work the bait in pockets, ease it over the pads, and drop it in another pocket.

Spoons

Retrieving spoons is a pretty straightforward endeavor since the action is derived from their size and contoured shape. Although spoons are primarily retrieved shallow, they can be fished at varied levels by letting them sink via the countdown method (count at a cadence of one second per foot) and then reeled steadily with an occasional twitch to alter the action momentarily. The heavier the spoon the deeper it sinks during retrieval. In retrieving spoons the most important factor is to establish the optimum swimming speed; in other words, reel the lure at the speed that produces the best wobbling action. A weedless type of spoon is mainly fished in freshwater in fairly heavy cover, such as vegetation, and is retrieved slowly, with occasionally an added pumping or twitching motion.

Diving plugs

You must know how deep any diving plug runs to be effective with it. Diving abilities depend on the lure, the diameter of line used with it, and the speed of retrieve. It is not necessary to crank the handles as fast as possible to achieve maximum depth with diving plugs. In fact, some lures lose depth when worked too fast. A moderate pace of retrieve will keep the lure as deep as it will go depending on your line. The heavier the line you use, the greater its diameter, which means it offers more resistance to the water and inhibits lure diving. The lighter your line, the deeper a diving plug will go. If you are flinging long casts, this will make a difference. Current, if it is present, will affect diving ability. Lures retrieved with the current or sideways to it don't run as deep as those worked into it.

Bottom scratching is usually critical in most fishing situations with diving plugs. Keep a plug rooting along the bottom, over objects, and along impediments. This is no problem with the right floating/diving crankbait. For the sinking version, let it settle to the bottom or count it down to a particular level and make your retrieve at a rate slow enough to keep the plug on or as close to the bottom as possible.

Floating/diving plugs are exceedingly buoyant, a feature that adds a different dimension to their fishability. If you stop your retrieve, these plugs will bob toward the surface like a cork. You can take advantage of this feature in your fishing techniques. A pull-pause action is easily accomplished by retrieving in the standard fashion and stopping momentarily, then repeating the procedure.

There are many places that are well worked with diving plugs, including open-water locales and structural objects. With objects, fish to, from, over, and around them, and don't be concerned about bumping the lures against them. Where possible, cast beyond targets so that when you retrieve, the lure will be able to get down to its running depth before it reaches the target. As with many lures, a key pointer for successful diving plug usage is proper positioning.

The bow angler is walking his stick bait around a bush, which is a skillful retrieval technique that often triggers a strike.

Surface lures

Poppers generally are worked slowly. The actual popping or forward chugging motion is made by jerking your rod up, or back, not by reeling line in, to achieve the proper movement. Keep the rod low and pointed toward the lure; this helps reduce slack to work the lure well and puts one in the best possible position to react to a strike. When you pop this plug you can do so with varying degrees of emphasis. Seldom is it worthwhile to jerk the rod hard so as to create the loudest possible commotion. If it appears that bass are feeding fairly actively, you can shorten the time between pops, but generally it is best to maintain long pauses, of several seconds' duration, between them. Obviously, poppers are time-consuming lures to fish, and do not cover a lot of area very well.

With **wobbling surface plugs** the common retrieval method is a straight, continuous motion. It is a worthwhile technique, however, to make the lure stop and go at times, or to give it a pull pause motion, particularly as it swims next to an object. Try to resist the urge to set the hook the instant a fish slashes at this lure and momentarily wait to feel the fish take your plug before setting the hook sharply. If the fish misses altogether, try stopping the lure in its tracks and twitching it a little, then moving it a bit and stopping. **Propellered plugs** are usually retrieved by using in a jiggling, jerking, pausing motion that is erratic and representative of a struggling or crippled baitfish. Point the rod down, utilize the rod tip to effectively impart action, and make your wrists do the work. Retrieve either quickly or slowly, the latter perhaps when prospecting for unseen fish and the former when casting to a school of fish.

A **buzz bait**, which is also a propellered creation, is at its very best in areas with thick cover. Worked on a steady, moderate retrieve, it is employed primarily for freshwater bass in emergent vegetation that is not too thick to prevent free lure passage, submerged vegetation that comes fairly

The key to walking the dog is an adroit combination of rod tip twitching and reel handle turning that makes a stick bait turn repeatedly from one side to the other.

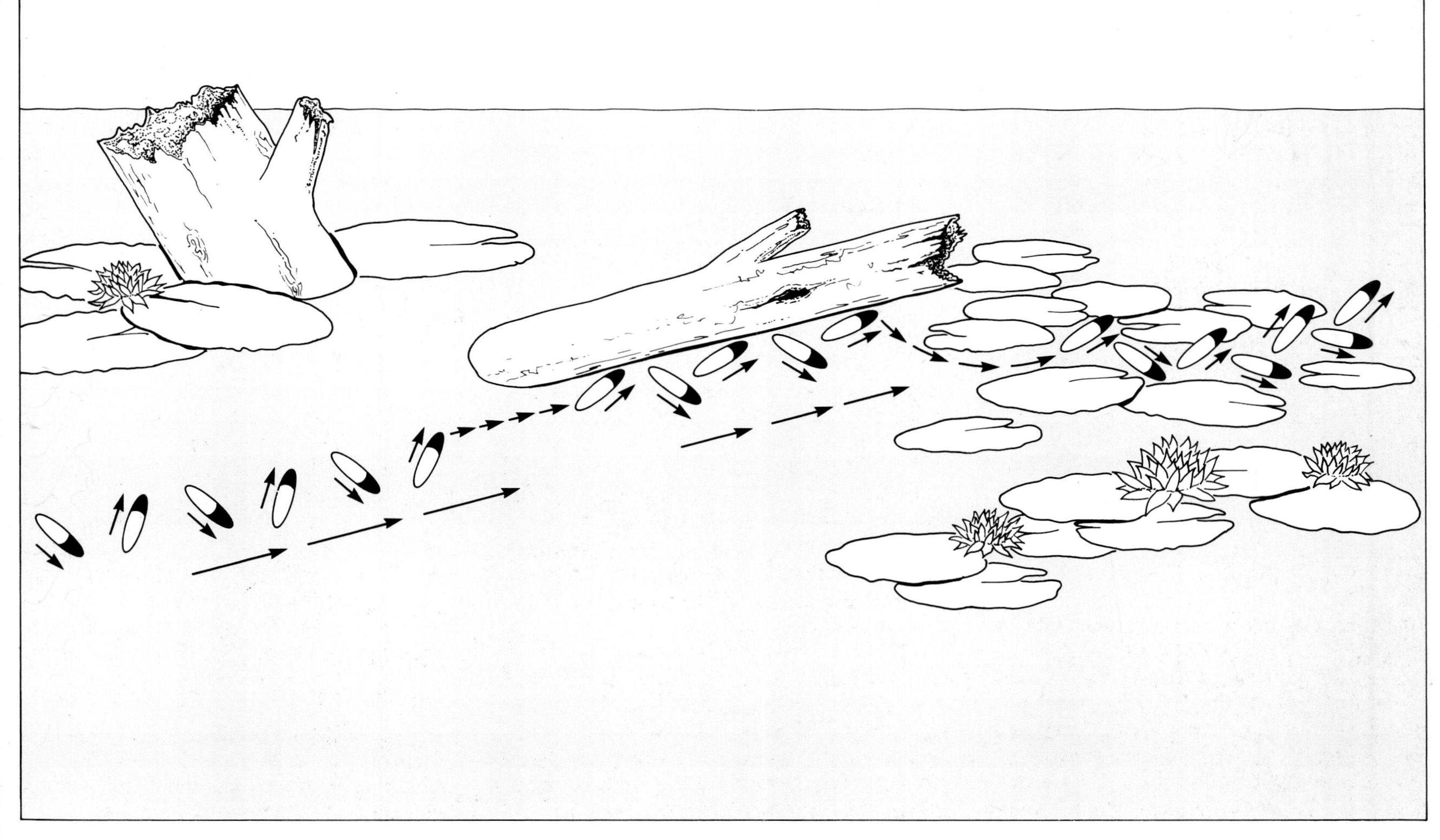

close to the surface, around brush, in timber, and around fallen wood. The closer you can work a buzz bait to such cover, the better.

A **stick bait** can't be tossed out with abandon and then cranked back in. The secret to its effectiveness lies in a masterful retrieval technique. All of the action must be supplied by the angler, making the stick bait foremost among lures for which retrieval skill is of paramount importance.

The principal stick bait retrieve, called 'walking the dog,' causes the lure to step from side to side. To accomplish it, begin with the rod tip at a low angle, preferably pointing toward the water. This permits a desirable angle of pull and allows the head of the lure to lurch in and out of the water most effectively. The all-important lure action is achieved through an adroit combination of rod-tip twitching and reel-handle turning. Make a continuous series of short jerks while simultaneously advancing your reel handle perhaps half a turn with each rod-tip twitch to take up slack. By slowing the pace, you widen the lure's path of travel; by speeding it up, you narrow it. A skilled stick bait angler can just about keep the lure in the same place, making it nod from side to side while barely moving forward.

An advanced technique of retrieving stick baits is one known as 'half-stepping.' This is the peak of stick bait retrieval skill and is a technique that can drive a fish wild. In the half-step, a stick bait moves repeatedly to one side instead of from side to side. To half-step a stick bait, first jerk the rod tip to bring the lure in the desired direction. Then barely nudge the rod tip, a maneuver that doesn't advance the bait, but causes it to turn its head just slightly outward. Now jerk the rod tip as before and the lure will dart back in the same direction it last headed. Nudge the rod once again, then jerk it. Again the plug will head inward.

Floating/diving lures These are most effectively worked in a deliberately erratic fashion to imitate a crippled baitfish, but this is one particular type of lure where the action you put into fishing it is directly proportional to the results.

The objective is to make a floater/diver gyrate as enticingly as possible in a stationary position. Keep the rod tip pointed low toward the water and use your wrist to move the rod. Jiggle the rod tip in a controlled, not frantic, fashion. Then jerk the lure back toward you a few inches. Then gyrate it some more, all the time reeling in an appropriate amount of line to minimize slack. This is not very difficult to accomplish if you have a rod with a fairly soft tip.

Another way to use this lure type is on a straight retrieve, allowing it to run

Drifting a visible dry fly on the suface is the usual picture that people have of fly fishing, but sometimes it is necessary to use a nymph, as this angler is doing, making a short drift near the bottom on the edge of the swift current.

Keeping his rod up, a summertime bass fisherman slowly crawls a plastic worm along the bottom.

a foot or two beneath the surface. This is more like using it in the style of a diving plug. Still another retrieval method is making it run just below the surface in a series of short jerk pause movements, running it forward half a foot with each motion. This retrieve is more in the style of darters, those plugs that float but have no significant surface action, and are used solely just below the surface.

Flies

The art of retrieving flies is a fairly precise one in many circumstances but is nearly always dependent upon a proper cast and often upon a delicate presentation as well. The latter is especially important in small stream or river pool fishing for wary trout, when a dry fly must alight gently and the line or leader should not slap the water to alarm the fish. In flowing water especially, where the drift of the fly is a major component of the presentation, the fly often must be placed in a proper place upstream in order to drift into the right location. Similarly, on a saltwater tidal flat, a streamer must be presented ahead of a moving or feeding fish in order to be retrieved across its path. This seems rather obvious, but the point is that in order to effect a proper retrieve, the fly must be placed properly at the outset.

In a stillwater environment, a dry fly is usually cast to a rising fish or to a likely fish lair, where it may be allowed to rest momentarily or be slowly skimmed across the surface by stripping line in short segments. In moving water, a dry fly is cast directly upstream or up and across stream and allowed to float with the current while slack line is gradually picked up during the float. Occasionally extra line will be flipped out to minimize drag (called 'mending'). Drag occurs when the fly floats either faster or slower than the current, and the ideal is to effect a drag-free float for the most natural-looking presentation.

Wet flies and nymphs, which are primarily used in current, are fished below the surface and often near or close to the bottom. They are primarily cast up and across current, sometimes more up than across in order to get the fly deep. Nymphs are fished on a tight line, often using a clearly visible strike indicator on the leader butt or end of fly line to detect strikes. They are usually fished on a free drift without drag but sometimes are jerked just a bit. Fish sometimes strike at the end of a drift as the fly line straightens and the angler is about to pull the fly out of the water to cast upstream again.

Streamer flies are meant to represent small fish, so they are retrieved in short darting or jerking movements, usually caused by stripping fly line in with your free hand. In current they are cast up and across stream, directly across stream, and downstream, and stripped while they drift. Elsewhere they are allowed to sink before the stripping retrieval begins, and this retrieval here may constitute foot-long strips, fine twitching movements, or short pulls.

Other so-called flies, fished on the surface, include an assortment of swimming or popping bugs. Poppers are fished with a pull pause line-stripping motion or the twitch of a fly rod tip. More vigorous strips produce loud noises while slight twitches produce light popping sounds. Sometimes it is worthwhile to fish these flies in quick darting motions. The same is true of swimming bugs.

Plastic worms Many people have trouble getting the retrieval down right when fishing plastic worms. To retrieve a plastic worm you should begin with your rod butt and arms close to your body, and with the rod held perpendicular to you and parallel to the water. Raise the rod from this position (we'll call it 9 o'clock) upward, extending it between a 45-degree and 60-degree angle, which would mean moving it from 9 o'clock to 10:30 or 11. As you raise the rod, the worm is lifted up off the bottom and swims forward, falling to a new position. Make this motion slowly, so the worm does not hop too far off the bottom and swims slowly. When your rod reaches that upward position, drop it back to its original position while at the same time retrieving slack line. Keep your motions slow. When you encounter some resistance, as would happen when crawling it over a log or through a bush, first gently try to work the worm along, and if this fails, try to hop the worm along with short flickers of the rod tip. The worm should usually be on the bottom, or right near it, although occasionally you may find it beneficial not to hug the bottom exactly, but to swim the worm slowly just off the bottom or above submerged cover.

JIGGING

A jig is not a throw-it-out-and-reel-it-back-in kind of lure, one that can catch fish in spite of the abilities of the person using it. A fisherman has to put some work into making a jig catch fish, and into being able to detect strikes. There is a bit of a knack to jigging, too. Good jig fishermen have that certain feel for what is happening to their lure, and are razor sharp at detecting and responding to strikes. To the inexperienced, fishing with such an individual while attempting to duplicate his success can be exasperating.

The key to jigging success is establishing contact with your lure, getting and keeping it where the fish are, and using the right rod to feel a strike. The greatest concern is often how deep you need to fish a particular jig, and how effective you are at doing that. Jigs excel at being on or close to the bottom, which is where the majority of jig-caught freshwater and saltwater fish are found. They also are productive for covering the area in between in vertical presentations.

It's usually important to maintain contact with the bottom, and to do so by fishing relatively slowly. Let the jig fall freely until the line goes slack. Reel up slack and lift the jig off the bottom. Once you are on the bottom, you need to maintain contact with it. Assuming that you have cast your jig out, let it settle to the bottom, and are now retrieving it toward you, you should keep it working in short hops along the bottom as long as the terrain and length of line out enable you to do so. If you are in a boat and drifting, the jig will eventually start sweeping upward and away from you and the bottom as you drift, unless it is very heavy, so you need to pay out more line occasionally until the angle of your line has changed significantly, then reel in and drop the jig back down again.

Choosing the right weight lure to use is critical to most types of jigging. The ideal is to have a lure that gets to the bottom and stays there under normal conditions, but which is not too large to be imposing to bass. Most anglers who fail to reach bottom not only don't use the right retrieval technique or compensate for wind or current, but also use too light a jig for getting down to the bottom under the conditions that they face.

Sometimes it is necessary to swim a jig by pumping it slowly and reeling, never actually letting it hop along the bottom. Other times it may be necessary to slowly drag it. When fishing a moderately sloping shoreline or point, for example, you should slowly pull the lure a little bit off the bottom, let it settle down while keeping in contact with it, take up the slack, and repeat this. When working a ledge, or a sharply sloping shoreline, slowly pull the lure over the structure until it begins to fall, let it settle, and then repeat. Don't hop the jig up quickly here, as it will fall out and away from the bottom and likely miss a good deal of the important terrain. With some jigs, such as grubs, it is sometimes a good technique to make them jump quickly off the bottom rather than make short hops. You can also swim a jig on the edges of cover by reeling it slowly across the bottom and giving it occasional darting movements with manipulation of your rod tip. The majority of strikes while jigging come as the bait falls back down, so be alert for a strike then and keep both a good feel, and an eye, on your line to detect this.

Establishing and keeping contact with the bottom is a critical element of jigging. Jigs should usually be fished slowly, and most strikes come as the lure falls.

Use short, slow hops to crawl a jig down a ledge.

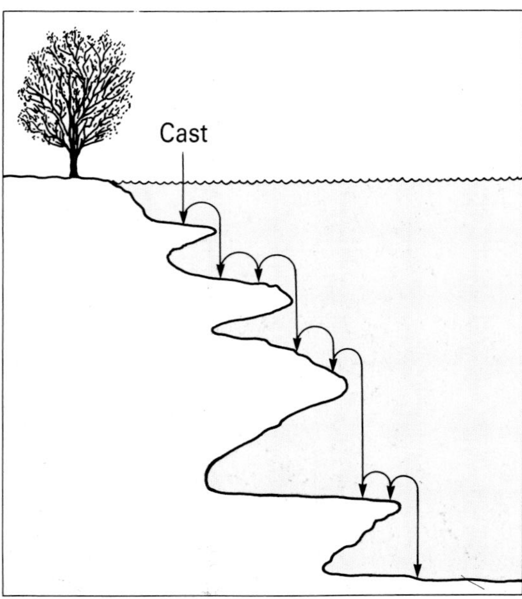

Jigs also have a lot of value in rivers and where there is current. In a fair amount of current you should cast upstream or up-and-across-stream, engage the line-pickup system as soon as the lure splashes down, reel up slack and try to keep the line taut by letting the jig drift or by reeling in slack to achieve a natural drift. You virtually fish a jig in quick water the same way a fly angler works a nymph, keeping slack out and rod tip up, and feeling the lure as it bounces along. In deep, swift current, you actually need to swim the jig a bit by pumping the rod tip.

Jigging vertically

This, of course, is especially useful when fishing through the ice or when angling for suspended fish in open water. Here, both leadhead jigs and metal or lead spoons are used and you needn't maintain bottom contact, though you might start at the bottom and jig your way upward. Sometimes it's necessary to get to a particular depth and regularly jig at that spot.

If you know what depth to fish you can let the desired length of line out and commence jigging, never reeling in any line and only paying line out if you begin to drift. Here's one way to know how much line you're letting out.

Reel the jig up to the rod tip, stick the rod tip on the surface, let go of the jig, and raise your rod tip up to eye level, then stop the fall of the jig. If eye level is 6 feet above the surface, your jig will now be 6 feet deep. Lower rod tip to the surface and do this again. Now you've let out 12 feet of line. Continue until the desired length is

In moving water, jigs are fished similar to nymphs, being bumped and bounced along rather than being hopped off the bottom. This angler will fish the back eddy and edge of swift water, but not the fastest current.

out. With a level-wind reel with a freely revolving line guide you can measure the amount of line that is let out with each side-to-side movement of the line guide, then multiply this by the number of times the guide travels back and forth. If you use a reel that doesn't have such a guide, you can strip line off the spool in 1-foot (or 18-inch) increments until the desired length is out. Another method is to countdown the lure's descent. A falling rate of one foot per second is standard and may be accurate for medium-weight jigs, but you should check the lure's rate of fall in a controlled situation first to ensure accuracy.

For some vertical jigging you may need to let your lure fall to the bottom, then jig it up toward the surface a foot or two at a time. Bring the lure off the bottom and reel in the slack, then jig it there three or four times before retrieving another few feet of line and jigging the lure again. Repeat this until the lure is near the surface. The only problem here is that you don't usually know exactly how deep a fish is when you do catch one, and you can't just strip out the appropriate length of line and be at the proper level.

Discerning a strike

When jigging, it can be difficult to discern a strike because so many fish don't slam a jig when they take it. Certainly some do, and there's no question then that a fish has struck, but in most light-jig usage where small fish are sought, something just a little 'different' happens that signals a strike. That difference is often barely perceptible. The job of detection is made even less obvious by the fact that most strikes come when a jig is falling, which is often when there is a slight amount of slack in the line. If you fail to detect the strike quickly enough the fish may reject the lure or you'll be too late to set the hook properly.

In a sense, it's good to tight-line a jig backward as it falls, but not with so much tension to make it fall unnaturally and stiffly. You need to slightly lower your rod tip as the jig falls, and when you feel something take the jig, set the hook quickly, keeping the rod tip high and reeling rapidly at the same time. A lot of jig-struck fish are lost because the angler, in reacting to a strike, raises his rod high but never gets the hook to penetrate the mouth of the fish. So the hook pulls out after a moment or the fish jumps and throws the hook easily. A forceful hook set that eliminates slack, coupled with constant pressure and rapid reeling, is the way to avoid losing fish on a jig.

Having the right rod is also a big factor, especially in freshwater where jigs are usually fairly light. Light jigs are rarely fished well on stiff, heavy rods, and vice versa; wimpy super-flexible rods don't make good jigging rods, nor do the pool-cue versions. This is where that elusive quality of sensitivity comes into play. A well-tapered rod with a fast tip is preferable, and it's good to keep the tip angled upward.

Vertical jigging, fishing a jig up and down below the boat as these two anglers are doing, is a good technique when fish are clustered or close to objects, or when drifting.

DOWNRIGGER TROLLING

No one disputes the claim that electric motors and sonar equipment have become nearly indispensable to legions of anglers who fish from boats. Much the same can be said about downriggers for those who troll. On big and small waters alike, boats of all sizes are sporting some type of downrigger, as people learn that controlled depth fishing –the hallmark of downrigger usage – is the way to go for many trolling situations in freshwater and saltwater.

Downrigging is fairly simple. Once you're on the water, you can be operating a downrigger and controlling angling depth in a few minutes. Here is how to get started.

Open the bail or push the freespool button on your reel and let your lure out to whatever distance you think it should be swimming behind the downrigger weight. Keep the reel in freespool with the clicker on if it's a level wind reel; loosen the drag or keep the bail open with a spinning reel. Bring the downrigger weight and line release close to the boat where you can reach them without stretching far overboard. Grab the line at the top of the rod and place it in the release (the device used with a downrigger weight that holds your line till a fish strikes), twisting the line first several times and setting the loop that is then created into the release. Set the weight back overboard if you brought it onto the gunwale of the boat or swing the downrigger boom back to trolling position so the weight can be lowered. Take your rod in one hand and make sure that the line is not fouled at the tip and that line will freely depart the reel spool. Use your other hand to lower the weight, either by depressing the down switch on electric downriggers or lightly releasing clutch tension or back-reeling manual downriggers. Stop the weight at whatever depth you want, as indicated on the downrigger's line counter. Set the rod in a holder and reel up slack so that the tip is bowed over.

Downriggers have become indispensable to many trollers, although they are used more frequently in freshwater than in saltwater.

That's all there is to the basic setup. The only thing you'll do differently each time you employ a downrigger is change the length of line between the downrigger weight or cable and the lure, and change the depth to which the weight is lowered. That depth can vary from just below the surface to as deep as the amount of line on your reel will allow. You determine desired fishing depth by checking temperature levels to see at what depth the thermocline or preferred temperature of your quarry might be found, and by watching a sonar instrument to find fish and locate structure.

Sonar is to downrigger fishing what headlights are to driving at night. The purpose of downrigger fishing is to control the depth of your lures and to place them in specific places and at specific levels. You use sonar equipment to find baitfish or game fish and the levels at which they are located, as well as the depth of the bottom and other aspects of underwater terrain. Without sonar you have to guess the depth to fish and the bottom depth of the water, and run the risk of snagging the weight.

How far back to fish your lures – called 'setback' – varies greatly, depending on the depth being fished and the species being pursued. As a general rule, the deeper you fish, the less line is needed between weight and lure, and the shallower you fish, the further you put the lure back. This is only a general guideline, as some fish can at times be caught shallow on short lines. Determining setback distance requires experimentation, as does the selection of lure type and color. Short setbacks, however, increase hook-setting efficiency, minimize possible conflicts with other boats in heavily trafficked areas, and make boat maneuvering easier.

When you place the downrigger/set rod in a holder it's important to reel in slack line, then pull on the line near the first rod guide while you turn the reel handle, to bring the line from rod tip to release as tight as possible without pulling it out of the release. The rod should be well arched in an inverted J shape to increase hook-up efficiency as well as alert the angler to a strike (the tip momentarily springs upward as the line is pulled out of the release). Also, the reel drag should be checked for proper setting and the clicker on levelwind reels should be engaged.

Fishing two or more downriggers

The number of downriggers used and their location determines what horizontal spread can be achieved with lures presented on downriggers. If you troll with two downriggers, you needn't be too concerned with rigging systems, other than to realize that you may want to keep the weights at different levels, use stackers or sliders to maximize your opportunities per line or per downrigger, and vary dropbacks lengths. The more downriggers you employ, however, the more you should be concerned with systems or patterns of operation, not only to cover the water well horizontally and vertically, but also to facilitate fish landing, minimize line crossing and lure tangling, and better appeal to some species of fish.

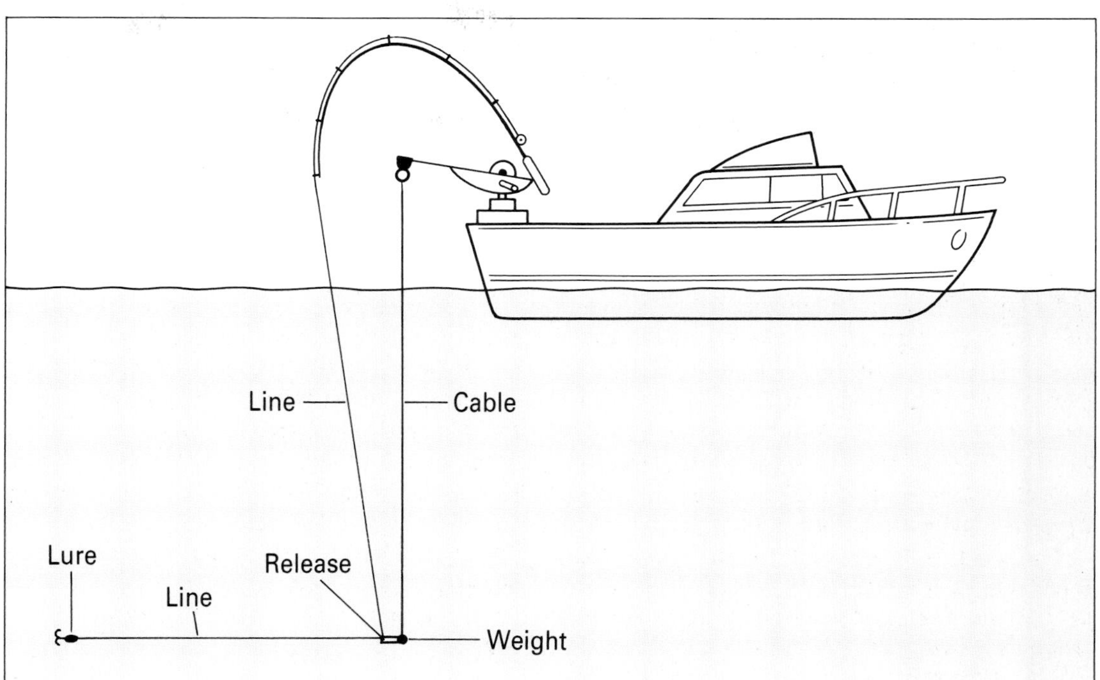

The principle of downrigging – fishing line connected to cable and weight via release mechanism – is one that works well for controlled depth trolling.

Boaters with four to six downriggers who fish large open waters can employ some variation of V patterns in terms of weight depth and lure dropback length to avoid inconsistent, possibly confusing, and perhaps troublesome lure and line placement. Regarding depth, in a V-Down pattern the innermost weights are deepest, the weights to either side of them are shallower, and the outside weights are shallowest. A V-Up pattern is just the reverse. An Equal-Depth pattern would see the weights all set at the same level. As for line-to-lure setback from the weight, in a V-In pattern the innermost lures are closest to the weight, the lures to either side of them are further back, and the outside lures are furthest. A V-Out pattern is just the reverse. In an Equal-Length setback, all lures are set at the same distance behind the downrigger weight.

Why would you want to adopt a pattern? Because you'll always know where your weights and lures are. The more rigs you troll, the harder it is to keep track of things, and when a hard-fighting fish strikes, and lines are cleared, in the confusion it can be easy to lose sight of what weight the successful lure was on, how deep that weight was, and how far the lure was set behind the release. When you know these matters, you can rerig immediately in a similar fashion.

It is important to minimize the possibility of lines crossing over one another and tangling. Realize that outside lures speed up and inside lures slow down on a turn. Outside lures keep swimming high while inside lures rise or fall; this varies with the type of lure used (floating plugs rise while sinkers fall). Some fishermen troll for hours without checking their lures, only to find that they have been dragging a tangle. The problem was the way lines were set and how that affected their movement when turns were made.

A V-Down depth system is preferred by many fishermen. Deepest lines are directly below the boat. Shallower lines are more out of the boat's direct path of travel with this system, perhaps where fish that are spooked by boat passage or deeply set downriggers may have moved. The V-Up system might

An angler sets his fishing line into the release attached to the downrigger weight; the distance between the lure and the weight varies with depth and type of fish, but is important.

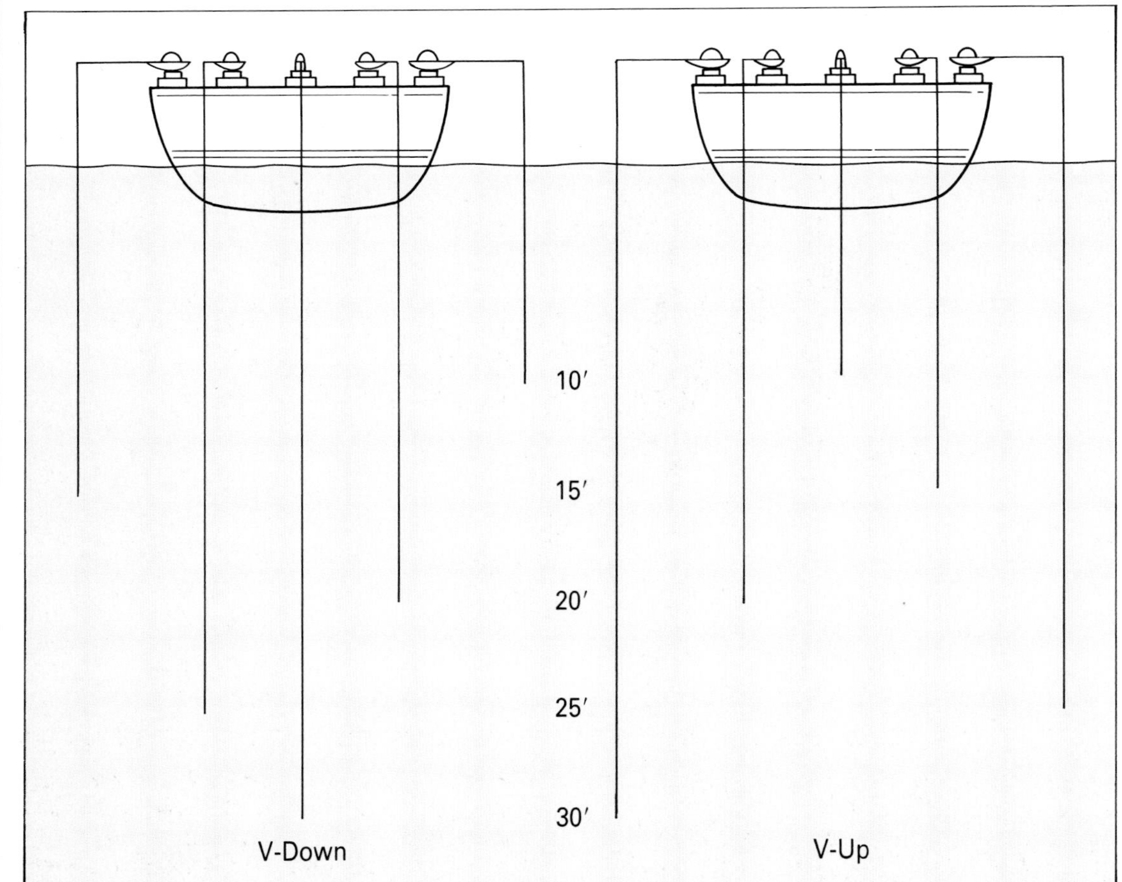

Boaters with many downriggers should stagger the depths that they fish, preferably using one of these two patterns.

be the better approach when you are after fish that are not spooked by the boat and may be attracted to its noise or to the prop wash. Coho and Atlantic salmon are two such fish. An Equal-Depth presentation may be useful when fish are only being caught at a very specific level, such as when they occupy a narrow-band thermocline, and when you are not trying to locate fish by scouring all depth levels.

With setback lengths, there is seldom much reason to use a V-Out system, and the V-In pattern is favored. When fish are caught regularly on lures trolled at a fairly specific mid-range distance behind downrigger weights (especially when depths are nearly the same), there is little reason to stagger them much, so Equal-Length setbacks can be used. With the V-In system, the inner lures will run under the outer ones when turns are made and fish that are located on sonar directly below the boat may move up and out toward the lures set further back. When used in combination with either the V-Down or V-Up depth settings, this setback system helps avoid line tangling when a fish strikes and releases deep lines from the release.

Naturally, you have to experiment with these patterns and see what's best for your type of fishing and boat. Where you only fish one or two downriggers, this is academic. Such patterns have their greatest use in mid- to large-sized boats, and the most common pattern is to use a V-Down/V-In combination. Keep in mind that depth and setback distances are relative. In a V-Down system the shallowest depth trolled might only be 12 feet, the intermediate depth 18, and the greatest depth 24, which is not really a significant variation, or it could see the same progression as 20, 40, and 60 feet. The same is true for setbacks. There are no limitations.

Stacking lines

It is possible to fish two rods off one downrigger, and this is particularly important for the small boater or single downrigger owner. You can even stack three. To set up stacked lines, rig the first line as you would conventionally and as described earlier. Once the first line has been placed in the release by the weight, lower the weight down 10 feet and attach the stacker release to the cable. Put the second lure out the desired distance and set the line in the stacker release. Place both reels in rod holders and leave the freespool clicker on, then place the boom in the proper position (if applicable) and lower the

In some waters, the bigger the boat the more downriggers that are used. This not only permits fishing many lures at one time, but affords an opportunity to stagger depths and distances behind the boat.

Below: This overhead view illustrates one pattern for setback – the distance that multiple trolling lines are set behind the boat.

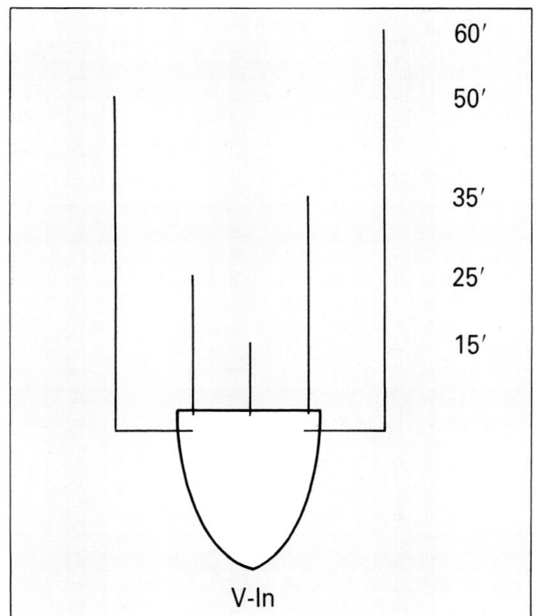

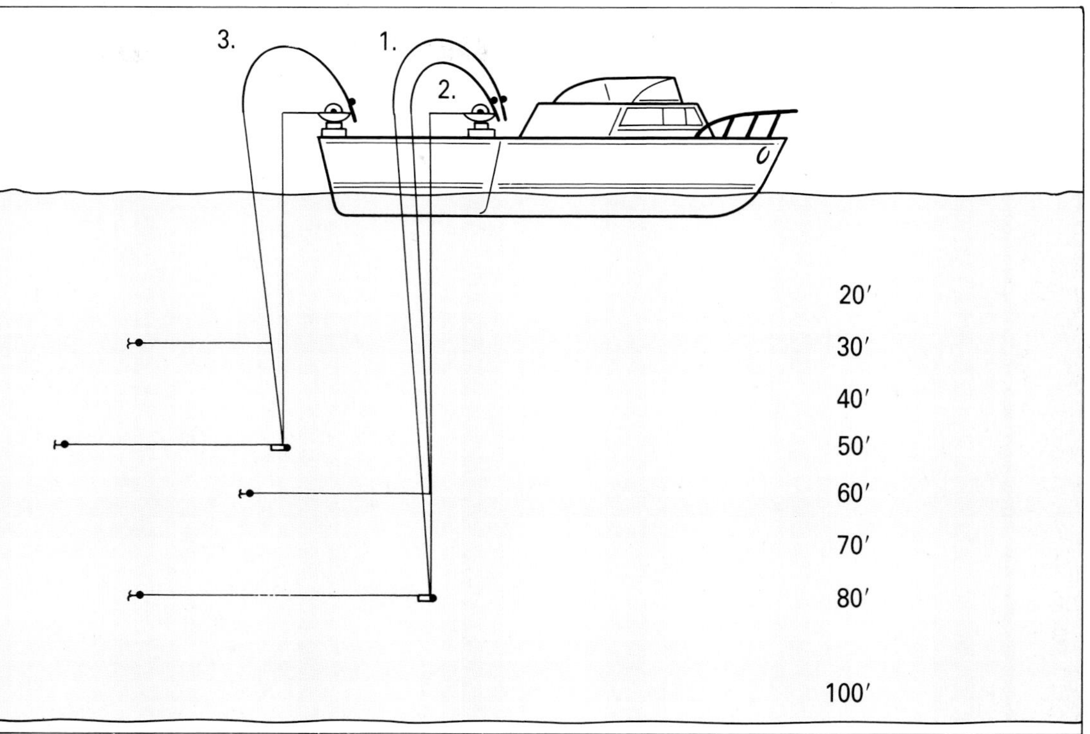

Above: Multiple lures can be fished off one downrigger as shown. Rods 1 and 2 each have a lure, which are stacked on one downrigger; rod 3 has two lures also, a slider fished midway down the fishing line, and the main lure at the depth of the downrigger weight.

weight down to the desired depth. The two lines are now spaced 10 feet apart. Be sure to place rods in holders so that the lower line will not tangle with the upper line if a strike is received and the fish immediately comes toward the surface. The setback for the upper line should be shorter than for the lower line, again to minimize interference if a fish strikes the lower one. The vertical distance between the two lines is optional, although it probably shouldn't be less than 10 feet. Where very deep water is fished, a difference of 30 to 50 feet may be useful.

Sliders

There is another option for fishing more than one lure on one downrigger, although it does not involve using two rods. This is to use sliders or cheaters. A slider is a lure that is affixed to a short leader and run down the fishing line. Slider rigs probably are of little value when the lower lure is fished less than 20 feet down, but are very useful when trolling deep, when fish may be scattered at all levels, when you are unsure what depth to be fishing but need to scour a lot of water, and when you have no idea what color lure to be using and need to wash a lot of different patterns.

There are techniques for fishing more than one lure off a single downrigger, but no matter what lures are used, proper depth and speed are critical.

FLAT LINE TROLLING

The simplest trolling of any kind is to run a flat line. This is put straight out behind the boat; there are no heavy ball sinkers, downrigger weights, diving planers, or other devices to influence the depth attainment of the lure. Anyone with a rod, reel, line, and a lure can run a flat line.

The key to productivity here is how long a line you fish and how you manipulate your boat to position your lures or bait. The clearer the water, the shallower the fish, the spookier the fish, and the more local boat activity there is, the longer the line you need. Lengths up to 200 feet may be used, as in freshwater trout fishing, but most trolling line lengths are under 100 feet.

Trolling even a long line straightforward for seemingly endless periods is boring, unimaginative, and unproductive. You have to regularly alter the lure's path of travel by turning, steering in an S-shaped pattern, driving in other irregular ways, or by increasing or decreasing the speed of the boat. This enhances your presentation by altering the speed and action of the lure, and making it appear less mechanical and more susceptible to capture.

As you are making a flat line trolling presentation, you have to consider where the fish are and how to get your lures in close to them without alarming them. Many fish that are in shallow water near shore or that are close to the surface in open water characteristically move out of the boat's path of travel. That is one reason why you seldom see fish on sonar in less than 15 feet of water. These fish, particularly schools, swim off to one side of the boat as it approaches. They may continue swimming away, they may stay where they are once they have moved, or they may return to their original location after the boat has passed.

If your lure is trailing directly behind a straight-moving boat, fish in the first two instances may never see your lure. If your line is too short, fish in the third instance may also not see it if they are slow to return to their position, or they may see it but associate it with the recently passed boat. This helps illustrate why a lure should be fished on a long line and how proper boat manipulation can bring lures into the range of fish that may not have been in the boat's path or that have moved out of it.

The true test of flat line trolling is to make such presentations in non-open-water areas. Near shore, around reefs or shoals or islands, along grass lines and weed edges, and so forth are hard places to reach effectively due to limited maneuverability, yet you may not have success if you don't reach them. Consider, for example, a lakeshore that drops off fairly sharply and which may have boulders or stumps submerged just under the surface. If you bring your boat too close to shore your motor may hit these structures. The way to deal with this when flat line trolling is to sweep in and out from shore, and plan strategically advantageous approaches to such areas as points, sandbars, islands, shoals, channels, and the like. You may have to troll by many of these more than once, from different directions, to effectively cover the area.

Flat line trolling is done by boats of all sizes and in all waters, but is particularly practiced in shallow water locations.

In shallow water it may be necessary to troll a long flat line in order to intercept fish that have moved out of the boat's path of travel.

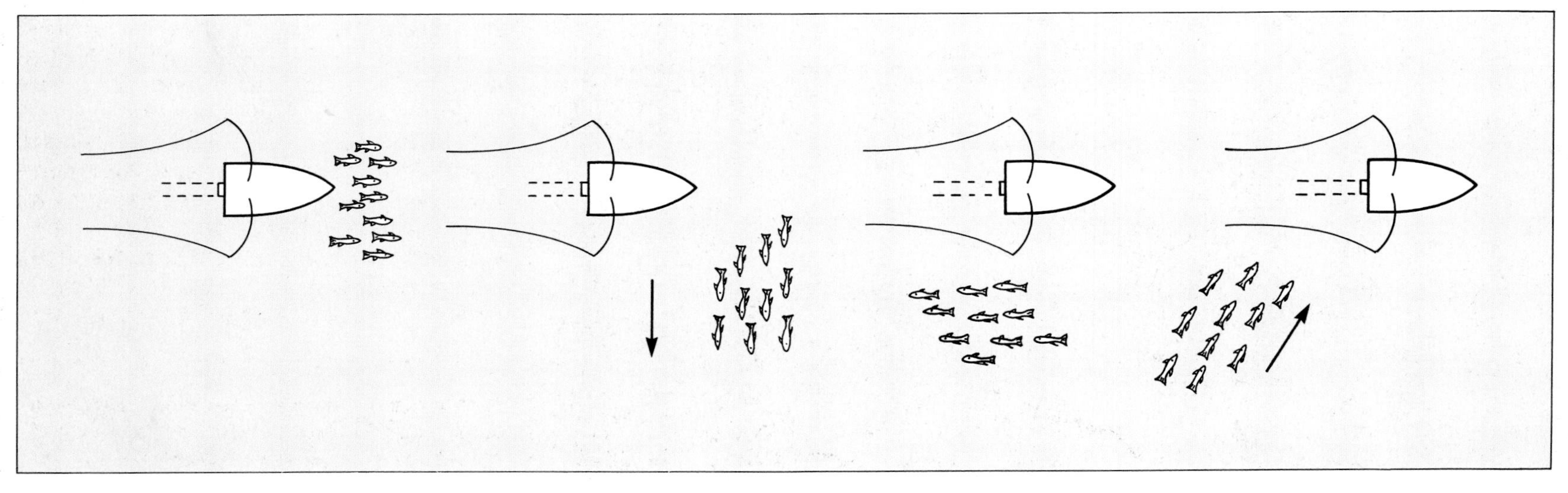

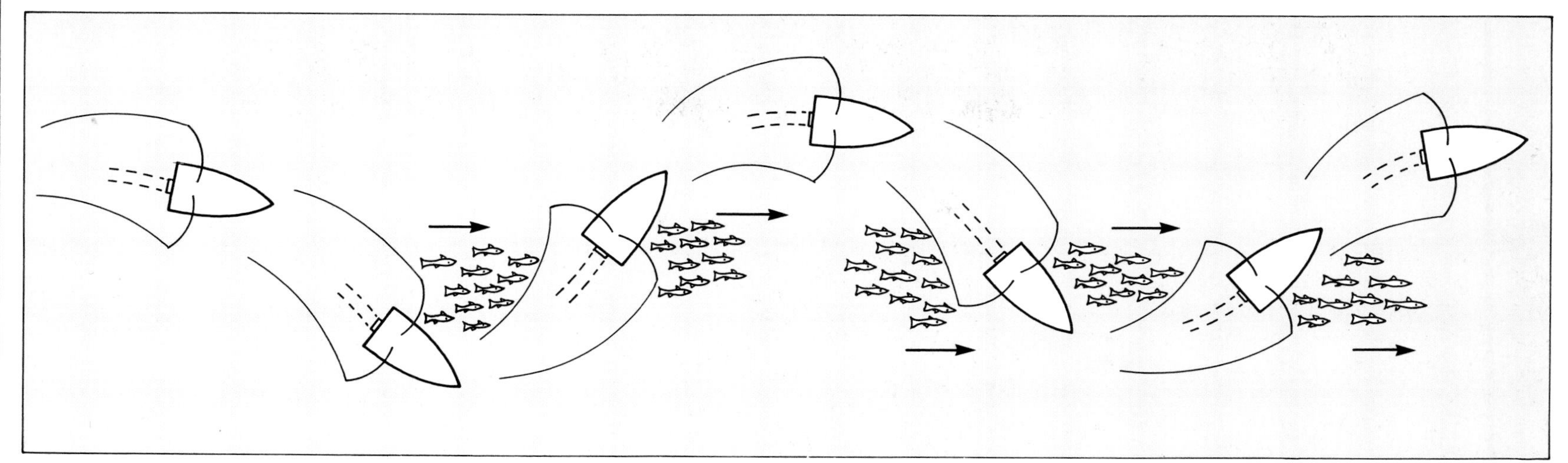

Above: Making S-like curves, particularly in shallow water, can be the ticket to bringing your lures into contact with fish, as well as favorably altering their behavior.

Side planers

There are devices that solve many of the difficulties of shallow trolling, and which make your presentations much more versatile than flat lining. These are side-planer boards. They are plastic or wooden surface-running planers that evolved on the Great Lakes for trout and salmon trolling. Side-planer boards work something like a downrigger on the surface. A non-fishing line or cable tethers the planer to the boat, and allows it to run at varied distances off to the side of your boat. One or more fishing lines are attached to the planer or tow line via release clips; you are free to fight a fish unencumbered when it strikes your lure and releases the fishing line from the clip. (Another type of planer, which is smaller, attaches directly to your fishing line, and pops free when a fish strikes. This side-planer has a calm water fishing advantage, but must be retrieved after a fish is caught, and makes hooking fish a little difficult.)

Side planers can be used in trolling for all kinds of fish, but are predominantly used in freshwater for trout, salmon, and walleyes. They vastly increase your presentation capabilities because they allow your lures to pass near fish that may have been spooked by the passage of your boat (or would be spooked if you ran your boat near them) or are in areas where you can't or don't want to take your boat.

How far you set the side planers out depends on how close you want your boat to shore, how far apart you want to spread your lures, how much room you have to fish, and how much boat traffic there is in the area, among other factors. Eighty to 100 feet out is a com-

A troller prowling the dropoff along a steep bank needs to weave in and out occasionally and not simply follow a straight line.

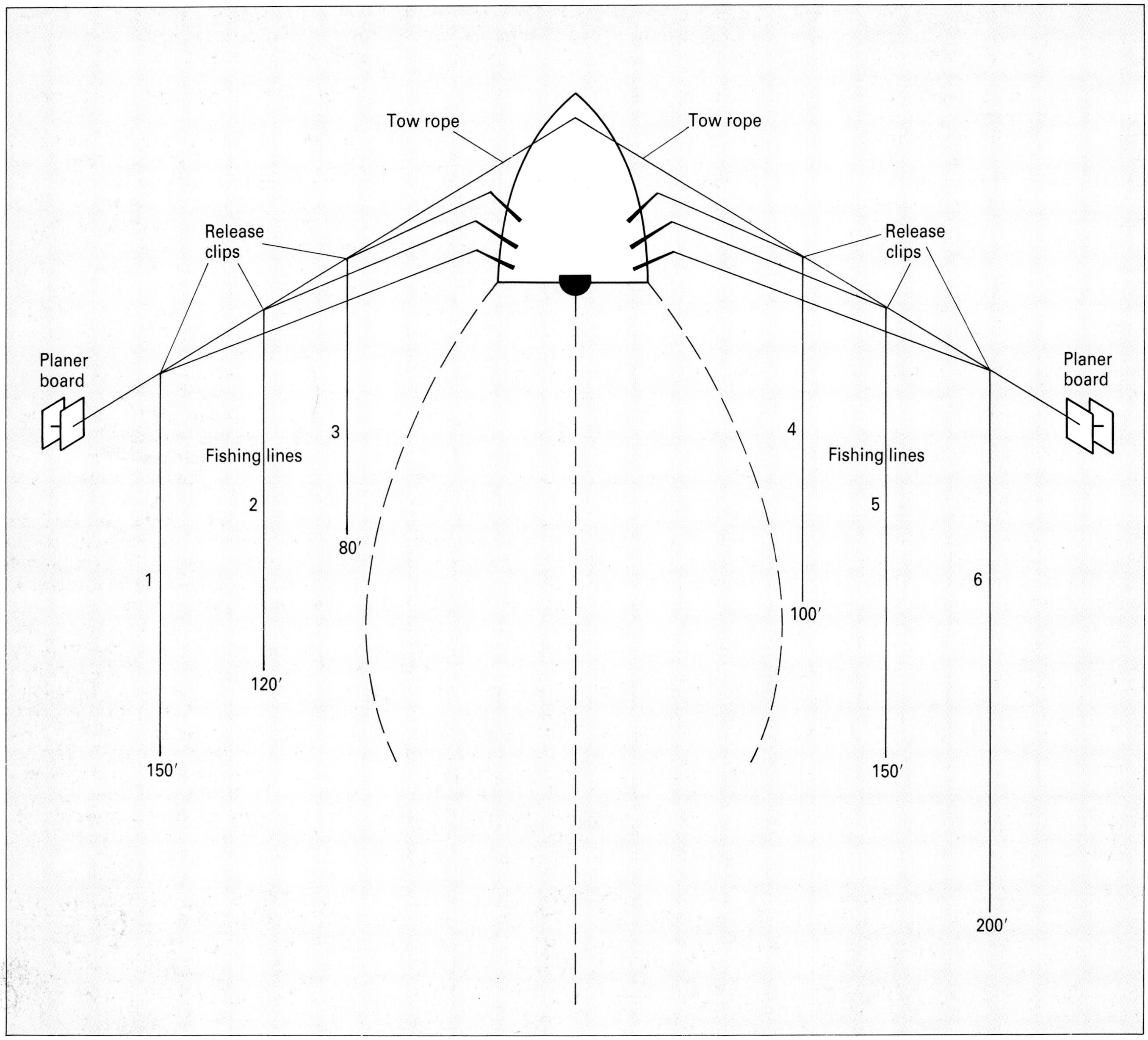

A large boat could fish six flat lines using this system via sideplaners. Note that the inner lines are short and under the outer lines when rigged, so there is no need to bring all rods in when a fish is caught. Fish are played in the dotted line area.

This view of a double-runner side planer in use shows how such a device can bring fishing line away from the trolling boat and permit the exploration of a greater swath of water.

mon distance. They can be run out as much as 200 feet if you have a high anchor point in your boat for the planer line (some fishermen use a 6- to 8-foot pole).

To use side planers you must have a method of tethering them to your boat and retrieving them. You can use manual downriggers for that, though this limits your range. Sideplaner booms and reels are generally used. Double-runner planers are becoming more common than single runners because they track well and handle rough water better.

You can run lures any length behind a side planer that seems feasible. Because the lures are trolled well off to the side of the boat, and behind a relatively unobtrusive planer, they often don't have to be run as far back as when using a flat line. You still need a lot of line on your reel, however, since your fishing line extends first to the release clip and then back to the lure.

With side planers, a host of fishing combinations are possible. When fishing near-shore areas you can run two or three strategically spaced lines off the shore side planer. On the open-water side of the boat you have the option of running a surface or diving lure on a long flat line, running a lure deep via the downrigger, or running one or more lures off the other side planer. Moreover, the amount of territory that can be covered is vastly increased. If you run two side planers, each 60 feet to either side of the boat, and have two fishermen in the boat, you might run four lines over a 40-yard span of water. If the bottom drops off sharply near shore, as it does in many trout lakes, you could be working over a few feet of water on the near-shore side of the boat, and over 40 feet on the opposite side, presenting your lures to fish that would not ordinarily see them, and which would not be frightened by the passage of your boat. (This example assumes that you can fish two lines per fishermen; in some states only one line per angler is allowed.)

Trolling strategies and boat manipulation techniques when using side planer boards are much like those described earlier for flat lining. When you turn, however, the outside planer board increases its speed and the inside one slows or stalls. Because the fishing lines are well separated, there is less chance of entanglement when you turn, particularly if all lines are nearly the same distance behind the boat. Although a lot of side planer board fishing is done with shallow-running lures, you can use whatever lures are appropriate for the conditions; moreover, by adjusting the tension of the line release, you can troll a hard-pulling deep-diving plug or a line with weights on it.

The white vertical objects in this boat are outriggers; though not in use here, they are another means of making flat line trolling presentations.

Outriggers

Large boats in saltwater, and some in freshwater, accomplish similar things, incidentally, with the use of outriggers, which are long rods that are extended out to the side of the boat and sport a release clip that frees fishing line when a fish strikes the following bait or lure. These originated in big-game trolling, but have been used to troll small lures as well. Lines can't be spread or separated as far with this system, and the angle of line from release to water entry is much greater, affecting lure depth.

Fishing several lines

When you're fishing several lines, you can experiment with their distance from the boat and the distance the lures are set behind the tow line or outrigger. When running two or three lines off one sideplaner or outrigger, don't put short lines on the outside. If a fish were to strike a short outside line, there's a chance that he'd cross over one or more of the inside lines after the hookup. Take this into account when setting lines out and try to arrange them so that a fish caught on the outside line will drop back clear of the inside lines, and then be played up the unfished center alley. If you have three lines on one side, and the outermost one pops, you can slide the inner lines out, then put the released line back out as the inside line. This is all accomplished without having to pull fishing lines and the planer in.

Calculating setback distance

To determine the length of line to set your lure out behind boat, sideplaner, or outrigger (downrigger, too) you can use one of several systems. With levelwind reels you can count the number of 'passes' that the levelwind guide makes across the top of the reel. Measure the amount of line that comes off the spool for one pass, then multiply that amount by the number of passes to arrive at a setback distance.

Another system, used with levelwind reels that possess a line guide that locks in an open position, and used with spinning and fly reels, is to count 'pulls.' Start with the lure or fly in the water, hold the rod in one hand and grab the line just ahead of the reel with your other hand. Pull off line in set increments, either as far as your arm will reach, or in 1- or 2-foot strips. Count the distance let out as you pull to arrive at setback length.

A third method is to 'sweep,' by putting the lure in the water, pointing the rod tip back at the lure, and sweeping the rod toward the bow of the boat in a measured length. As the boat moves ahead, bring the rod tip back and then sweep forward again. If your sweep is 6 feet, multiply that by the number of sweeps you make to approximate setback length. Sweeping is a bit less accurate than using pulls or passes.

BACKTROLLING

Backtrolling is a premier small-boat tactic used in freshwater lakes and rivers, primarily by walleye, steelhead, and salmon fishermen, and it is a precise method of boat control for slow lure or bait presentation. In lakes, backtrollers use a tiller-steered outboard motor in reverse or a transom-mounted electric motor (with lower unit turned so that the stern goes back when the motor is technically in a forward position), and move very slowly stern-first to maintain precise position around points, reefs, weed lines, sandbars, and along dropoffs.

By using sonar, a backtroller can maintain position along specific depths, nearly hover over selected spots, and maneuver his boat to use whatever wind direction is present to position his boat in such a way as to keep his following bait in the proper and desired place. This is especially vital when a school of fish are packed into one small spot.

In many rivers, precise boat control and lure or bait placement is achieved by floating, drifting, or trolling slowly backward downcurrent. In some places this is also referred to as backtrolling. In others it is called 'Hotshotting,' which is a derivative of the West Coast technique of using a Hotshot plug for river trout and salmon, or 'pulling plugs.' And in still others it is called 'slipping.'

Whatever you call it the idea is to have your boat pointed bow upstream, using motor or oars to control the downstream progression of the boat. The boat moves very slowly – it actually drifts – downstream, and at times remains stationary in the current (some boaters anchor once they have caught fish in a spot), while lures are fished at 50- to 80-foot distances behind the boat. The lures dangle in front of fish that the boat has not yet passed over, and this is a big difference compared to upstream trolling, where the boat passes over fish and alerts them to your presence, possibly spooking them. Additionally, lures that are slipped downstream ahead of the boat approach the heads of fish, instead of coming from behind them and swimming past their head. Lures are usually fished in the channels and deep pools where bigger fish lie, and waver in front of fish for a much longer period than they would if cast and retrieved or if trolled upstream and away. The fact that fish have a better chance of being undisturbed and of seeing a more natural presentation (a small fish, for instance, struggling against the current and being slowly swept downward) makes this a highly effective river fishing technique.

Most of this downstream drift-trolling is done with diving plugs for fish that take them. Some fish, such as shad, don't take plugs and you must use shad darts (a form of jig) or tiny spoons fished behind torpedo-shaped bead chain sinker. Others respond well to bait; winter-run steelhead, for example,

With splash boards in place to keep water from slipping over the transom, a fisherman puts his tiller-steered outboard motor in reverse gear and moves backward for slow, precise positioning.

Slipping slowly downriver as these anglers are doing allows for precise lure positioning.

are caught with pencil-lead-weighted spawn sacks, single-hook salmon eggs, or worms. Many different attractions, including plugs, spoons, spinners, flies, and bait, can be used, depending on the circumstances.

When slipping, it's important to manipulate the boat properly in order to maintain precise lure position. The location and depth of your offering is critical to river fishing success. The lure must be on or close to the bottom, so you need to use the appropriate amount of weight or design of lure that will achieve this.

Pools are the major locale that is fished with this technique, and often the boat needs to be positioned far enough upriver so the lure slowly works from the head of a pool down through the tail of it; it's not good enough to boat down to a pool and then hold position, as the fish you seek may have been located at the head of the pool. When working from side to side across the river, you should realize that it takes a while for a trailing lure to catch up to the boat position; when you sweep close to a bank, for instance, hold that position because it takes time for the lure to get over to the bank. If you were to sweep in and out quickly the lure wouldn't get as far to either side as you might like.

Another point to remember is that you want to slip backward in a slow, controlled fashion. When you stop rowing or throttle the motor back, a floating plug rises, a spinner doesn't spin, weights sink, etc. This is because there is now less pressure against those objects. Slow, controlled slipping keeps lures working best and draws more strikes. Boat control is maintained with oars, especially in rafts, johnboats, and river drift boats (McKenzie River style dories), or with small tiller-steered outboard motors.

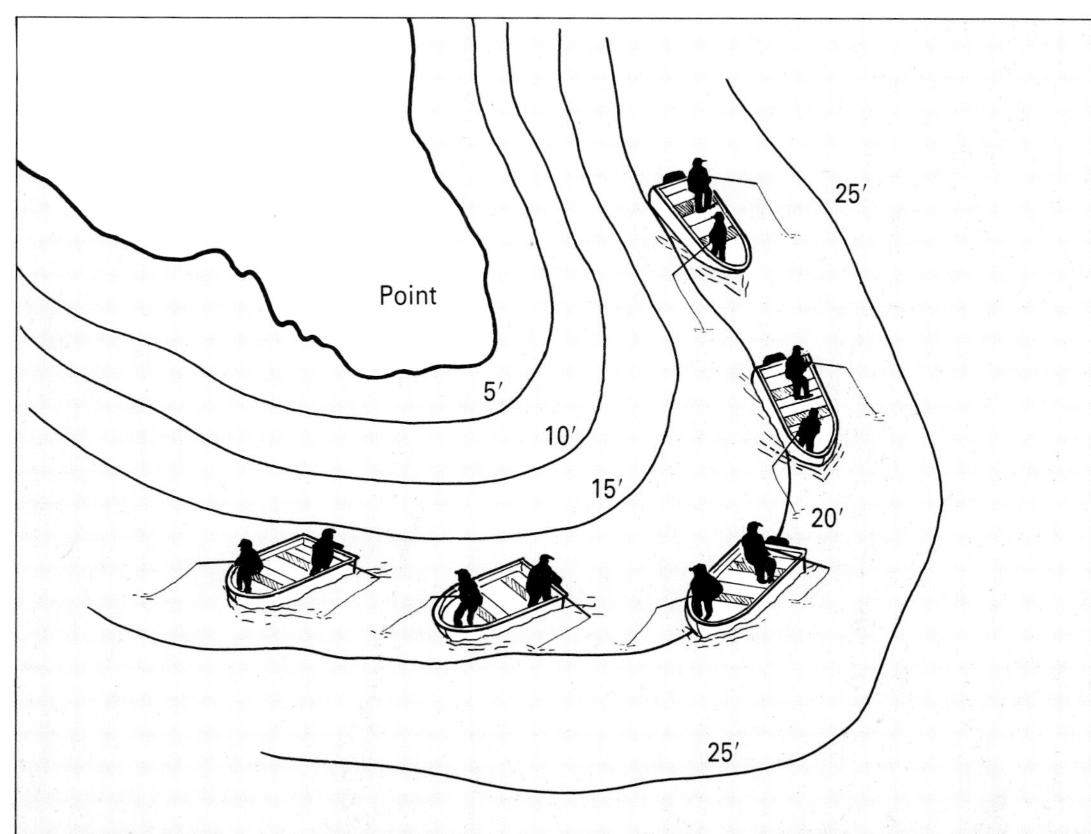

Precise positioning and control is the main attribute of backtrolling.

BIG GAME TROLLING

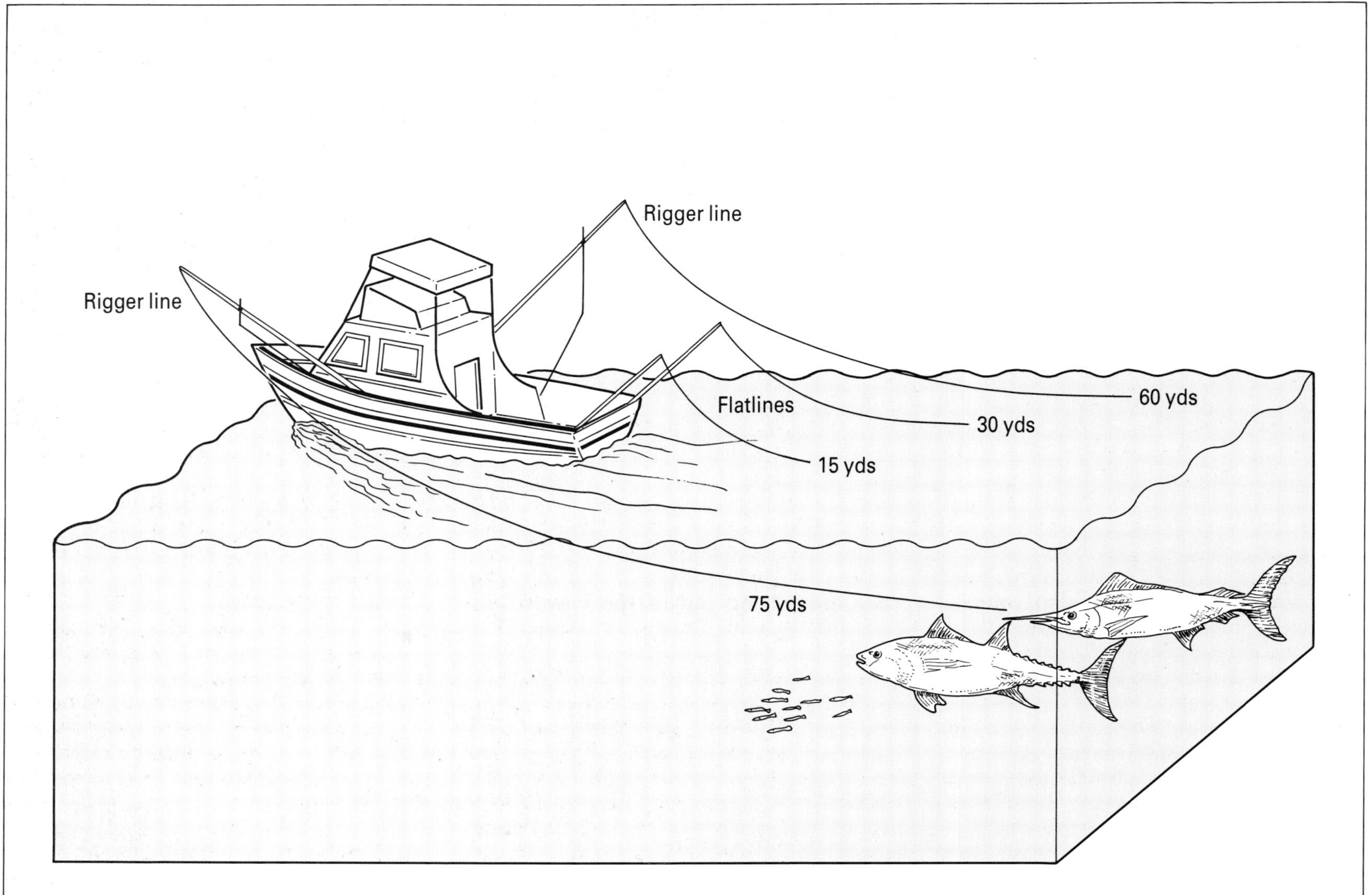

Both outrigger and flat lines are used in big game fishing, with offerings set at staggered depths.

The offshore surface trolling practiced by big-game anglers is different from any other type of trolling, not only because the species involved are large – primarily billfish and tuna – but because this activity involves high speed fishing, the use of large natural baits or lures, precise rigging methods, and a particular hooking technique. Although the quarry generally include blue marlin, white marlin, striped marlin, sailfish, swordfish, yellowfin tuna, and bluefin tuna, smaller species, such as dolphinfish, wahoo, and bonito, are often caught as well when trolling offshore.

Although this trolling activity is a surface one, lures and baits may be trolled either as below-surface swimmers (although just slightly below the surface) or topwater skippers. Thus, there are skipping and swimming presentations. The swimmers should stay below the surface at all times, except for popping through an occasional wave. Skippers primarily bounce along the water and wave tops, occasionally darting through a wave or diving under the surface momentarily and resurfacing and skipping. A fast boat speed, in the range of 6 to 10 knots, is required, depending on size of bait, type of sea conditions, and direction relative to the waves. Higher speeds are used when only artificials, such as feathers or Kona head-style trolling plugs are employed. Speed is also gauged by the working action of the offerings; where rigged natural baits are used, it is critical that these work properly to be effective, and this requires a combination of proper rigging and trolling speed.

Natural baits vary with the size of the principal quarry, although baits of different types and sizes are often used in order to attract whatever game fish might be available. These items include balao, mullet, and similar sized bait for smaller game fish (such as sailfish, white marlin, and dolphin), and mackerel, bonito, large mullet, and similar sized fish for large game fish. Most of these are used for skipping, although they can be rigged for swimming as well; feathered trolling plugs are often run as swimmers, however, and fished in conjunction with baits or skipping plugs.

Most of the time, offshore trollers fish with four lines. On bigger boats they may run six. Outriggers are generally used to troll one or two lines per rigger; one or two flat lines are run from reel tip to the water directly in the wake of the boat. The flat lines should be set shallow, one only 30 feet back and the other just 10 or 15 feet further. Outrigger-set baits should be 15 to 20 feet beyond the deeper flat line. Both flat and outrigger lines are effective, and it is not uncommon for a big fish to strike more than one, or even all, trolled baits or lures.

A lot of smaller fish, plus tuna, are hooked at the moment of strike in offshore trolling. The combination of a hard strike and swift boat motion work to set the hook automatically, although it is advisable for the angler to set the hook again as insurance. Billfish sometimes strike viciously and hook themselves immediately, but more often, and especially with natural rigged baits, they don't take the offering that hard, so it is necessary to give the fish slack line for a few moments before setting the hook. This slack line is called a 'dropback.' The angler (or mate in the case of a charter boat) quickly takes the rod that has been struck out of the holder and applies light thumb pressure (to avoid a backlash) to the lever drag reel for a short time as the boat continues moving swiftly ahead. When the angler determines that enough time has passed (several seconds at least), he points the rod tip toward the fish, puts the reel into gear, waits a microsecond for the line to get taut and to feel resistance, and then sets the hook hard and fast, perhaps more than once. How far to dropback is a matter of intuition, partly based upon the size of bait (longer for big bait) and the species of striking fish, if known.

It pays to be constantly watching trolled baits or lures to determine the type of fish that strikes; this is one of the reasons why big sportfishing boats have towers, which are also referred to as 'tuna towers', or flying bridges. It also pays to react instantly when there is a strike. Billfish usually bring their dorsal fin and/or bill out of the water before striking, so you know that some dropback is probably necessary.

If the fish doesn't have the bait when you dropback, raise the rod tip upward and reel furiously to bring the bait forward. Sometimes the striking fish, thinking that his prey is escaping, will return and strike this offering or one of the others. Once a fish is on, the other baits or lures are retrieved and rods are placed out of the way so all attention can be directed to playing the hooked fish.

Sometimes offshore fish, particularly billfish, will come into the boat's wake and trail a lure or bait but not strike it. This is referred to as 'raising' a fish, and it happens quite frequently. Offshore fish are pelagic wanderers and are often curious. While they spend some time on or close to the surface, most of the time they are a considerable depth below cruising for food, and are attracted to the engine noise, the wake of the boat, and the action of the baits. Why they don't strike remains a mystery, but the offshore trolling game is both a matter of attracting fish to your offering as well as searching for fish to present your offering to.

A balao rigged on wire leader is one of the baits used in offshore trolling, and for which a dropback hook-setting procedure is often necessary.

Fast boat speeds, heavy tackle, blue water, and lures or baits that skip along the surface or dart just under it are the characteristics of offshore big game trolling.

Obviously this fishing isn't done just anywhere, although depending on geographic locales it may be as close as a mile from shore (southeast Florida's Gulf Stream) or as distant as 50 miles off the coast (New Jersey's Hudson Canyon), in what is often referred to as 'blue water,' where the water coloration turns from murky or greenish to sparkling blue. This is warm water angling and the fish are usually located in well-known areas where there is a sharp dropoff, such as a canyon, on the onshore floor, or a pinnacle rising up from deep water. The fish are nomadic here, but are attracted to irregularities on the surface, too, including floating weeds or other objects and rips or eddies. They search for baitfish, and big-game trollers should always be on the lookout for signs of feeding fish. Birds are often the giveaway here, and since big-game trollers cover a lot of territory in a day, they stand a good chance of seeing birds working somewhere in the distance. Gulls and frigate birds actively dive for wounded or mutilated baitfish that have been left by ravaging gamefish. Head for a commotion of diving birds quickly, and fish the outskirts of that activity. A lone frigate bird (also called a man-o'-war bird) may indicate a big fish. Also look for splashing baitfish or cruising game-fish. Some species, such as billfish and marlin, can actually be seen cruising the offshore surface waters and it is desirable to intercept them with the trolled baits.

OTHER TROLLING TECHNIQUES

The old and the new is juxtaposed here, with a wire line outfit set next to a microprocessor-equipped electric downrigger.

While flatlining and downrigging are the most popular methods of trolling, there are alternatives to using a downrigger to get deep, or to simply using a lure or bait behind a nylon monofilament line or a fly line. These include:

Running an object on a weighted line Similar to the previous method, this simply involves using some type of weight (drail, split shot, keel, bell, or other type of sinker) to get a lure or bait deeper than it would achieve unaided. The element of knowing actual depth fished is dependent on boat speed, line size, current, trolling line length, amount of weight, and so forth.

Running an object behind a lead-core line In this system, the weight of the line causes the object being trolled to sink. Depth achieved depends on how much lead-core line is let out. Lead core is marked or color-coded at intervals; how much line you troll essentially determines how deep your lure will run, depending also on speed and lure type. While this can be a more precise method of fishing than using an unweighted flat line, it primarily puts the lure or bait at a general trolling depth, and it is not as comfortable to use, since lead-core line is strong and is bulkier than nylon or Dacron. Lead core isn't as supple as those products either, so it doesn't transmit the fight of a fish quite as well.

Running an object behind a wire line This is probably the least practiced and least popular trolling tactic, although still used in freshwater by some lake trout and musky trollers and in saltwater by a few striped bass, bluefish, and deep reef trollers. As with lead core line usage, the weight of wire line causes the object being trolled to sink, and the amount let out determines the depth to be achieved. Wire can't be fished on any rod or reel, requires stout tackle, is subject to kinking, crimping, and spooling difficulties, and does nothing to enhance the sporting nature of fish being caught because the tackle blunts the fight of the fish. It does, however, telegraph every movement of a fish quite well because of its high sensitivity.

Running an object behind a diving planer A diving planer is fished off of a very stout rod, because it pulls so hard when trolled, and is used with fairly heavy line. Such planers dive quite deep on a relatively short length of line, and the amount of line trolled essentially determines how deep the planer will dive. The planer trips when a fish strikes, so you don't have to fight it as well as the fish.

Running an object behind a releasable cannonball sinker system This is a deep-trolling system. Where a large cannonball-shaped sinker is used to get down, with the sinker being released and dropping to the bottom when a fish strikes. You lose a lot of lead weight in this system, and need stout, heavy-line tackle. You also don't often know the depth you're fishing when you're off the bottom.

Each of these systems can suffer from imprecise depth control; in other words, you often don't know exactly how deep you're fishing. Veteran trollers using these systems, however, have overcome that problem and have learned to have more mastery over their depth placement than inexperienced anglers. Getting a lure or bait down to the proper level is the key to any trolling system.

This diving planer sports a release pin that trips when a fish strikes; the planer can also be adjusted to guide it to swim to the left or right.

Right: A diving planer, hanging from the rod behind this angler, accounted for the salmon he is holding.

10
11
Trilene

DRIFTING

Many non-anglers seem to think that fishermen are basically lazy people who sit out in a boat with their feet propped up and a line dangling over the side waiting to get lucky. Some anglers are like this, no doubt, but others who look pretty laid-back will fool you, and there are a lot of times when those who seem to be doing little, if nothing, have an uncanny knack for achieving success. Drift fishing from a boat, for instance, appears to be about as lazy a fishing method as you can find, but there may be more to it than meets the eye.

There are times when it is advantageous to drift with live bait or lures, such as when the fish appear to be spooked by engine noise. But the haphazard drifter, who pays little regard to how deep he is fishing, where he is headed, and what he is using, is not likely to do as well as the drifter using carefully selected tackle and making a calculated approach.

If you are drift fishing with live bait, for example, pay attention to the type of live bait rig that you use, and to the sinker. Bank, dipsey, pencil lead, and split shot sinkers are commonly used in live bait drifting. While split shot are often used for suspending bait at specific depths, the others are essentially used for keeping contact with the bottom, are good in deep water, and cast well. Split shot are preferred for light tackle. Dipsey sinkers are also used with light to medium tackle and where bait is suspended off the bottom above the sinker.

A very popular bait-fishing rig, used for drifting as well as for trolling, and which is especially useful on perch, walleyes, and bass, is a spinner rig, which features a small spinner ahead of a worm, with a fixed sinker or sliding sinker above it. A spreader rig, which is very popular in saltwater and used strictly for fishing on the bottom, is also conducive to planned drifts. This T-shaped rig utilizes a springy wire for the horizontal section, with a nylon leader to the hooks, a heavy weight extended vertically below the wire, and fishing line extending from above. Another popular bottom-drifting bait rig features a three-way swivel attached to a bell sinker and a leadered hook.

Some fishermen who cast lures use a wind-aided drift to their advantage in combination with occasional electric motor use to help maintain a desired position. In plastic worm fishing for bass, for instance, one can successfully work an open weedy area this way with a variety of lures. Plastic worms, in fact, are especially good for some slow drifting work, and can be fished on a slow retrieve that is combined with a drift. Generally, however, the best lure to use when drifting in saltwater or freshwater is a jig, either with a soft-plastic attachment or strip of live or dead bait.

In order to properly drift over a particular stretch of water, be that a salt-

Early morning anglers drifting a river for trout are little different from other drift fishermen; all need to use the right amount of weight to keep their bait offering tumbling at the proper pace as well as proper boat positioning.

water flat, pass, or tidal rip or a freshwater bank, you have to plan the approach properly, taking wind and current into consideration. Drift fishing is usually done on the windward side of the boat, particularly in deep water; it is preferable if the boat is in a position broadside to the wind, but this is not possible with some boats. Be sure to note where you start a drift and have success, as you should return and redrift over productive stretches. The longer you drift, and the more the wind shifts, the harder it will be, especially in open water environs, to return to the proper place or to achieve the desirable drift.

River drifting

This is popular, too, and there is little haphazard about it. Using electric motors, outboard motors, or oars, boaters try to effect a downstream boat movement at a pace much slower than the speed of the current, allowing them to cast lures and baits and work them better or longer (or present them more often) in likely places. This is especially effective for salmon, steelhead, trout, bass, and walleyes.

The most critical aspect of river drift fishing is proper bait or lure presentation through boat control. A premier method of doing such is called 'slipping,' and it entails moving slowly backwards downstream while in complete control of your craft, in such a way as to allow passengers and boat operator to fish at ease. To do this, point the bow of your boat upstream and accelerate the outboard motor in forward gear. With the bow placed into the current, throttle the motor down to a point where your boat has begun to move backward downstream. The thrust of the motor is not enough to keep you going forward, and your boat slowly drifts backward, stern first. The boat moves very slowly, sometimes almost imperceptibly, and you have precise control over your position and rate of descent.

With the motor at a steady forward thrust, the boat backs downstream with ease as you cast and retrieve. Cast upstream and retrieve slowly downstream. Upstream casting allows you to present lures in a manner similar to the movement of natural bait in current. The bow of the boat is always pointed into the current. It is a position easily held, providing you don't allow eddies and backwaters to entrap your boat, and you can readily move across current as necessary.

Most river anglers who fish from shore, incidentally, are drift fishermen, though they don't think of it that way.

Casting across and slightly upstream, then drifting lure or bait with the flow, is a common technique for wading anglers fishing in current.

The standard procedure for casting to nearly every river species, regardless of whether you are using lure, fly, or bait, is to cast across and upstream and then allow the offering to drift or swim naturally in the current. Proper presentation is one of the keys to success here, and it is effective presentation that makes drifting a worthwhile technique in various forms of fishing.

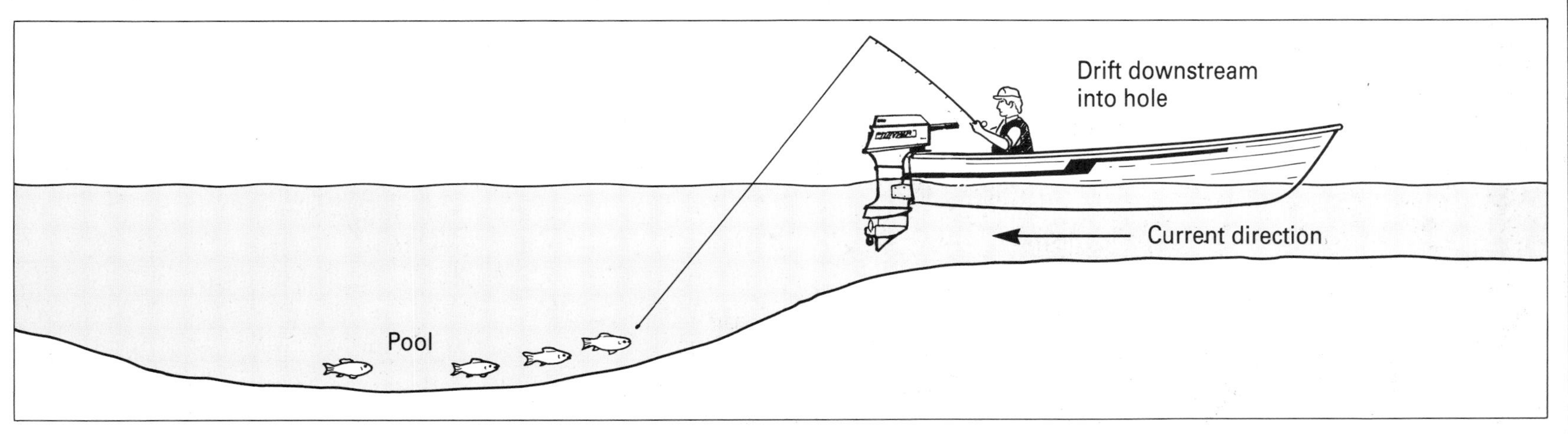

Slow, controlled drifting downstream can be done with an outboard motor under low power. More effective presentations are possible in good locales with this technique.

INTANGIBLES

Fishing is a sport with a lot of intangibles, all of which have some influence – albeit varying and usually difficult to measure with absolute surety – on the angler's success. Certainly some anglers are more astute than others, some are plain luckier than others, and some are blessed with more natural talent. There are some things in fishing that are intuitive by nature, things that many successful anglers do routinely, and which make them successful yet also separate them from those who are merely adept. Yet every angler can improve himself if he desires to do so and is willing to make the effort. Consider these intangibles.

Observation

Are you an observant fisherman? Do you see fish that swirl after your lure or follow it to the boat? Do you notice when schools of birds are working baitfish that are being plundered by larger gamefish? Are you able to spot fish lurking near cover in clear shallow water? Do you notice the infrequent telltale signs that denote the presence of fish?

It's true that the average angler misses a lot of what's going on around him on the water. Sure, it's easy to see fish rising to take surface flies in a river pool, or notice a school of fish that are busting the surface in great commotion, but it's much harder to watch for the smaller things. It helps, of course, if you spend a lot of time on the water; many anglers aren't observant enough simply because they are infrequent fishermen who have to get adjusted to aquatic goings-on every time they go out.

Nonetheless, some anglers are much better than others at seeing fish or spotting activity that indicates the presence of fish. One of the easiest ways to become more observant is to watch your lures better when you retrieve them. You'd think that an angler would always be watching his lures closely to be able to respond to a strike. But people become lackadaisacal and inattentive, especially when the action isn't fast, and they often fail to notice something that might be instrumental in helping them be successful.

Some freshwater fish, notably bass, are prone to swirl after shallow-running or surface lures and create a sizable boil in the water after they miss the lure in an apparent attempt to stun it. Fishermen who aren't watching closely don't see the boil and cast elsewhere, though they might have been able to catch that fish or at least note its location for a later visit.

Some fish are prone to follow lures close to the boat. Pike, pickerel, and musky do this often enough that it's a good move for anglers seeking these species to watch their lures as they are retrieved at boatside and be on the lookout for fish to materialize almost as the lure is pulled out of the water. Other fish, including lake trout in shallow water and barracuda on saltwater flats, may behave similarly, though you'll never notice if you aren't paying close attention.

One of the tricks for spotting shallow-water fish is to look not at the

Sight fishing on a shallow saltwater flat is made more difficult by cloud cover, wind, and the nature of the bottom.

surface but below the surface and at the bottom. When you focus on the bottom, try to look for something that stands out as being different, and whose movement contrasts with some bottom locales enough for you to detect it. When you see the wake of a moving fish, realize that the forward edge of the wake is behind the fish. Therefore you take this into account when you are making a cast that is intended to intercept that fish.

Sometimes it's important to be able to see fish before you cast to them –such as shallow-water trout or salmon fishing or flats fishing for bonefish – because you have to be able to approach them without alarming them. Other times it's important to see certain objects that might be harboring fish. Polarized sunglasses are a big help here; glasses that offer wrap-around side-view protection are best. A cap with a wide bill and dark underside is also a good aid.

Obviously much of this applies to relatively shallow-water fishing and to casting, but being observant pays off in all kinds of angling, even if it isn't always possible to see the fish you seek. Changes in water color, rips, reefs just below the surface, near-surface vegetation, shade, current flows, or little splashes that might indicate baitfish are some of the many indicators that, if observed, may help you catch your quarry successfully.

Changes

Making a change – especially knowing when to make a change – is one of the real tricks to fishing success. This is true in fly fishing for stream trout, casting for bass in a lake, trolling for inshore saltwater fish, and in nearly all aspects of angling.

Some changes, like moving to a new place on a given body of water, seem obvious. Other changes, like lengthening a downrigger trolling line a few feet, are subtle. Changes involve places, techniques, and tackle, but they are often at the core of fishing success. The ability to make the right change to adapt to particular fishing circumstances is one that too few anglers possess. It especially proves helpful when fishing is tough.

One of the reasons why people don't make changes is that they become complacent. They develop pet lures, favorite holes, or specialized techniques, and they either stay too long with those things when they aren't producing, or they are uncomfortable about breaking new ground and doing something that is out of their ordinary routine. Even when the fish don't respond, these anglers continue doing the same thing; they either hope that the fish will turn on and be receptive to the old tactic again, or they try to force-feed them. This stick-to-itness can be a self-perpetuating problem, and an angler who isn't well rounded will miss some very good fishing as a result.

Not so evident are the salmon just in front of the shaded water in this creek. Many anglers would have looked quickly there and thought they'd seen rocks, passing by about half a dozen big fish.

Unfortunately, there are no commandments for when to change or what changes to make. Good anglers, regardless of the species they pursue, often do this intuitively. There is no substitute for experience in this regard, because the fisherman who has done a lot of varied angling under a wide set of circumstances can recognize conditions that he has successfully dealt with before, and be able to adjust better when faced with them anew.

Because there are so many variables that affect fishing success, it can be hard to develop confidence in different lures/techniques, etc., which is why it's a good idea to do some experimenting when the fishing is very good. That's how you can learn a lot. Sometimes when the catching is good in one locale, the fish suddenly shut down. Perhaps they get used to seeing a certain lure. Sometimes changing to a different color of the same lure, or simply to a different type of lure, will bring about action once again. But changing when the action is hot is one way to learn a little more about what to expect

Left: Making a change in location, lure, or technique is often intuitive, but one of the little things that contribute to angling success.

out of your lures and what to do under given circumstances, so on another occasion, when you sense a need to change, you'll know what to do.

The ability to make a change, of course, especially where lures are concerned, often makes change happen. Some casting anglers, for example, keep several rods ready so they can quickly pick up a different lure than they had been using and cast to a spot with something else or with a lure that may be more appropriate for that location. Different places call for different lures, and sometimes you go by a place while changing lures and don't get a chance to cast at it unless it's easy to do so and you're ready.

You can facilitate some lure changing by employing a good quality snap. And you can avoid wasting time rummaging around in a tackle box looking for the right lure to try by having a few likely lures in holders or lying along the side of the boat (fly fishermen often keep favorite flies handy on their vest pocket.

Another reason to have alternate lures ready, and to use more than one lure in a given place, is obvious the lure you are using at the time you go by a likely fish-holding locale may not be the one the fish want at that time. By making casts with several different lures, you are simply being a more thorough angler. That takes a little more time than using one lure and then leaving, so it means that you have to spend your fishing time wisely by concentrating on good locations.

Big-water trollers who fish out of large boats and are able to run many lines simultaneously have a clear advantage over other anglers because when they are hunting for fish in open water they can try different lures, trolling line lengths, and colors all at once. This is like building a house yourself or building it with a crew of four; you can do it both ways but one gets the job done quicker. When such trollers have success they can fish more of the same type or color of lure and be still more effective. Thus, they are able to narrow the many angling variables down much more quickly than other small-boat anglers or casters.

And there are plenty of variables that affect angling:

Lake conditions, water temperature, water color, water level, type of habitat, disposition of fish, time of year, fishing pressure, current, tides, and so forth. That's why it's tough to say with absolute certainty that one thing alone contributes to fishing success on a given day. As a result, there can be a lot of changes to make in all kinds of fishing.

Maybe on a given day you don't need to change place or lure. Maybe you have the right lure but your line is too heavy and the lure isn't getting as deep as it needs to or doesn't have the best action or you can't cast it as far as necessary. You might need to change to a lighter strength line. Maybe while fishing you have several strikes, but don't hook the fish, or you see several fish that swirl after the lure but don't take it. That's an indication that the fish are not overly aggressive and you need to fish slower and use a trailer hook. Maybe you're trolling and you see fish on your sonar that come up as if they are looking at your lures but they don't strike. That's a good time to change boat speed, increasing or decreasing it to make the lures behave differently. This tactic often triggers a strike. Things that you do to alter the working of your lures, whether trolling or casting, are changes that may bring success.

Right: Conditions can change rapidly while fishing, and sometimes success belongs to those who are able to use different lures and techniques accordingly.

Brute

Confidence

No matter what type of fishing you do, confidence is one of the most influential aspects of angling. It is a quality that can't be bought, and which you can't dupe yourself into possessing. It is also a state of mind, since there are some anglers who have spent a lot of time on the water, yet still lack confidence.

Primarily you acquire confidence through learning and doing – by developing an understanding of the habits and habitat of your quarry, by mastering the intricacies of your tackle, and by slowly putting together the pieces of the fishing jigsaw puzzle. Hopefully, good advice and tutelage when you first start fishing will serve as a big help in upgrading your angling proficiency,

There is no substitute for experience, and confidence is an intangible factor that is a product of experience and which helps fishermen be more productive.

and, if so, your confidence will soar. Just going out and catching a couple of fish (preferably the species that you are deliberately seeking) is a big boost to the neophyte's confidence. So is having, and knowing how to use, good equipment.

Too many anglers, particularly novices, lose their concentration and conviction when the fishing is slow. They unreasonably expect to catch fish easily, and when they don't do so, or their favorite places or techniques don't produce, they lose interest, become sloppy or lackadaisical, or simply are flustered. Faith in your abilities, in your equipment, and in your knowledge of where to seek various species of fish has to be acquired through experience, which is why few beginners can stand shoulder-to-shoulder with most veterans.

Ted Trueblood, the late and venerated writer for *Field & Stream*, thought that enthusiasm was one of the keys that separated consistently successful fishermen from unsuccessful or occasionally successful fishermen. In that magazine, in February 1961, he commented that consistently successful anglers and hunters were enthusiasts. 'Because such a man is enthusiastic,' said Trueblood, 'he does everything a little bit better than another who may be more or less indifferent or who doesn't honestly believe that he will kill any game or catch any fish . . . I think the difference stems primarily from the thought and effort each individual puts into his sport. And the enthusiast, the person who has faith and hope . . .does the best he can all the time. And it pays off.'

Although Trueblood noted that success breeds confidence and more success, he also noted that there are ways to help your confidence along even when fishing is poor. Changing lures, for example, has an important psychological effect on the angler, giving him 'new faith.' Changing locations, and taking a rest to prevent fatigue and discouragement, were others.

Every move that a good fisherman makes is related to confidence – in the selection of which lure to use; area to fish; in the placement of his casts; in judging when to stay in, or leave, a particular spot; in determining what type of retrieve to employ; and so on. Because he is confident he concentrates harder on what he is doing, and is generally more attentive.

At the same time he realizes that not every cast will produce a fish, nor will every day be a good one. He realizes that fish are unpredictable creatures and that he can't always figure them out, which is probably why he likes the sport in the first place. Yet, top-notch anglers are always convinced that there's a fish waiting to snare their very next cast, and that they're going to catch the fish. That's confidence.

Don't overlook the effects of feeling positive about your abilities and about your understanding of the world of fishing. Perhaps your greatest tool is not in a tackle box, but in your head.

SETTING the HOOK

Anglers devote a great deal of thought to where they fish, what they fish with, and how they use the things that they fish with, but they devote comparatively little time to what happens immediately after the strike of a fish.

On face value, hook setting is a rather subjective virtue. It is harder to set the hook on some fish than on others, and there are enough variables – whether the fish is swimming away from or toward you, whether you are sitting or standing, whether you are using a stiff or limber rod, etc. – to make a non-studious appraisal very risky. Indeed, few anglers have an accurate notion of how much force they generate when they set the hook to the best of their ability. Actually, the average fisherman is quite inefficient when he punches the hook home, as tests using instruments that gauge the force applied have demonstrated.

Consider that you may not set the hook as efficiently as desired at all times, especially when caught unawares by a strike or hampered by a bony-mouthed or strong-jawed fish, or that some other factors (such as a bow in the line while river fishing or having a striking fish run toward you) will impede your effort, and you see that it is imperative to do all that you can to execute the best hook set possible time after time.

Below: Just rearing back will sometimes set the hook and catch fish, but it is often not enough, especially with large fish, fish that jump, and fish that have tough mouths.

This starts with proper technique. Hook-setting effectiveness has little to do with your physical stature or with brute strength. If you doubt this, tie a barrel swivel to the line on any fishing rod, and have a friend stand 40 feet away from you holding the swivel clenched between his thumb and forefinger. Raise the rod slowly and apply all the pressure you can to try to pull that swivel out of his hand. If you don't jerk back violently, you can't pull it out.

Effective hook setting has to do with timing and hook point penetration. Pulling back on the rod with steady pressure after you detect a strike is not how you should set the hook, although this is how many anglers react to a strike even though they think they have done something more definitive.

There are two recognized and effective techniques in hook setting, one with a no-slack approach and the other with a slight, controlled amount of slack.

With a no-slack hook set, you lean toward the fish, reel up slack till the line is taut, and then punch the hook home. This is accomplished in the blink of an eye, and it is crucial that you only reel slack up till the line is taut but not pulling on the fish; if you tighten up the connection to the fish so far that it feels tension, it may quickly expel your offering. You acquire this timing through experience.

With a controlled slack-line set, the line is not reeled taut to the fish, but nearly so, and the hook is punched home quickly to provide shock penetration. The theory here is that you get better hook point penetration from a snappy shock force than from a tight-line pull. Try pushing a nail into the wall with the head of a hammer rather than by striking it sharply with the hammer, and you'll see the significance.

In either method there is a common denominator of speed, particularly rod tip speed. But that alone isn't the key. A principal reason why many people are ineffective at hook setting is not their inability to respond quickly, but the way they use their body and contort themselves while doing so. Hook setting is not a whole-body maneuver, but an exercise of wrists and arms.

Right: Good hook setting procedure is mostly a result of wrist and forearm movement. The arms shouldn't be waved over the head, but the rod should be brought up into the chest.

Back and legs have little to do with this. Someone thin and short might deliver more hook setting force and better hook penetration than a much larger and more powerful individual.

It also helps a great deal if you are prepared for what is about to happen before it happens. Start by keeping your rod tip down during the retrieve. With the tip down, you're in the best position to respond quickly to a strike, even, as often happens, if you are distracted from what you're doing when the strike occurs. If there is little or no slack in the line you can make a forceful sweep up or back when you set the hook, and then be in immediate control of a fish to begin playing it. When working some lures, however, it is necessary to keep the rod tip up to work the lure properly and readily detect a strike. When setting the hook you can compensate for a high rod position by bowing the rod slightly toward the fish while reeling up slack; this enables you to get a full backward sweep and be in the proper position for the beginning of the fight.

Hook setting should be a quickly accomplished maneuver. When a fish strikes, the angler reacts reflexively, bringing his rod back and up sharply while holding the reel handle and reeling the instant he feels the fish. The position of the rod is important. The butt is jammed into the stomach or mid-chest area and the full arc and power of the rod is brought into play, without having hands or arms jerk wildly over your head. In order to countermand line stretch it is important to be reeling hard and fast the moment you set the hook.

Nylon monofilament lines have about a 30 percent stretch factor when wet, which in part explains why you can deliver more force when a short nylon monofilament line is used rather than a long one (also with a dry line versus a wet one). By comparison, a low-stretch braided Dacron or cofilament line, if it had other desirable fish line qualities, would be better for hook setting over all distances, though you would still generate more force on short lengths.

Good hook-setting procedure, however, doesn't end once you have reacted and feel the fish. Like a golf swing, the follow-through is usually important and sometimes critical. The line must remain tight; people who bring their rod tip back behind their head or raise their arms up high often put some slack momentarily into the line when they bring the rod back down in front of them. Not having to do this is the advantage of keeping the rod in front of you, and also of reeling continuously until the fish is firmly hooked and offering some resistance.

There are a few other points that enter into the matter of hook setting. The type of rod that is used can aid or impede your efforts. Generally speaking, limber rods decrease your ability to generate hook-setting force while stiff rods increase it. The soft and somewhat spongey response of a limber rod does, however, make it harder to break the line and to cast light lures, so there are functional tradeoffs. A stiff rod can aid strike detection, but it could lead to breaking light lines if the hook is set particularly hard. Is there a difference in hook-setting effectiveness between types of rods? Less so than we like to think. The difference is really one of rod action.

Light lines can pose hook-setting problems, incidentally, especially for those who are accustomed to heavier tackle and jaw-breaking hook sets. Again, that's usually a problem of using a rod that is too stiff for the line. Where light line is used, you need a rod with some cushioning effect. With a medium- or light-action rod that is used with light line, and the appropriate drag setting that must necessarily be employed, it's almost impossible to break the line when setting the hook. You can prove this to yourself when you're hung up on some obstruction while using such tackle; try setting the hook to break the line and you'll find that it's just about impossible to do so.

If your line has a belly or bow in it, as it might when river fishing or when a fish takes your offering and runs laterally with it, you may not have time to take out all or most of the slack when you set the hook and still not alert the fish, so this is where you might execute a slack line snap, being sure to keep the line tight after the hook-up. Fly fishermen using light tippets and fishing in current don't want to muster

After you set the hook you have to follow through, keeping the rod tip up and applying steady pressure on the fish. In the case of strong-running fish, let the drag do the work and let the fish run while keeping a tight line.

much force anyway, so they'll use this method. A line that is impeded by some obstruction, is also hard to deal with, since your hook-setting force is directed more at that impediment than at the fish beyond. There isn't much you can do about this situation except realize the problem and regularly check your line for damaged spots that might be a problem later.

Below: For good hook setting and fish playing, keep the rod tip angled down on the retrieve when possible (1); react swiftly, keeping the rod butt in the chest area and the line tight (2); keep the rod tip up throughout the fight (3); keep slack out of the line (4); and guide the fish away from the boat or other objects (5).

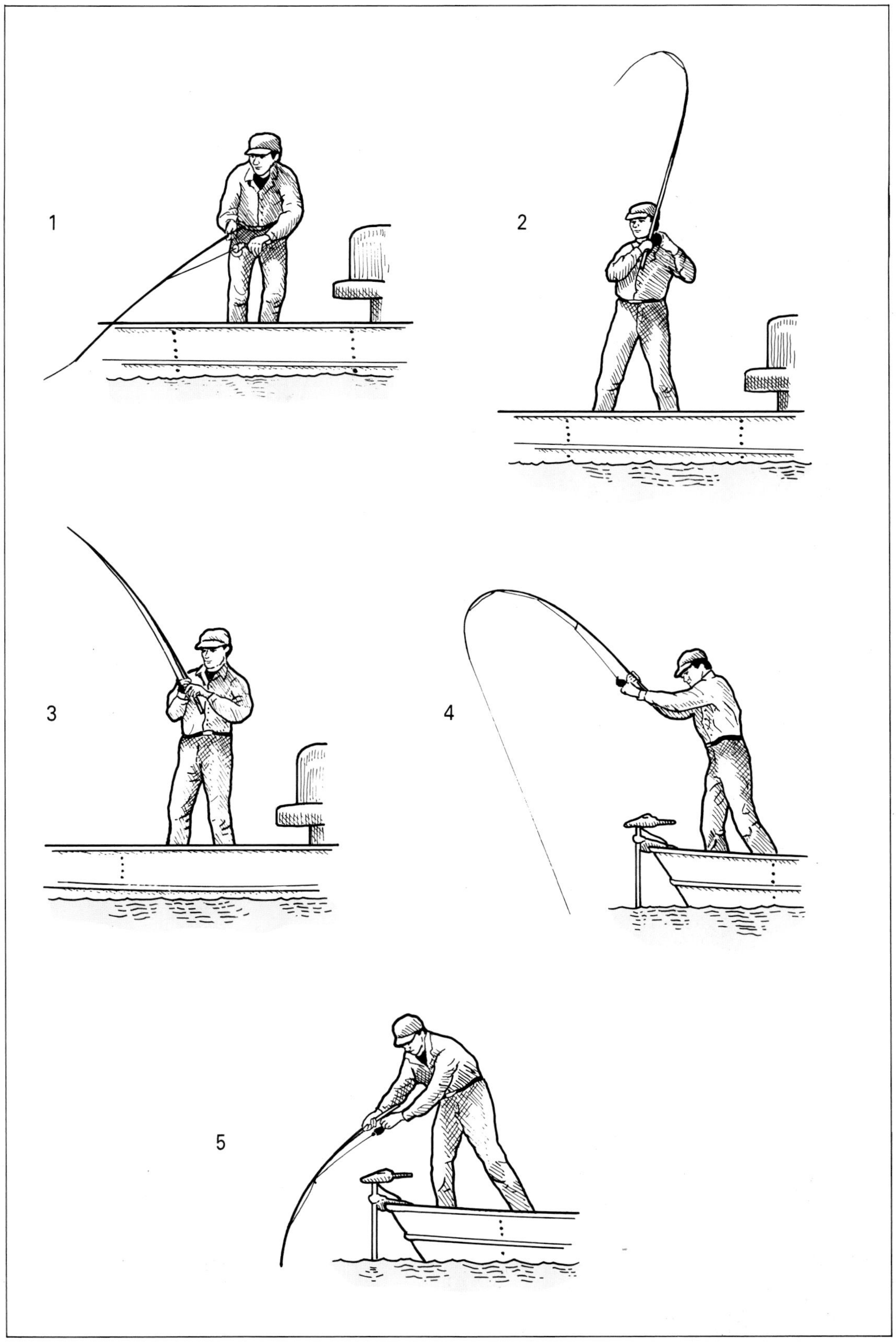

Above: Usually when setting the hook, you should keep one hand on the reel handle, and reel at the same time as you drive the hook point in. This angler, using a long limber rod and ultralight line, is exhibiting good form.

Drag slippage can also be an impedance to hook setting. Some anglers who use bait-casting tackle put their thumb on the reel spool when setting the hook so they can prevent slippage, but it is best to have the drag set precisely for the line strength so you don't have to do this.

One way to deliver better-than-average hook-setting force is to set the hook with both hands on the rod, one on the handle around the reel and one on the foregrip. Most anglers set the hook with one hand on the rod handle, and the other on the reel handle. Usually this is adequate. There are special circumstances, however (such as big-game offshore fishing), that necessitate using two hands to reef the hooks home. There are also a few occasions when it is desirable set the hook two or three times in rapid succession.

What about when trolling? The fish already has the lure when you pull the rod out of its holder; should you set the hook then? It depends on the situation and fish. Where the quarry are large and hard-mouthed, yes. When using very light line or angling for soft-mouthed fish, no, because you run the risk of pulling the lure out. In either case you will still have to concentrate on keeping pressure on the fish and not making a mistake when playing it.

Paying attention to these matters will help you be more efficient at setting the hook. It you want to put this information to work for you in the best way possible, however, be sure to sharpen new and used hooks. The primary benefit of having a sharp hook is to gain penetrating effectiveness. Maximum penetration translates into optimum hook-setting efficiency and better hook retention, which ultimately mean more fish hooked and landed.

PLAYING FISH

While fighting a strong fish, this angler will pump it by lowering the rod while simultaneously reeling, then bringing the rod back to its present position and repeating.

Many of the large fish that strike are not caught because a lot of anglers don't know how to properly fight and land fish that put up more than token resistance. The following information about fish-playing techniques will help you catch any fish that does its share of tugging and scrapping before being subdued. You should employ these to reduce the chances of losing fish.

Playing, or fighting, a fish starts with hooking them well (see p.110). From the moment that you set the hook, the position of the rod is important. The butt should be jammed into the stomach or mid-chest area and the full arc and power of the rod should be brought into play.

Throughout the fight, keep the rod tip up and maintain pressure on the fish. The position of the rod butt remains unchanged. Reel the line in while lowering the rod, then pressure the fish as you bring the rod back up. This technique is used for all but the smallest fish; it is often referred to as 'pumping,' and is critical when fighting a large or strong fish and/or when using light line.

Often when a fish is fairly close to you it is still energetic. Continue to keep the rod high. This is a time to be directing the fish. If you're in a boat and the fish streaks toward it (perhaps to swim under it) you could be put at a disadvantage, particularly when using light tackle. You must reel as fast as possible to keep slack out. If the fish gets under the boat, stick the rod tip well into the water to keep the line away from objects and possibly being cut.

You should anticipate that a fish will rush the boat and should be prepared to head it around the stern or bow. In some cases a companion can manipulate the boat (especially with an electric motor) to help swing the stern or bow away from a fish, which is a smart maneuver that can aid the playing of a large fish. If possible, go toward the bow or stern to better follow or control the fish. Don't hang back in a tug-of-war with a large, strong fish; use finesse rather than muscle.

When a fish swims around your boat, keep the rod up (sometimes out, too) and apply pressure to force its head up and to steer it clear of the outboard or electric motor and their propellers. (Sometimes it's best to tilt motors out of the water.)

At times it may be necessary to change the angle of pull on a strong and stubborn fish, perhaps to help steer it in a particular direction, or to make it fight a little differently. Apply side pressure then, bringing the rod down and holding it parallel to the water, and turning your body partially sideways to the fish. Fight it as you would if the rod was perpendicular to the water.

With very large fish that get near the boat but are still energetic (tuna, billfish, big salmon, etc.), or with big fish that stay very deep below the boat and can't be budged by the fisherman, it may be necessary to move the boat a fair distance away and rather quickly, letting line peel off the drag. This changes the angle of pull on the fish and usually helps bring it up from the depths.

In current, a big fish that gets downriver and through rapids where an angler is unable to follow, may return upriver if the angler releases line from his reel and allows slack line to drift below the fish. The line below the fish acts as a pulling force from downstream (instead of ahead), and may cause the fish to head upstream again.

With some species of jumping fish (tarpon, in particular), and when using fly tackle, it is necessary to slacken the tension when the fish jumps by bowing the rod toward it so the jumper cannot use taut line as leverage for pulling free of the hook. Sometimes you can stop a fish from jumping by putting your rod tip in the water and keeping a tight line, which changes the angle of pull and may stop a fish from clearing the surface.

Eventually the fish is next to you and may be ready for landing. If it still has a last burst of energy, however, this will be a crucial moment.

Because of the short distance between you and the fish, there will be a lot of stress on your tackle. You must act swiftly when the fish makes its last bolt for freedom.

As it surges away don't pressure it. Let it go. Point the rod at the fish at the critical moment so there is no rod pressure. A large fish will peel line off the drag, which, if set properly (and does not stick), will keep tension on the fish within the tolerance of the line's strength, and provide the least amount of pressure possible. As the surge tapers, lift the rod up and work the fish.

If you are alone and without a net, you must be careful when landing the fish. Keep a taut line, extend the rod well back behind and over your head, and reach for the fish with your other hand (landing it by hand with some species, or gaffing or netting others). In this position you are able to maintain some control over the fish, even if it is still active, and avoid creating a momentary slack line situation that may give the fish its freedom.

Generally, fish-playing activities take place in a short period of time. When playing most hard-fighting saltwater fish and nearly all freshwater fish, the action is often fast. Your reactions must be swift and instinctive, and your tackle, particularly line and reel drag, must be capable and of good quality.

Fighting large, strong fish requires constant effort by the angler, and sometimes quick maneuvering by the boat captain.

You may need to relax tension as a fish jumps, or point the rod at it to reduce line stress and drag tension when it surges away.

In saltwater, however, such large fish as tuna, billfish, tarpon, shark, and some deep-water dwellers, will require up to several hours to land, depending on the size of fish, tackle employed, and skill of the angler. In such long fights, it is imperative that presure constantly be applied to the fish, as they can regain strength with just a little rest. All tackle is put to its severest test in such a situation. The maneuvering of the boat is often a critical factor in the outcome.

Reasons for losing fish

Many fish are lost somewhere between being hooked and being landed, and often this is a result of the way in which the angler plays the fish. A big fish, for example, will often run for cover or some obstruction and an angler must do his best to prevent the fish from getting to those places. Within the capabilities of your tackle, take the fight to the fish; don't sit back and be casual.

Line breakage is often the reason for losing large fish. Certainly it is possible to have purchased an inferior quality line, but more often breakage is due to line that is old and poorly conditioned, or line that is worn and weakened. Fishing line isn't good for angling indefinitely. Old line, especially if it has been left in the sunlight for a long time or it has been severely stressed in the past, needs to be replaced. Line that is frayed or sports little nicks or burrs has lost a good deal of its strength; check it occasionally and cut off affected sections.

When you have a line problem, did the main stem of the line actually break or did the knot slip or break? Poorly tied knots weaken fishing line, causing you to fish with line that is not as strong as you expect and that is unable to take the strain of playing a big or hard-pulling fish. Many anglers don't tie fishing knots as well as they should, and some don't realize that there are knots and then there are fishing knots (see p.26).

Another reason for losing fish is an improper reel drag setting. When the drag is set too tight, line won't freely come off the spool under the surges of a strong fish. This feature, which is akin to shock-absorption, helps prevent overloading the line, causing shock breakage. When the drag is set too loose, however, there is not enough tension on the fish, so a middle ground, based on the strength of line and fishing conditions, is best.

Playing a large fish that has run downriver may require moving downriver, too, to keep the fish from spooling off all line or cutting the line on some obstruction, but also to be able to fight it from a better position.

LANDING FISH

Landing a fish by net, gaff, or hand is just the culmination of the act of fighting and playing fish, but it's also where a lot of anglers have trouble, especially when large, strong fish are involved.

Perhaps the greatest mistake of new anglers is reeling a fish right up to the tip of their rod when the catch is at boatside, as if they are going to spear it; better to leave a few feet of line between the rod tip and fish to direct it to a net or swing it onboard. Applying too much pressure on an active fish near the boat is another mistake. Finesse, not muscle, is the secret. The key to properly landing fish is to employ common sense, anticipation, and finesse.

An easy way to boat small fish that are well hooked is by simply lifting them aboard with the rod. This is only practical for small- to medium-size fish caught on tackle that is sturdy enough to permit it.

Landing fish by hand

This is a tricky maneuver for some species, but a practical and desirable method for those that have no teeth. Fish that are small, and that are to be released immediately, are best handled at a minimum, leaving them in the water while unhooking them.

Toothless species, like bass, snook, and stripers, can be landed by grasping the lower lip, provided the fish is well tired before the attempt is made. Simply insert your thumb over the lower lip, with remaining fingers outside and underneath. This immobilizes the fish and is good for unhooking as well as landing. Be sure not to plant your thumb on the hooks of the lure.

Netting fish

For other species, particularly large ones, netting or gaffing is required. Most small fish don't need to be netted but some, such as scrappy stream trout, are often netted because they are difficult to land by hand. Proper netting technique is as much a matter of knowing what not to do as it is knowing what to do. Under most circumstances you shouldn't put the net in the water and wait for the fish to come close. Nor should you wave the net overhead where a fish might see it. A net in the water or moving above it is foreign and alarming to fish. It's best to keep the net solidly in hand at the ready, either motionless or out of sight, until a fish is almost within reach.

Don't attempt to net a fish unless it is within reach, and not if it is going away from you or appears to be able to go away from you. The fish should ideally be headed for you so that it must continue forward, or that if it turns you may still be able to move the net in front of it. As a general rule, don't try to net a fish unless its head is on the surface or just breaking to the surface. A fish that is up on the surface has little mobility, and cannot do as much as one with its entire body in the water, particularly if the fish isn't played out.

Don't try to net a fish from behind. If a fish is completely exhausted you may be able to net it from the side, but the most desirable position is from the front. And don't touch the fish with the rim of the net until it is well into the net. Touching fish, particularly if they are still lively, often initiates wild behavior.

If the fish acts wild, it could roll on your line and break it, or simply snap

Some fish – without teeth – can be landed readily by hand.

Net a fish head first and try to get it fully into the net before attempting to lift. Many fish are lost because they are only partially into the net when the angler tries to hoist them into the boat.

it from the force of its getaway rush. Therefore, resist taking a stab at a fish that may be technically within reach of your extended net, but not in the best position for capture.

A major problem that occurs when anglers try to net a fish that is in a poor position to be netted, or when they don't get a fish coming squarely into the net, is snagging a multihooked lure on the mesh or webbing of the net bag. This is one of the surest ways to lose fish, particularly those that are heavy and cannot be readily hoisted into the boat or scooped up in the now-tangled net.

The angler can help the netter by making an effort to get the fish's head up so that it is near or on the surface and not deep in the water. When the fish comes up and is being worked toward the net, the fisherman should back up in the boat, put more pressure on the fish to gain line, raise the rod high to keep the fish's head up, and tell the netter that the time is right, attempting to lead the fish closer as the netter goes into action. The angler should be prepared for miscues, too, when his fish is to be netted. It is a good idea to back off a bit on the reel drag, or perhaps open the bail of the reel, when a fish is brought into the net. If it flops out, runs through it, or charges away, there may be a lot of pressure on your tackle, so anticipate this possibility and don't count the fish as caught until it is solidly in hand.

Netting a fish by yourself is often a tricky chore, made more difficult by the influence of current, wind, and tide. Bringing a fish to net or boat as quickly as possible may not be feasible when you are alone and have a large fish, and it is often necessary to play the fish out thoroughly before you can slip the net under it. Try to get the fish to within several feet of the tip of the rod, then raise the rod high over and behind your head while you reach for the fish with net extended in your other hand.

Netting efforts are sometimes more arduous in fast-moving waters because fish are usually below you and it is hard to get big fish back upcurrent and positioned for proper netting. Another problem is that when you don't gain on fish in current, they rest momentarily and recoup enough strength to prolong the battle or give that last extra

With rod high and behind him, an angler uses good technique to get a large trout into his net.

Gaffing is done with many large and toothy fish, especially in saltwater, and a sharp hook and firm, careful action bring best results.

kick just when you think you have them. For this reason, those who net a fish for someone else in swift water usually get a reasonable distance downriver, in a position to land a tired fish as it wallows near the bank, still resisting the angler but unable to swim off with vigor.

If it isn't feasible to try to land a fish because the net is too small or because you are without a net, you always have the option of landing it by hand or beaching it. In either case the fish must be thoroughly whipped and under your control before you can do so.

Gaffing fish

Fish that are netted usually can be released alive if desired. Gaffing is another option for landing fish, however. Gaffs are primarily used in saltwater; most gaffing is done for fish that are to be kept, although some fish are released if gaffed in the mouth.

Like netting, gaffing isn't terribly difficult, although fishermen sometimes have trouble. In essence, you gaff a fish by getting the point of the gaff in the water beneath the fish and then strike upward sharply. Being too excited or being too lackadaisical can causes problems. When gaffers flail wildly they often miss the fish or, worse, strike and break the angler's line. Poking the fish with the gaff instead of ramming it home is likely to make the fish act wild, perhaps causing it to surge enough to break free.

It's important to firmly but surely gaff the fish and follow through with the upward motion by lifting the fish out of the water. Most fish to be kept are gaffed in the midsection, which, of course, initiates bleeding and may ruin some meat. Fish to be released can be gaffed in the lower jaw, preferably by putting the gaff point through the inside of the mouth and out the lower jaw (rather than coming from outside to inside). This is done when the fish is thoroughly played out. Obviously, the point of the gaff must be razor sharp to do the most effective job. The point should be covered when the gaff is not in use.

RELEASING FISH

If you can remove a hook from a fish while it is in the water, that will enhance its survival. Generally, the sooner a fish is released after capture, the better.

Though anglers as a group release more fish voluntarily today, they also release more fish out of necessity. There are many more situations in which anglers (especially in freshwater) must release fish slot limits, minimum size limits, fish caught during closed seasons, catch-and-release waters, fish that may not be kept in any size, fish that should not be consumed, etc. Thus, there are many more fish being released because they have to be released.

Proper care of the fish you want to, or must, release goes a long way toward helping perpetuate quality angling, as well as marking you as a sportsman, in the real sense of the word.

The suitability of a fish for release is sometimes affected before it is landed. When very light tackle is used, or when exceptionally large or strong fish put up a lasting and determined fight, fish will be exhausted upon landing and harder to rejuvenate. Such a fish experiences shock, probably from the buildup of lactic acid, which increases the fish's need for oxygen; if placed back in the water immediately, it may turn belly-up and sink out of sight. It may not right itself, and then will not recover. This is as true for small fish as for large ones, though the latter may take much longer to revive.

Whether fish are tired or not, the best thing for their survival is that they never leave the water, a feat that few fishermen do often enough. In some instances, fish can be shaken off at boatside by leaving some slack in the line and jiggling the rod tip. This is especially true if single-hooked and barbless lures are used. Wading fishermen can accomplish this easier than boat or bank anglers, but it is possible to unhook some fish in the water by grasping the hook with needle-nosed pliers and pulling the barb out.

A minimum amount of handling is desirable in all cases, particularly in warm water or warm weather. If fish must be taken out of the water, be conscious of their inability to breathe and of the length of time that they are forced to forego oxygen while being unhooked. Don't let them flop onshore or in a boat if you intend to release them; their protective mucuous coating can be removed, increasing the possibility of an infection that will be grotesque and life-threatening. Don't grasp fish tightly around their midsections to prevent movement during the unhooking process, as this can cause internal damage. Don't put your fingers in their eye sockets or grab them by the gills, although you can carefully slip a finger between gills and gill plate to hold a fish (this is advisable for toothy species), as well as hold some fish by the lip (bass, stripers, crappie, etc.). Don't keep fish that are to be released on a stringer or cooped up in a warm, poorly oxygenated container or well; you're cutting down their survival chances significantly by doing this. In a well or container, cool water and abundant oxygen are vital. And don't cull – replacing a fish on a stringer or in a well with another – unless you are keeping an injured fish and releasing a healthy one. Generally a fish that has been detained is not as suitable for release as one that has been freshly caught.

While it is seldom beneficial to keep fish in so-called livewells for later release (as opposed to instant, on-the-spot release), there are many people who do this in freshwater. In this case, it is good to use Catch and Release, a granular chemical that stabilizes fish, causing them to require less oxygen, and which fights fungus infection and mucus loss. Using ice, non-iodized salt, and some drugs (available from aquarium supply stores) are other measures that can be taken to aid fish that are detained for a long period prior to release, though this is something that relatively few anglers need to be concerned with.

When releasing some fish and keeping others, keep the ones that are caught in deep water rather than those caught in shallow water. Fish caught in deep water are usually harder to revive than those caught in shallow water, so be thoughtfully selective. Keep a fish that is bleeding rather than one that is not; bleeders, particularly those hooked in the gills, are less likely to survive than unharmed fish.

By not using bait you can significantly reduce the chances of killing fish that you must, or want to, release. However, when it is not prudent to remove a bait hook from a deeply caught fish (because you may damage internal organs and/or cause bleeding), cut the line or leader and leave the hook inside. The hook will eventually corrode (bronze, blue, and gold hooks corrode much faster than cadmium or stainless, and all hooks corrode faster in saltwater). This may not guarantee the fish's survival, but the odds will be increased significantly.

Be particularly careful with netting. A net can remove some of a fish's mucous coating and scales. Also, a plug-caught fish often gets enmeshed in a net because some of the loose hooks catch in the webbing during the netting process. As the fish thrashes around he pulls against the stuck plug, which can bend the hooks and/or tear the mouth of the fish where it is caught, prolonging release efforts. Fish caught on single-hooked lures are much easier to release, whether landed by hand or net. Hooking-mortality studies have shown that single- and treble-hooked lures are about equal in terms of causing fish mortality, but it can take longer to remove treble-hooked lures from a fish, and in the case of fish that are netted, this may really cause problems. Barbless hooks, therefore, if fish are to be netted, make sense. (Incidentally,

Right: Easing a fish back into the water is preferable to tossing it back. Fish that have fought particularly hard and are very tired may need some coddling in order to regain their strength before swimming away.

there is a way to determine the weight of a fish without having to keep and kill it – multiply the length by the girth squared, then divide by 800.)

While it may not be harmful to toss some fish back in the water, it cannot be helpful either. A gentle release, head-first, and after having certified that the fish has pizzazz and will scoot away, is desirable. It may be necessary to take the fish by lip or tail and lead it around head-first so that water flows through the gills. Keep the fish upright, minimize vertical holding, and don't let it go until the fish tries to pull away from you.

Seeing a fish swim off is no guarantee of its survival. That's merely short-term survival. What the long-term survival, or delayed mortality, may be is open to speculation, but it certainly depends on the treatment of the fish prior to and during the release.

Below: Leading a fish head-first, to force water through its gills, will help revive it. In a river, face the fish upstream and release it into the current.

From Catchin' to Kitchen

The key to enjoying fish isn't necessarily having a particularly good recipe or using a certain method of cooking. Once the fish is in the kitchen, you can increase or decrease its palatability, but if you harbor any hope of enjoying its fullest taste and nutrition, you must give it proper attention from the moment you catch it. The advantage that anglers have over people who buy fish is that they get this food as fresh as it can possibly be found, and they control its preparations and treatment. The end results will only be as good as you want them to be, and make them.

Care on the water

Once you've caught a fish that you're going to keep, you have to decide what to do with it. Where are you going to put it? On the floor of the boat? On the pier? In a tub or bag? That's okay – if it's cold out, if the sun isn't shining on it, if it will only be there for a few minutes, or if you don't particularly care what it will taste like.

Keep fish out of the sun and preferably in a cool, or iced, environment. The hotter the weather, the quicker fish can spoil.

The worst you can do is pay no attention to fish you've just caught. Leaving fish exposed to air and sun for a long time is undesirable, as is leaving fish ungutted overnight. Unaerated livewells, livewells filled with warm water, and stringers that are overcrowded or trolled or hung in warm surface water do not aid the edibility of fish they contain.

Ideally you should clean fish immediately after they've been caught, then put them on ice. But that isn't always practical. Maybe you can't clean fish at the place where you catch them. Or you simply don't want to stop fishing to do so. Or you don't have ice, or a fillet knife, with you. Do so, however, as soon as possible.

Air and water temperatures are keys to good fish care. The warmer both are the harder it is to keep fish alive and/or fresh till you stop fishing or reach the place where you will be cleaning and storing them, and the sooner you need to begin preparations. Do whatever you can to keep fish protected from heat and warmth. At the very least that may mean putting them in the shade, stopping fishing after a reasonable length of time to clean them, covering them with a wet cloth, or taking care to keep them alive in a protected, cool place.

A stringer or rope is the most common way to contain whole fish until you bring them home or to the landing site. If you string fish, make sure they are allowed to breathe so they stay alive. Don't run the stringer through the gill. Put it through the lower jaw (and in the case of big fish or weak stringers, put it through both jaws). Try to keep the stringer away from gasoline in the water or any other substance that might affect the flavor of the fish. Take the stringer out of the water when the boat is underway at full speed, and try not to leave it out of the water for a long time. If you're going a long distance, stop for a minute and put the stringer back in the water. Whether in the water or boat, keep stringered fish in a shaded locale.

There is merit to killing some fish immediately, even if you have the option of keeping them alive, and also to keeping some fish alive rather than killing them. Some fish that die slowly, and struggle and bruise themselves in the process, won't taste as good as they might if they were simply dispatched

with a couple of quick blows to the top of the head with a billy and stored temporarily in an appropriate environment. Still other fish are pretty hardy, and if you have the option, for example, of keeping them alive in cool water rather than dead under a cloth on the floor of the boat, opt for alive.

Remember that once fish are dead, the inevitable natural process of spoilage through bacteria growth begins. Fish are among the most perishable of foods. With this in mind, it sometimes pays to use a livewell to contain fish, especially if the water is cool and if there is constant water circulation.

If you're not keeping fish alive, and you have an ice-packed food or beverage cooler, you should place freshly caught fish in the cooler for later cleaning. You can leave ungutted fish on ice all day and clean them at the end of the day without sacrificing freshness or taste. Plan for this eventuality at the beginning of the day by obtaining ice before going fishing. For short-term storage, cube ice is best, because you can cover fish fully with it.

You can tell when fish have lost their freshness if they are dried and shriveled, if they smell, if their eyes are glossy, if the skin is bleached, and so on. Fish that exhibit these conditions may be edible, but the manner of handling has contributed to some loss of freshness and therefore tastiness.

Cleaning

How you clean fish depends to some extent on the species, its size, and how you expect to cook it. Some fish, especially small, pan-sized species, need only to be gutted and scaled for frying. Larger fish that will be baked require the same treatment. Fish to be pan-fried or sauted should be filleted.

The best you can do is to eat fish soon after they have been caught; a fish fry shore lunch cannot be topped for freshness.

If you'll be baking the fish or if you want the skin, you'll need to remove the scales. (A few fish, such as small trout and salmon, don't need scaling.) Scaling is best accomplished when the fish is whole, and by working from tail to head. You can use a fillet knife blade to scale fish, though a spoon, a tooth-edged scaler, or some equivalent implement will suffice. If you're at an outdoor cleaning station, which can be found at some piers, landings, marinas, and fish camps, you might be able to run water on the fish to facilitate scale removal and keep them from flying all over. In any event it's best to scale fish outdoors.

If you aren't going to fillet a fish, you

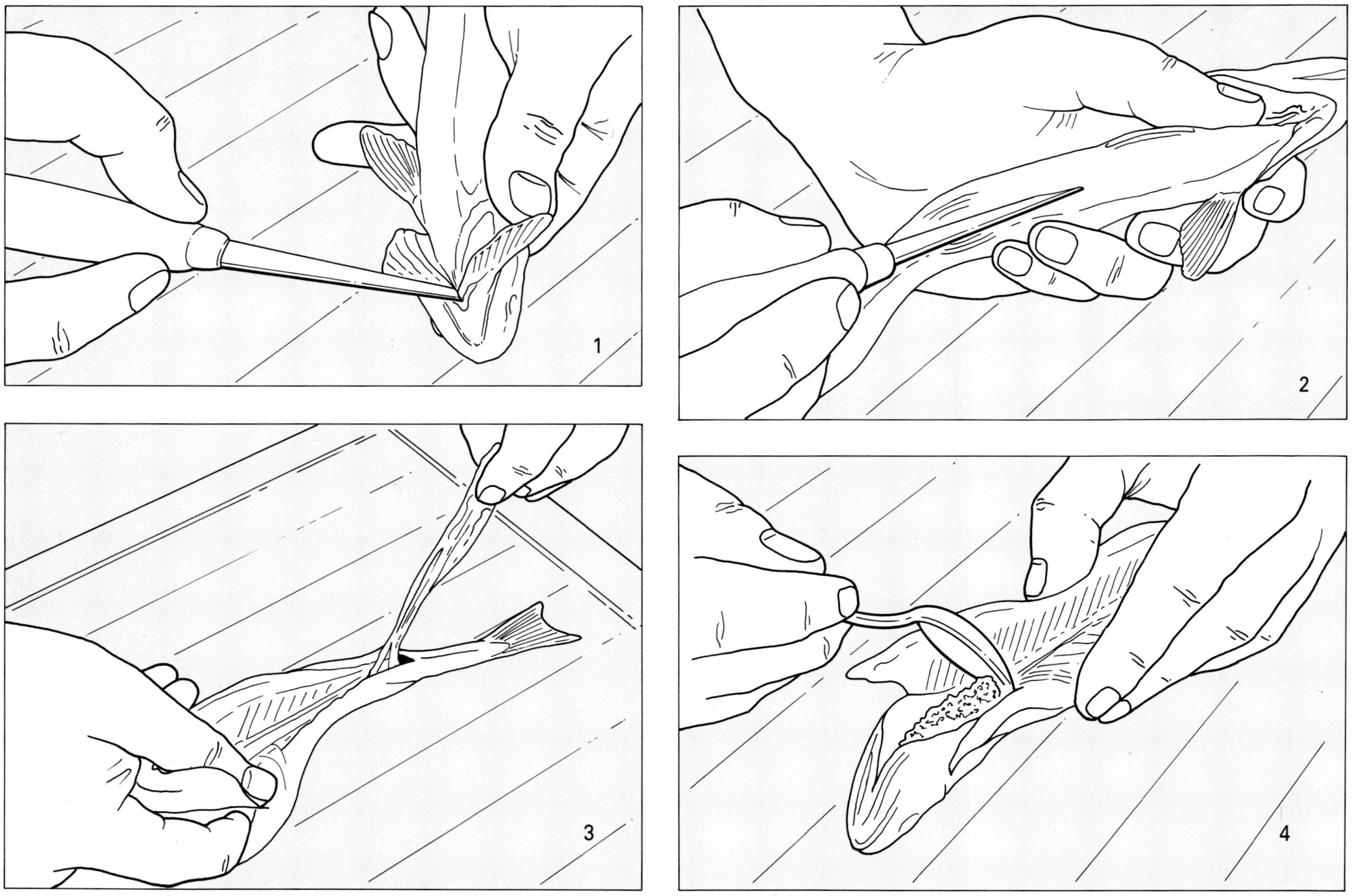

Small trout are a fish that are easily cleaned while astream. Start by turning the trout belly up and cut away connective tissue between gills and throat with a thin-bladed knife (1). Insert knife tip into vent and run the blade up to the throat (2). Grasp head and pull the gills toward the tail, pulling the entrails with it (3). Scrape out the bloodline with thumb nail or spoon and rinse fish with cool water.

need to gut it by removing the entrails from its body cavity after it has been scaled. Insert the point of a sharp knife blade in the anal area and move it forward until it is near the base of the pelvic fin. Clean out the contents of the body cavity, being especially careful to completely remove the bloodline (kidney) recessed in the cavity.

Cut the head and tail off if they aren't needed. For small fish that will be pan-fried, you should remove the dorsal and anal fins; slice along each side of the base of these fins, then pull free. Flush the cavity with clean cool water. At this point, a fish that has been gutted and scaled is ready for eating or freezing.

Generally the quickest method of

Filleting, as this angler is doing, is the preferred method of cleaning most fish, especially those to be fried. Small fish, and those to be baked, may be gutted and descaled.

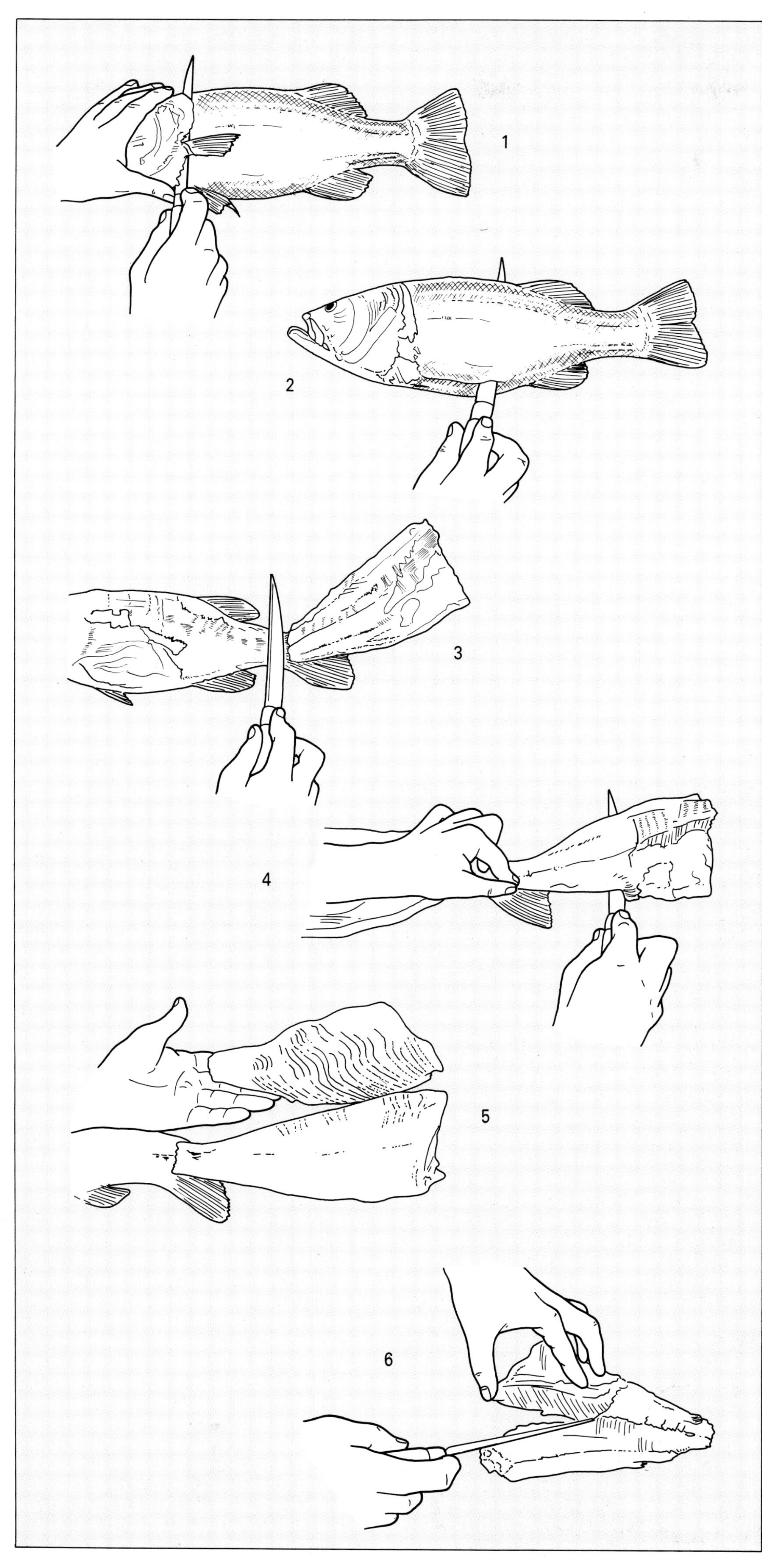

cleaning fish is to fillet them, which removes the rib cage bones that anguish many reluctant fish-eaters. When properly done filleting causes little loss of meat, and is accomplished easily. One of the keys to good filleting is having the proper instrument. A sharp, moderately flexible blade with an upwardly turned point is best. A 7- to 8-inch blade is standard for most freshwater fish and the average smaller species of saltwater fish. A smaller blade would do if you filleted nothing but pan-sized fish, while a longer blade is helpful for big-bodied fish.

The first filleting step is to make an angled cut behind the pectoral fin down to the backbone. Reverse the direction of the blade so that it is facing the tail and lying flat on the backbone, and slice back toward the tail along the backbone. A smooth cut, rather than a stop-and-go sawing motion, is best.

If the fish has been scaled, cut through the skin at the tail.

If the skin is to be removed in the filleting process, do not cut through the tail, but slice to the end without severing and flop the meat backward. Angle your knife through the meat to the skin, then slice along the skin, separating the meat while exerting pressure on the skin with your free hand. If you accidentally cut through the tail, freeing the fillet from the carcass, you will find it a little more difficult to remove the skin. In this case, press the thumbnail of your free hand on the tail of the fillet (or use a fork), and skin it with your knife hand.

Now, with either scaled or skinned fillet, cut behind the rib cage, slicing the whole section away. Use the same procedure for the other side of the fish. Rinse fillets and prepare for the freezer or for eating. This filleting technique can be used on nearly all fish, except those with additional Y-shaped bones.

There are some other fish that require special dressing treatment. Catfish, for example, pose problems to many people, yet can be simply dressed. To skin and gut small catfish for pan frying, make a thin slice on the top of the fish, from behind the adipose fin up to the dorsal fin, and continue with a vertical cut from the dorsal fin down to the backbone. Put the knife aside, grab the head with one hand and body with the other and bend the head down to break the backbone. Hold the body portion firmly, with finger over the broken backbone, and pull the head away from the fish toward the tail, removing skin and entrails in the process. Cut the tail off and rinse the fish.

To fillet a fish, make an angled cut behind pectoral fin down to backbone (1); reverse knife and slice toward tail along backbone (2); stop just short of the tail (3) and then separate flesh and skin (4 and 5). Slice rib cage away and rinse fillet.

Left: Some species, like these catfish, require a little different treatment. Small catfish are usually skinned for frying whole.

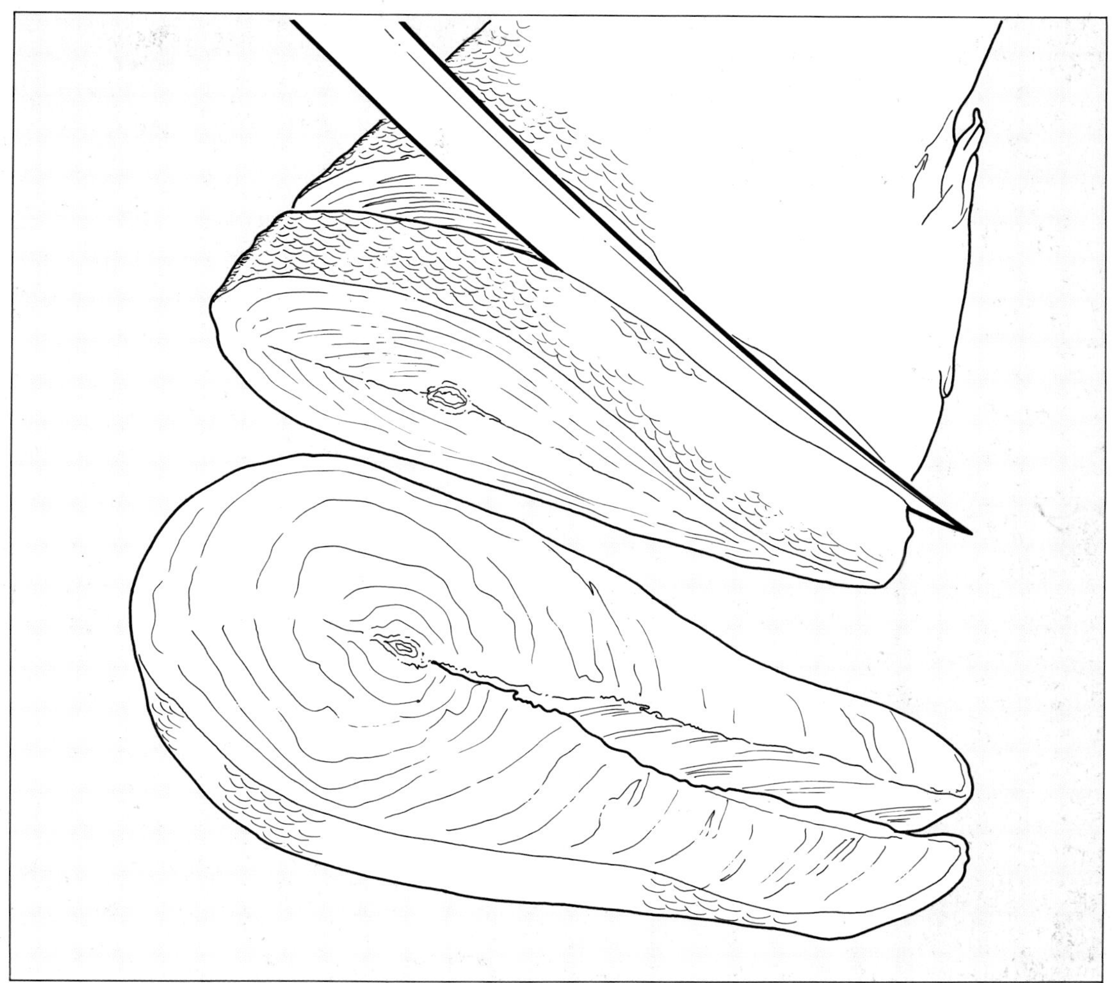

With larger catfish it's best to slice the perimeters of the skin. Hold the head firmly. Slice completely around the fish behind the pectoral fin. Slice along the top of the fish and around both sides of the adipose fin, then slice along the belly and around both sides of the pectoral fin. Use a pair of snub-nose pliers to grasp the skin near the pectoral fin, and pull back firmly toward the tail to remove it. Repeat on the other side. Sever the head and tail and remove entrails. You can now fillet the fish, keep as is, or steak it.

Steaking fish for frying or broiling is a good way to deal with large specimens. To steak a fish, scale and gut it first, then make a slice on both sides of the fins and pull them free. Cut the head and tail off and make the steaks about 1-inch thick. A fillet knife won't do an adequate job of steaking fish. Steaks should be neatly cut, not ragged and hacked. Use a butcher's knife, or cleaver, for steaking.

A final suggestion about cleaning fish: Some fish contain a dark lateral line that has a different flavor than the rest of the meat. If you fillet these fish and remove the skin, you can also slice away this dark flesh. For some fish that have a fairly high fat or oil content (such as bluefish and lake trout) it's a good idea to trim the belly section. With Great Lakes salmonids, and occasionally other fish, slice off a little of the back tissue and as much fatty belly tissue as is evident. These portions are known to harbor the principal concentration of pollutants such as PCBs. By trimming this flesh you can minimize the amount of potentially harmful chemical (not detectable by taste, incidentally) that you consume. This procedure is recommended by many state health and fisheries agencies for a wide range of fish in many different waters.

Below: These large fillets still need some attention before storage. The rib cage will have to be sliced away from the flesh, and each fillet will be rinsed in clean water to remove dirt and blood.

Care in the kitchen

If you bring home fresh fish that will be eaten in a day or two, you can wrap them tightly in freezer paper and foil, or in a sealable plastic bag, and place them in the refrigerator. Let them stay like this no more than two days, and then only if they were refrigerated the same day they were caught.

For longer storage, fish must be frozen. Remember that fish are very perishable, so they must be wrapped properly, and won't stay fresh when frozen for extremely long periods of time. Fatty or oily fish should be eaten within a few months of freezing. Other fish should be eaten within six to eight months for best taste, and frozen smoked fish can last up to a year. Generally, however, it's wise to eat fish as soon as possible. By labeling and dating packages you can consume stored fish on a rotational calendar basis, using the oldest fish first.

You can store fish simply in one tight wrapping of aluminum foil for a short period. But if they're in the freezer like this very long, they'll develop the white-tipped symptoms of freezer burn, plus it's easy to puncture or scrape corners of foil packages and expose the contents. Better to double- or even triple-wrap fish using wrapping paper, foil, and/or freezer paper. The delicatessen wrap, in which the ends of the paper are brought over the fish to meet one another and then are folded together several times, ensures a good seal.

Be sure to pack fish so there is enough for yourself or your family for a single meal, and, if possible, put wrapping paper in between fish or fillets to make them easier to separate and thaw. Also, label each package by writing on the outside with an indelible marker (or put a piece of masking tape on the package and label that).

Another method of storing fish is freezing in blocks of water in plastic containers, empty milk cartons, etc. If you don't have much food in your freezer, or only put a few fish in it occasionally, you might try this.

SPECIES

AMBERJACK

With the exception of tuna, amberjack are as hard-fighting a fish, pound for pound, as is found in saltwater. Any angler who has engaged in a tug-of-war with a large amberjack knows well how his forearm muscles have been strained and how his back and shoulders ache after the duel.

There are many fish in the jack family, and a host of North American amberjacks, all of which have thicker and longer bodies than their relatives. The foremost amberjacks, however, number two: the greater amberjack, which is found along the southern Atlantic coast, and the California yellowtail, which is found along the southern Pacific coast. The California yellowtail is generally referred to simply as 'yellowtail,' although there are other species of that name, and also as 'California amberjack,' which is a different and less popular fish. It does have a light yellow lateral stripe. The greater amberjack is the largest of the species. Both are especially popular with party and charter boat anglers, as well as with private boat anglers.

It takes fairly stout tackle to land large amberjacks such as these yellowtails.

Amberjacks are a wide-ranging fish and likely to be found in various locales, providing good fishing from spring through summer. They are most commonly associated with such intermediate to deep habitat as reefs, rocky outcrops, wrecks, buoys, and other structures. They usually band in small groups, and it is typical to catch an amberjack and have others follow it to the boat. Leaving it hooked or tethered may keep the school around and provide further success.

Amberjacks are fast swimmers and voracious predators that feed on small fish, such as sardines and anchovies in the Pacific, and on crabs and squid. Fishing with cut or live bait is very popular, as is vertical jigging with bucktails or metal jigging spoons. Lures are sometimes adorned with a strip or chunk of meat.

They take a lure or bait very hard, and there is seldom question as to whether a strike has been received. When fishing in deep water, it is often critical to muscle a big amberjack immediately after the fights begins, as they usually head deep for cover and, if successful, will break the line on a rock.

It is a chore to turn a big amberjack immediately and get it coming away from the cover. Amberjack are hard fighters that make determined runs and fight all the way to the boat, even when brought up from deep water. A strong rod and fairly heavy line are often needed, and some fishermen, who hook an amberjack while deep fishing for snappers and groupers, find that they are overmatched when an amberjack comes along.

Amberjacks, especially yellowtails, are found near the surface at times, too, and casting bait or plugs, spoons, and flies is possible, from a boat or from shore. Trollers use deep-diving plugs in appropriate places as well.

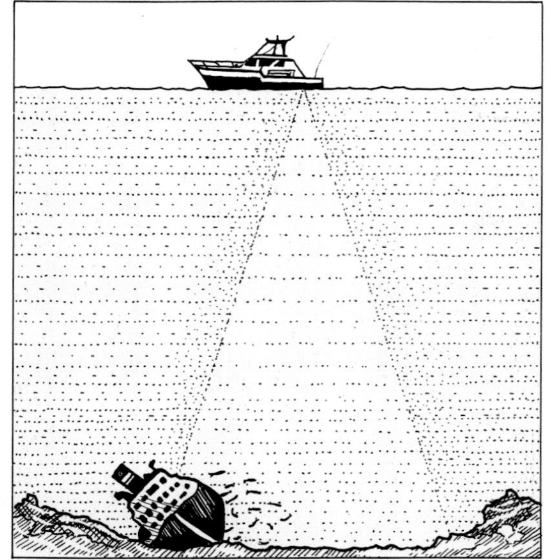

Saltwater anglers use sonar to help locate wrecks; these usually have a variety of fish around them, including amberjack in tropical waters.

BARRACUDA

Long, slender, silvery, and fearsome-looking, the barracuda is often a fish that won't be around when a fisherman wants to catch it, but can be a nuisance when he's looking for something else. Nonetheless, barracuda are able battlers that often strike savagely and frequently jump out of the water when hooked, yet they are an under-rated saltwater gamefish.

There are several forms of barracuda in North America. The great barracuda, which is found primarily in warm water along the southeastern coast of the U.S. as well as in the Florida Keys and the Caribbean, is the most prominent of these and the largest-growing; the West Coast hosts the smaller Pacific barracuda.

Barracuda are primarily found in shallow water close to shore, and around such locales as mangrove edges, bridges, and jetties. They are also found away from shore, however, around reefs, wrecks, oil rigs, coral heads, and the edges of dropoffs. Many a blue-water troller has ventured a little too shallow inshore and been rewarded with a barracuda when he was seeking other game. However, large barracuda are often found in or near deep water and by themselves, while smaller barracuda may school.

For a fish with a ferocious reputation, barracuda can actually be timid. They are alert to the presence of anglers and boats, yet they are known to closely approach divers. They will follow a lure for quite a distance, but they'll scoot off as the lure nears a boat. For this reason, when casting it's good to make fairly distant casts beyond a barracuda to give it a chance to follow and strike the lure without being alarmed.

Barracuda eat whatever fish is available, with needlefish, small jacks, and mullet among the mainstays. They are best caught on flashy, erratically worked items such as plugs, spoons, and surgical tube lures. Fly fishermen can take them on streamers, too. A quick speed of retrieve is favored, however, regardless of lure. Barracuda often follow a lure that is worked at a slow or moderate speed and not strike it, or will ignore one that stops altogether, whereas an increase in speed, even if it means going from fast to faster, can be provocative.

Casters often ply the shallows and flats looking for barracuda, most of which lie motionless waiting to pounce on unsuspecting prey. Using light- to medium-action spinning, bait-casting, or fly-casting tackle provides the best sport.

There is a lot of trolling done for these fish, too, although usually with heavier tackle and usually concurrent with the pursuit of other fish. Plugs, spoons, trolling feathers, and rigged bait are used here.

Barracuda have a prodigious array of teeth and should be handled with care; wire leaders should be used with lures. Great barracuda are known to host a toxin in their flesh which sometimes produces ciguatera poisoning when consumed, although this does not occur with every fish nor at all in the Pacific barracuda.

The toothy barracuda prowls inshore and reef environs and is caught by a variety of methods.

BASS

There are a lot of species referred to as 'bass' in both freshwater and saltwater. Some are truly bass and some aren't, but in any event this section will encompass largemouth bass, smallmouth bass, striped bass, white bass, and sea bass.

Largemouth bass

Largemouth bass are the most avidly pursued and popularly desired freshwater fish in North America. Widely distributed, and classified as a warmwater species of fish, largemouth thrive in relatively fertile lakes and are most active in 60- to 80-degree water. They are found in creeks, ditches, sloughs, canals, and many little potholes that have the right cover and forage, but they principally live in reservoirs, lakes, ponds, and large rivers.

These fish orient toward cover, usually toward bottom, and most of their preferred food is found in or near objects, such as logs, stumps, lily pads, brush, weed and grass beds, bushes, docks, fence rows, standing timber, bridge pilings, rocky shores, boulders, points, and the like. Their main forage is primarily shiners, bluegills, shad, alewives, and minnows, as well as crayfish.

Although some trolling and some live bait fishing is done for these fish, the overwhelming angler preference is for casting, using primarily lures, but also flies; pinpoint presentations are more important in largemouth bass fishing than in most other forms of freshwater fishing.

Largemouth bass are found in many environments and are usually oriented toward the bottom and some form of cover.

Lures that catch these fish don't necessarily have to closely resemble actual forage, although at times this is helpful. However, there is no single species of fish for which more lure types are useful and for which there have been devised more individual lures or colors of lures. Many of these overlap in application and technique, while others are suitable only to particular conditions and require specialized usage.

For shallow-water fishing, floating/diving plugs and spinnerbaits get the call. In the plug category, minnow-imitating balsa or plastic lures that float at rest and dive only a foot or two on retrieve are traditional, proven baits. Spinnerbaits are excellent lures, particularly in the spring when fish are shallow, and also when fishing vegetation, and they can also be used quite effectively in deeper water, crawled slowly across the bottom or jigged.

For medium-depth angling (4 to 12 feet) most bass fishermen employ a straight-running, dive-to-the-bottom-on-retrieve lure. Bottom-hugging crankbaits are manufactured in shallow-, medium-, and deep-diving versions, all of which are determined by the size and shape of the lip protruding from each one. Medium and deep divers are usually the most useful to bass fishermen, and these come into play in spring, parts of summer, and fall in many locales. Worms and jigs are also highly effective bass baits in this depth range.

For deeper fishing, the bass angler

Because bass are primarily found around some form of cover, anglers will make repeated casts to likely objects, such as a large stump, covering it from many angles.

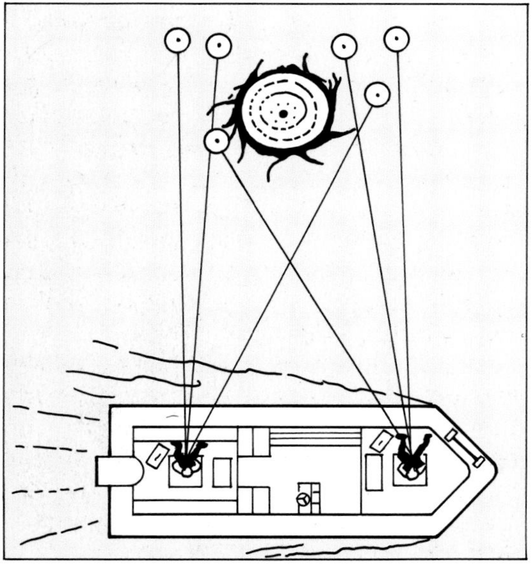

When casting to vegetation, such as these lily pads, concentrate on isolated patches, deep holes, points, and irregular edge features.

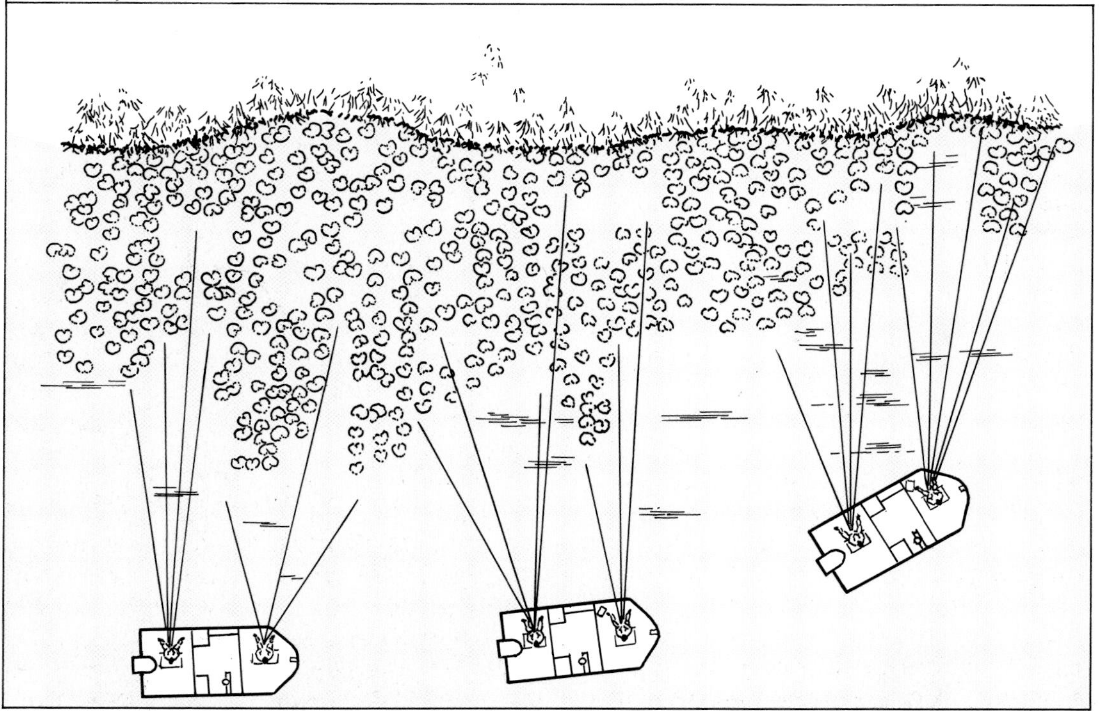

No fish responds to more types of lures than a largemouth bass; the plastic worm that caught this largemouth is visible in the photo.

without a plastic worm, or who doesn't know how to use it, is in for a rough time. It is a fact that bass seek the comfort of cooler, deep-water temperatures in late spring, summer, and early fall, and plastic worms are probably the most effective lure at these times and are widely used. Jigs, particularly jig and pork combos, can be fished extremely effectively in very deep water, as well as along rocky, sharp-sloping bluffs and shorelines, and on underwater mounds. Super-deep-diving plugs are also a candidate for deep-water work.

Surface fishing is a favored largemouth technique, but one that is generally less productive than below-surface methods at most times. Surface lures run the gamut from soft plastic floating baits to wood or plastic plugs that twitch, wobble, chug, sputter, etc., as well as fly-rod poppers.

The most popular time to fish for bass is in the spring, when largemouths are shallow and close to shore. It is generally understood that bass are harder to catch in the summer than in spring or fall. Good summer fishing can be had, however, by putting in time, searching, making good presentations, and working thick cover or deep-water structure.

There isn't one outfit that will adequately handle all aspects of largemouth fishing because it involves a range of fishing conditions, lure styles and sizes, and fishing methods. Medium-duty tackle and 6- to 14-pound-test line can be assigned to handle the majority of bass fishing circumstances.

Smallmouth bass

There is no freshwater fish of equal size that pulls harder or fights more tenaciously than a smallmouth bass. It is an ideal fish to play on light tackle; it has discriminating habitat and food preferences; and it is challenging to pursue.

Smallmouths typically inhabit rocky terrain. Their native, and primarily northern, range is typified by somewhat infertile, natural, rocky-shored, cool northern lakes. Their expanded range now includes southern impoundments with shoreline and deep-water rock structure. In lakes, smallmouths are located around rocky points, craggy cliff-like shores, rocky islands and reefs, and riprap shores. They prefer golf ball- to brick-sized rocks, but larger rocks, including boulders, are also suitable. In rivers, they are found around boulders, rocks, gravel, stone, shale, and such obstructions as fallen trees and uprooted stumps, large blasted stones, current-diverting structures, and bridge pillars and pilings.

Smallmouths hold in these places because of the availability of such food as minnows, crayfish, hellgrammites, nymph larvae, and leeches. Where crayfish are abundant, however, they are the principal food for smallmouths, and among bait fishermen, soft- or hard-shelled crayfish are the premier offering.

A variety of lures are used for smallmouth bass, with jigs being perhaps the most effective of all artificial enticements. Jigs can be fished plain or tipped with a small piece of nightcrawler. Any jig that looks like it might represent a crayfish or hellgrammite, acts erratically, and is darkly colored, is a contender. Small hair- and soft-plastic-bodied jigs, including grubs and curl-tail models, predominate, but heavier jigs sporting a rubber-tentacled skirt and pork chunk have a strong appeal to large fish.

The second-ranking smallmouth lure is a crankbait. Not surprisingly, these diving plugs look somewhat like crayfish in their swimming action, size, and, when used in brown-and-white, color. Crankbaits can be productive for cast-and-retrieve use all season long if smallmouths aren't too deep, and are especially valuable in the spring. Intermediate and deep runners are generally best, and should be fished fairly slowly and in contact with the bottom. A pull-pause action is easily accomplished by retrieving in the standard fashion, and is highly effective.

While jigs and crankbaits account for most lure-caught smallmouth bass, there are times when other lures may be successful. Lake smallmouths may be taken with spinnerbaits when they are in shallow rocky environments close to shore, when they are on shoals

Above: Smallmouths usually dwell around rocky environments and feed heavily on crayfish.

to feed, and when they are on beds in sparsely covered terrain. Spinners have been traditional smallmouth catchers, particularly in northern flowages. Surface lures are mainly applicable for smallmouths when the fish are shallow, and there's a variety of these lures that are worth trying.

Some trolling and drift fishing is done for smallmouths, incidentally, usually in deep water. Fly fishing has merit, too, with flyrodders using nymphs, streamers, and popping bugs.

Light- and medium-duty spinning gear will handle the majority of smallmouth bass fishing situations. Light (6- and 8-pound) and ultralight (2- and 4-pound) lines are practical, even desirable, because smallmouths are residents of open water, and when hooked do not have to be powered away from obstacles other than the bottom. Also, in many regions they inhabit relatively clear, deep lakes and are an especially wary fish, so delicate presentations involving light, thin-diameter line, small jig lures, and corresponding rod and reel combinations, make light and ultralight tackle a fundamental part of smallmouth fishing success.

Top right: A hard-fighter, smallmouth bass are a good light tackle fish.

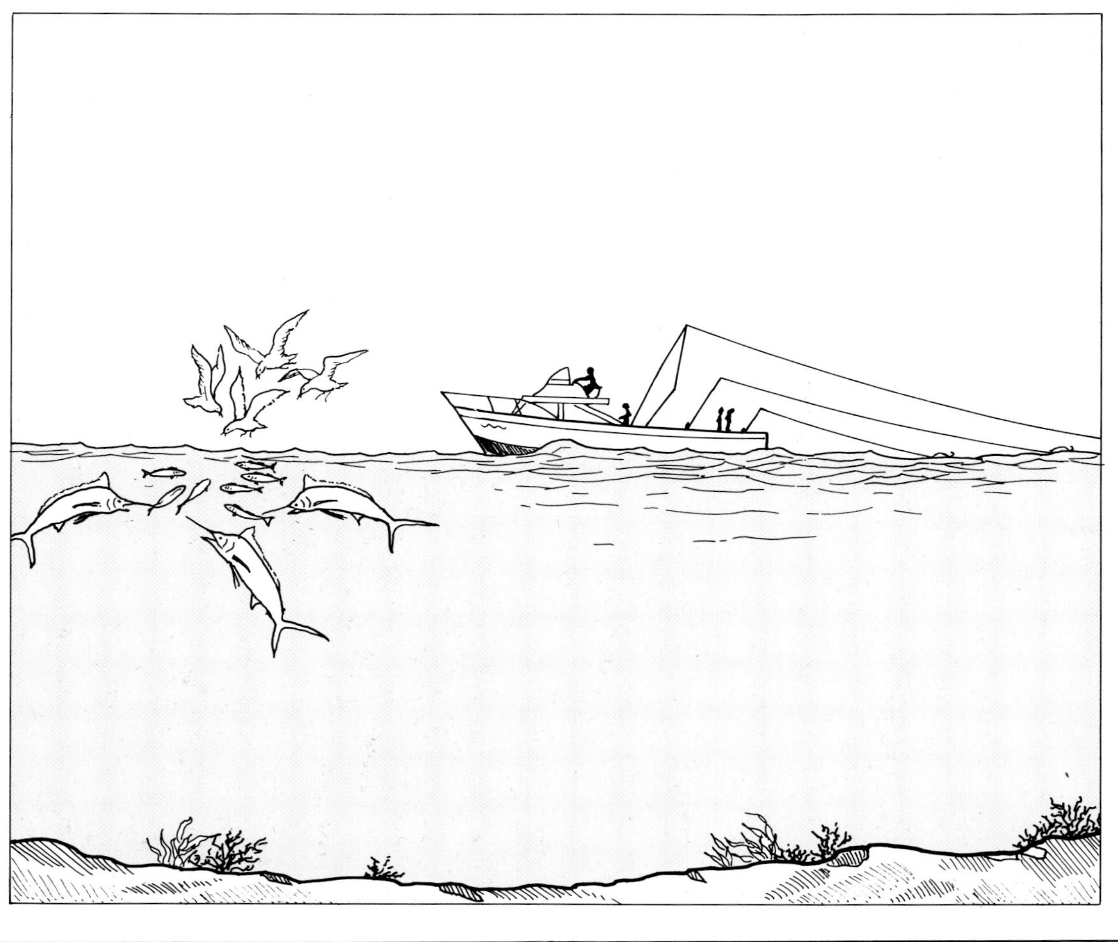

Right: Big game fishermen become good bird watchers, as a school of active, diving birds may be a sign of baitfish being pursued by sailfish or marlin. Trollers will circle the perimeter of the action, but not boat through it.

Striped bass

Striped bass are one of the foremost anadromous fish in North America. In their natural saltwater habitat, they live in the ocean and migrate up rivers to spawn in freshwater. In saltwater, stripers are found all along the Atlantic and most of the Pacific coast, although their numbers are currently depressed and sportfishing is restricted or curtailed in many locales. They have historically been one of the most important saltwater sportfish, but in recent years have provided only a fraction of angling attention.

Stripers are thriving, however, in landlocked environs in several dozen states, where they use large lakes or reservoirs as their ocean and each spring migrate up tributaries to spawn. In freshwater, hybrid stripers have become enormously popular and exhibit many of the same traits as their pure-strain striped bass parents. These sterile fish, which are a cross between the female striped bass and the male white bass, are known to many anglers simply as 'hybrids,' or as 'whiterock bass' or 'wipers,' and they are the most popular and successful of all hybrid fish. Fishing for freshwater stripers has increased in popularity, and now provides the bulk of this continent's striped bass angling activity.

The most popular times for striper fishing are spring, during the spawning run, and fall, when there is frenzied schooling action. In saltwater they are often fished a lot at night.

In saltwater or freshwater, these fish are predominantly open-water nomads and vigorous, if not gluttonous, eaters. In freshwater they consume primarily threadfin or gizzard shad, plus alewives or small panfish in locales that do not have shad. In saltwater they feed on menhaden, herring, anchovies, crabs, and shrimp, among other items. They grow large, over 40 pounds in freshwater and over 60 in saltwater, fight very well, and are a prized table fish.

The methods of catching stripers include using live bait, jigging, casting, and trolling. Casting is done to schools of fish that are ravaging large pods of baitfish near the surface (observed by watching for bird activity); to fish in the tailrace waters below a dam; and to inshore fish in the surf by beach or jetty anglers. Live bait is still-fished while the boat is at anchor or slowly adrift, usually using a fair amount of weight to keep the bait at the proper depth and right below the spot where you have positioned it. Cut bait, in the form of chunks or strips, is sometimes

Once only found in saltwater environs, striped bass have become a popular, major freshwater quarry.

effective, but fresh lively bait is usually preferred. Jigging is primarily done when stripers are holding in deep water in a defined area, using $^1/_2$- to 2-ounce bucktail jigs and jigging spoons. Trolling may be practiced the most, either flatlining or downrigging, using a range of plugs.

Long rods, in the $8^1/_2$- and 9-foot category, are popular for casting, trolling, and bait fishing, especially if large fish are to be encountered. Bait-casting reels with large line capacity, a solid drag, and a freespool clicker are most popular, using 17- or 20-pound line, though lighter line and other light tackle, including fly rods, are used in appropriate circumstances.

White bass

White bass are a popular, important freshwater gamefish in many regions of North America, particularly south of the Mason-Dixon line and in large river systems. Also called 'sand bass,' 'sandies,' 'stripes,' and 'silver bass,' they are truly a member of the temperate bass family, which also includes yellow bass, white perch, and striped bass. Unlike their striped bass relatives, white bass aren't heavyweight fish. However, their savage strike and vicious darting fight surely place them in the middleweight division.

These are a schooling fish, and it is common to catch quite a few white bass in one location. The average size white bass is about $^3/_4$ to $1^1/_2$ pounds in most places, and a 2-pounder is considered large; generous limits and fine-tasting flesh make it desirable to keep a good number. Light tackle is highly suitable for these fish, which are aggressive, tugging fighters. Spinning or spin-casting rods loaded with 4- to 8-pound line are ideal.

White bass feed primarily on small shad or minnows. Lures that correspond to the size and likeness of these baitfish are best. This includes small crankbaits, white bucktail or marabou jigs, silver jigging spoons, spinners, sinking lures, and tailspinners, but also small stick baits and buzz baits. Some fish are caught trolling, but jigging, casting, and live bait account for most success.

In the spring, white bass run up tributaries to spawn and provide a lot of action. Spring white bass runs are renowned on many large lakes and river systems, and this movement seems to generally take place once the water temperature in the tributaries exceeds 55 degrees. Late in the summer and into fall there is some exciting angling for schools of white bass that are feeding near the surface on shad. There are many fish in such schools and they are literally frenzied while tearing into the baitfish. Many boats follow these schools and enjoy fast fishing. Shallow, wind-blown, gravelly points are also a prime fall white bass locale. In rivers, look to those areas where streams enter, where bridge pilings disrupt current flow, above wingdams, along riprap, downstream from lock-and-dam structures, and on rocky points.

Sea bass

The term 'sea bass' is a widely used one in saltwater, sometimes referring to such species as striped bass or grouper. Two fish that are commonly associated with this category are the white sea bass of the Pacific and the black sea bass of the Atlantic, both of which are abundant and popular sport and table fish.

Black sea bass are caught from New England to Florida and seldom weigh more than 5 pounds. They are a bottom-feeding fish that congregate around hard, rocky, ocean floor areas, as well as such objects as reefs, wrecks, rocky outcrops, and shellfish beds. They feed on clams, shrimp, worms, crabs, and small fish, and most angling is done with bait.

Smaller black sea bass are found fairly close to shore, perhaps where the

A plentiful fish usually found in schools, white bass provide fine sport and good eating.

bottom depth ranges from 20 to 50 feet, in channels, bays, and inlets. Larger fish are usually further from shore and deeper. Most angling is done from anchored boats, either jigging with 2- to 4-ounce metal jigs, or stillfishing with bait.

Black sea bass have a fairly good-sized mouth and can take a relatively large bait. Where bigger sea bass are likely, a large piece of clam or squid or a small whole fish might be used for bait, although smaller baits, such as a worm, shrimp, or small piece of clam, are used inshore. It is practical to use a two-hook rig, with the lower hook left on the bottom and the upper one 2 to 3 feet off it. Sea bass can be nibblers and bait stealers, so it pays to keep an eye on your bait.

Sinkers used vary with conditions. Usually bank sinkers are employed, and they range from perhaps 3 ounces in shallower water to 8 ounces in deep water where current is swift. Medium-action boat rods and 15-pound line is the normal tackle used to catch these spirited fighters. They are predominantly caught in the spring and summer, incidentally, and they migrate easterly as the water gets colder.

White sea bass are actually members of the weakfish family and have the tender mouth usually associated with those species. Found along the Californian and Mexican coasts, these fish are usually found in kelp beds that are in fairly shallow water near shore. Like their Atlantic counterparts, they feed on small fish, crustaceans, and squid, but they grow much larger, and consequently fairly heavy tackle is used.

A lot of fishing for white sea bass is done on or near the bottom using live bait or cut bait while drifting or anchored. However, these fish will roam the water column and are caught at other levels as well, sometimes by casters tossing plugs, spoons, or other lures, and sometimes by trollers.

Sea bass are bottom feeders, usually caught on some form of bait. Shown is a black sea bass.

BILLFISH

Billfish is a common term used to collectively address a number of billed pelagic big-game fish that seasonally inhabit tropical and temperate environs. In North American waters these include sailfish, swordfish, blue marlin, striped marlin, and white marlin. These are all highly respected for their sporting virtues, elusiveness, and difficulty to catch. They are among the premier game fish in the world.

These fish overlap in range and share many common features, most obvious of which is their long bill. The bill is rather prehistoric in appearance, but is used to swat, and sometimes even impale, food. Fast swimmers, billfish characteristically rush after prey, which is also usually moving rapidly, and stun it, then return to consume it. This behavior gave rise to the standard trolling tactic of dropping back free line to a fish that has taken a whole or strip bait or lure, as described in the previous section. Nowhere is this more necessary, however, than in billfishing.

Another common feature is the fight. Although billfish vary greatly in size, they all battle hard and impressively. They usually jump, sometimes often, high in the air and in a spectacular tail-walking fashion over the surface, with head shaking violently back and forth. There is no more impressive sight in sportfishing. They are swift fish, too, and make long sustained runs; large billfish will take up to several hours to subdue because they have exceptional endurance. Their initial runs cannot be slowed, and throughout the battle, there will be plenty of pumping and hard work on the part of the angler to retrieve line that has been stripped off repeatedly.

Billfish wander at various depths, but are generally most active near the surface. They feed on a variety of schooling and migratory fish, including mackerel, tuna, herring, bonito, balao, needlefish, flying fish, and squid. Many of the same species are used for trolling, as well as dolphin, bonefish, and mullet, either rigged whole or as a strip bait, and trolled on the surface or just under it. The size of the bait usually conforms to the size of the anticipated quarry. With blue marlin, for example, you might troll large whole baits, but for sailfish or white marlin, a strip bait or small mullet or balao would generally be sufficient. Often the types and sizes of bait are mixed, as different types of billfish may be encountered in a given day. Big-game trolling plugs, such as Konaheads, and trolling feathers are also used.

Most fishing is done by fast trolling on the surface, and although a lot of billfish are taken blindly, anglers look for visible, wandering billfish while trolling in order to intercept them, and they see fish come into the boat's wake and look over or trail the trolled offerings before striking or vanishing. The boat captain will watch the water ahead and to the sides for the upper tail and dorsal fin of nearby billfish, while the mate and anglers watch the wake for a high dorsal fin looming in behind a trolled offering.

There is some live bait drift fishing done for billfish, and a minimal amount of slower, deep downrigger trolling.

With rod attached to a shoulder harness, a stand-up angler strains to pump a marlin up from the offshore blue-water depths.

Billfish can be taken on a fly, usually by first locating a fish and trolling a hookless teaser, which excites the fish and is then pulled away from it so a large streamer can be cast in its place.

Sailfish

Although they are the smallest member of the billfish clan, sailfish are among the most popular with anglers because they can be taken fairly easily by experienced anglers on light tackle, including spinning rods and fly rods. There are Atlantic and Pacific sailfish, and some disagreement exists as to whether these are the same or different species. Pacific sailfish grow considerably larger on average, however. Nonetheless, the usual fish is between 5 and 7 feet long and weighs between 30 and 65 pounds. Sailfish are distinguished, of course, by their high first dorsal fin.

These billfish usually travel alone or in small groups, primarily offshore, but occasionally in shallower near-shore waters. They are often found on the edges of reefs and dropoffs or current eddies, and are fought by most fishermen while standing up. Twenty- and 30-pound outfits are used for trolling, but lighter gear is readily employed, and more enjoyable.

Blue marlin

In terms of size, tackle, and stamina, blue marlin are at the other extreme. Found on both coasts and in the Gulf of Mexico, they may grow in excess of 1,000 pounds, and are the premier North American marlin. A blue water-fish, they are seldom found close to shore, and are highly migratory.

Most blue marlin caught on sportfishing tackle weigh between 150 and 400 pounds, and it is an awesome sight when such a fish, or a larger one, spears through the surface in the distance and leaps high in the air. It may do this repeatedly, then run great distances, sound deep, and resist capture

All billfish can be acrobatic, sometimes with spectacular effect. This sailfish being battled by a light tackle angler clears the water very close to the boat.

till the angler is weary. Large baits and trolled plugs are the normal offering, pulled at 4 to 8 knots, and tackle ranges from 30- to 130-pound outfits, employed on both flat lines and outriggers.

Striped marlin and white marlin

Found in Pacific waters and most abundant in North America off southern California, striped marlin do not grow as large as blue marlin, but are revered for their acrobatics. No billfish jumps more often, and striped marlin are likely to make successive greyhounding leaps across the surface. White marlin, found along the Atlantic Coast and in the Gulf of Mexico, are more like sailfish in size and fight. They are more frequently caught than blue marlin, and are often found in near-shore environs. Whites are a good light-tackle billfish; 20- to 30-pound outfits and 2/0 to 6/0 reels are commonly used.

Swordfish

Not a light tackle fish, these large creatures attain blue marlin size and are ferocious fighters. They are less readily caught, however, than other North American billfish despite being most widely distributed.

Also called 'broadbill,' swordfish do have a flattened bill that is wider and longer than other billfish. They are pelagic and usually travel alone in continental shelf waters, and can be found at varied depths. They are often located in very deep, and cool, water, but will bask on the surface and may be spotted there with the upper tail fin out of the water. It is that characteristic that used to make them susceptible to harpooning. Occasionally they are spotted by trollers, who maneuver to make a careful presentation to them. Swordfish are finicky and wary, however, and are difficult to tempt into striking.

An effective swordfish technique is drifting at night with bait, using chemiluminescent light sticks that glow brightly as attractors. Baits are set at staggered levels, some very deep. Squid is the favored bait, but various fish are also used.

Because of their size, stamina, and fighting abilities, which include leaping, deep diving, and rolling, swordfish tackle is usually in the 80- to 130-pound range, with heavy leaders. Although they are fine eating, many of the broadbill caught by sportfishermen are tagged and released.

Having just caught this blue marlin, the fishermen will tag it, revive the fish, and then release it.

BLUEFISH

Bluefish are one of the most voracious fish in saltwater, a quality that endears them to sport fishermen.

The bluefish is one of the most awesome of saltwater fish because of the vicious way it attacks its prey, particularly when it is schooled and rampaging through a pod of baitfish. So savage is their behavior that they have been likened to the notorious piranha and given the monicker 'chopper,' and have the oft-noted distinction of occasionally being a menace to bathers at beaches. Indeed, they have been known to run themselves up on the beach when frenziedly chasing bait in the surf wash. On the other hand, they are an enormously popular quarry of sportfishermen because they are strong fighters that put up a long battle, even though they are typically caught in the 5- to 12-pound range (though they get larger). They will also jump if not caught on very heavy tackle.

Historically bluefish tend to be cyclic in abundance, but in recent years they have heavily populated the inshore waters of the East Coast. They range widely through the world, but in North America are found only in Atlantic waters, though they are distributed from Florida to Nova Scotia. Bluefish are basically a deep-water species that migrate westward to inshore waters, where they are most abundant in spring and fall, and lately through the summer as well. They are a bit unpredictable, however, as they roam widely, at times being well offshore and at other times being up in the surf. They will also wander into marshes, brackish rivers, and estuaries, although these are usually the smaller fish, called 'snappers.'

Named for their bluish-green back, bluefish are easily detected when they are marauding schools of baitfish, because there will be birds working the slick that is created. Casting, jigging, and trolling in the perimeter vicinity are standard tactics then. At other times, however, blues are a little harder to locate, usually being found deep, around tide rips, and in places where the water is unruly, particularly inshore on a moving tide. Bluefish feed on a wide range of small fish, usually preferring what is most available, but they can be selective feeders and will also scrounge the bottom for sand worms and eels.

As with largemouth bass in freshwater, bluefish succumb to a host of angling techniques and terminal items, in large part due to their aggressiveness. This is true for the boat as well as shore angler. Trolling may be the most employed boating technique, using diving plugs, thick-bodied spoons, and surgical tubes; a fast speed is preferred. Drifting and jigging is popular where bluefish are known to be located, using metal jigging spoons and bucktails, sometimes tipped with a piece of meat. Live bait works better than dead, but some anglers chum for blues and successfully drift hooked pieces of cut bait amidst the chum. Casters use a variety of plugs, as well as streamer flies when the fish are thick. Shore, surf, and pier fishermen can stillfish with bait in current or cast surface or diving plugs and squid-imitation spoons. There should always be movement to the offering, as still lures or bait go untouched.

Tackle varies widely, from heavy boat rods for trolling and deep jigging to light spinning tackle and fly rods. The reel drag should be of good quality, and a gaff should be employed for fish that are to be kept. Bluefish have extremely sharp teeth, so anglers should take great care when handling these fish. Many an angler has been hurt, when unhooking a lively blue.

BONEFISH

Its scientific name means 'white fox,' and how appropriate that is. For the bonefish is indeed a wary, elusive creature, one that usually must be stalked stealthily, and which bolts with startling speed when hooked or when alarmed.

One of the most coveted of all saltwater fish, bonefish don't grow particularly large; 2- to 5-pound fish are commonly caught and a 10-pounder is notable. Large bonefish are more likely to be found alone or in small groups, but small fish usually travel in schools. They are mainly found on the eastern coast of Florida, the Keys, and the Bahamas in warm tropical water.

Although some bonefish are caught accidentally in deep water, the exclusive habitat explored by anglers is shallow tidal flats and shoals. Bonefish feed on these flats, scouring the bottom for small clams, crabs, worms, and shrimp. Their mouth is under the snout to facilitate feeding, and bonefish are often first detected while feeding with their body tilted in a head-down, tail-up manner, with all or part of the tail fin protruding through the surface. These are referred to as 'tailing fish.' Bonefish also sometimes stir up the bottom when rooting along, and this cloudy mudding can be a telltale indicator to the observant angler.

The shallow flats, which range from less than a foot up to several feet deep, is where any fish is most vulnerable, so bonefish have good reason to be skittish. Engine noise will send the fish scattering and boaters prefer to pole silently along in search of fish, staking the boat and fishing from the boat or by foot when bonefish are spotted. People with waders walk on hard bottoms and carefully approach the feeding fish.

Bonefishing is primarily sight fishing, so this species, in effect, is stalked. Unless their tails are poking through the surface, the silvery form off a bonefish can be surprisingly difficult to see, even in the shallowest water. Polarized sunglasses aid through-the-water vision and are virtually a necessity. Calm water and bright sun help visibility as well. When bonefish are spotted, the angler maneuvers into position to intercept the fish with a judicious cast.

If the cast object lands on top of the fish or a school, the fish will dart away. So the lure, fly, or bait should be cast 6 to 10 feet ahead of the feeding or cruising fish and slowly stripped in. At the strike and hookset there is an explosion in the water, and instantaneously the bonefish streaks across the flats toward the security of deep water. It is not uncommon for a bonefish to strip 80 to 100 yards of line off the reel in a scorching run, and the angler must have the drag set properly and keep the rod tip up high so the line avoids mangrove roots, grass, and other flats objects that could cut the line or leader.

Bonefishing is primarily done with fly or light spinning tackle, using a 6-to 7-foot spinning rod or 9-foot fly rod and reel with adequate line capacity. Six-pound nylon monofilament line is just right for spinning use. Small streamers and jigs are the primary artificials, in pink, white, and yellow colors, and shrimp, clam, and conch meat are popular baits. Some bonefish anglers anchor or stake their boat and chum with crushed shrimp. The end of an ebb tide and the beginning of a flood tide are usually best for the sake of spotting shallow fish, but a slack flood tide can produce for anglers who fish waist-deep water by casting blindly with small jigs.

A fish primarily caught on shallow tropical flats, bonefish are highly revered for their wary nature and strong fight.

BONITO

There are a number of bonito and related species that are popular among saltwater anglers in both the Atlantic and Pacific Oceans, although there is often considerable confusion over fish identification. Bonito are actually part of the mackerel family, and in North America the most important members are the Atlantic bonito, also known as the common bonito, which is found all along the eastern Atlantic, and the Pacific bonito, which is found most frequently off the California coast.

These are pelagic fish that exist mostly in temperate waters offshore and which are usually found in fairly large schools, primarily from late spring till fall. They feed on small mackerel, squid, and other schooling fish, and don't grow very large; 3- to 6-pounders are average. Because of their size, they are often used as trolling bait for big-game fish.

A related species with similar range in the Atlantic Ocean is the little tuna. This is commonly called little tunny or false albacore, as well as simply bonito, and it resembles Atlantic bonito in shape, color, and average size, though it has more vermiculated wavy markings along the length of its back. Another related species is the skipjack tuna, which is known as oceanic bonito, oceanic skipjack, and striped tuna. It has dark longitudinal stripes along its lower body, and inhabits tropical waters.

The fish are commonly referred to as school tuna, and they look and act much like small tuna, being found in large, actively feeding, and migratory schools which are occasionally found fairly close to the shore. They are often preyed on by tunas and by billfish.

Bonito are often caught while trolling with bait or lures for larger quarry, and, when caught on the heavier tackle used for that sport, they are understandably overmatched. However, when caught on light tackle they are a robust battler, diving, surging, running, and generally doing their best to stretch the fishing line.

Light tackle may be kept handy for use while trolling and coming upon a school of bonito (when bigger baits are retrieved and light rods, equipped with a jig, spoon, or plug, are used), or it can be employed when drifting and live bait fishing or when chumming and using cut or live bait. A light- to medium-action spinning rod, 7- to 8-feet long, with 10- to 15-pound line, is about right, going even lighter for more of a battle.

When trolling deliberately for bonito, skipjack, and little tuna, a fast boat speed is usually best, as are trolling plugs and feather jigs. These fish aren't put off by the wake of a boat or engine noise, so flatline length can be relatively short.

Bonito are found in schools and can provide fast open-water action.

CARP

Although many North American freshwater anglers have a distinct affinity for certain species of fish, they often have a clear dislike for others, and carp usually top the list of the latter. Carp, which are imported fish of European and Asian origin, don't get much respect because they seldom take artificial lures or standard natural baits, and have a tendency to roil the water when feeding and spawning. However, they are a fish that can grow quite large and that will provide a strong fight.

Although attempts have been made to eradicate carp in North America, they have not been successful because these are hardy, durable fish. They can live in lake and river waters that will not sustain other fish species, including places with little oxygen, and can withstand extreme changes in water temperature, although they are not active in cold water.

Carp spawn in shallow bays, stream tributaries, or flooded fields and marshes from mid to late spring or early summer, and are quite noticeable then as they thrash about and disturb the water. Often their backs are exposed, providing an obvious target for spear fishermen or bowfishermen. At other times of the year they are frequently seen leaping out of the water or rolling or finning in shallow water.

Look for carp primarily in shallow water, realizing that they can find bait better on a sand or gravel flat than in thick weeds. In back waters, work narrow, open areas between deep-water locales. Carp funnel through these while feeding. Carp scour the bottom when feeding, often uprooting water plants in the process. They consume much vegetation, as well as insect larvae, crustaceans, and small mollusks, and are often found quite shallow.

In large lakes and reservoirs, and in slow-moving back waters, carp anglers fish with worms, corn, grubs, marshmallows, potatoes, and dough balls. In rivers, anglers use these same baits but also live crayfish and hellgrammites. Sometimes carp are caught accidently on artificial lures, usually on a small dark jig that is tipped with a piece of worm, or on a small diving plug. Dough balls are the most popular item used specifically for carp; these homemade concoctions are made from corn meal, flour, syrup, anise oil, vanilla extract, etc., and rolled into a ball.

Tackle for carp varies. Ten-pound line is adequate, as is the standard tackle used in casting for such species as bass or walleye. Lengthy rods with long handles are used by shore fishermen, who prop these into rod holders while waiting for their bait to be hit.

Carp favor shallow, heavily vegetated environs in lakes and ponds, and are a forceful fighter.

CATFISH

Angling for catfish has long been one of the primary fishing activities in North America, even though these fish are often overlooked in the popular press. Catfish are abundant in most areas and are highly valued on the table.

Catfish are whiskered creatures who travel close to the bottom of North American waterways. Some catfish species grow huge and fight hard, and all scavenge almost anything old or new to eat. While they are occasionally taken on artificial offerings, they are commonly caught on live or dead bait, more often the latter, including malodorous offerings known as 'stink baits,' as well as nightcrawlers, hellgrammites, shrimp, clams, and crayfish.

Channel cats may be the most popular of these fish. They have a varied natural diet, but prefer a fresh frozen chicken liver or gizzard shad as bait. Look for channel catfish at current cuts in rivers, stream mouths, gravel and rock bottoms, deep-cut river banks, shallow ripple areas with a hard bottom, river channels, and lake reef edges. They are a renowned bait stealer and are sometimes difficult to hook, and they are extremely sensitive to line pressure.

Uglier than the channel, the flathead catfish grows larger, up to a humungous 100 pounds (35-pounders are not unusual), and is found predominantly in rivers, followed by big reservoirs and lakes, as well as directly below dams in the tailrace waters.

The flathead's diet consists mostly of fish and crustaceans. Anglers often take these huge catfish on deep-diving crankbaits, jigs tipped with sucker minnows, or large live bait left to lie on the bottom. Though flathead take just about anything, they prefer live fish. Small, 1/2- to 1-pound live carp and river suckers, hooked through their noses with a large, 4/0 to 6/0 single hook, work well.

Blue catfish are fewest in number among the catfish clan and are spread over the smallest area, but they grow as large as flatheads. They prefer rivers and large dam impoundments and are often found working the lower river estuaries and backwaters. Blue catfish are noted for striking the worst of stink baits, but their diet consists of just about anything.

Bullhead catfish, known as 'bullheads' or 'horned pout' and found in both black and brown varieties, are a popular catfish for many pond and lake anglers. They don't grow particularly large as a rule, and anglers catch them while stillfishing with an assortment of baits. Catfish are mainly nocturnal, and, on the whole, anglers spend as many hours working all catfish species after dark as they do during daylight hours.

Anglers after the larger catfish use very heavy tackle. This may be required when fishing in waters that are filled with snags, brush, logs, and other debris, but a medium-weight bait-casting or spinning rod and 10- to 15-pound line will do the job in most circumstances.

Catfish are the foremost bottom-feeding freshwater fish; some species, such as this flathead, grow quite large.

ARCTIC CHAR

Salvelinus alpinus, as the Arctic char is known to the scientific community, is a rather puzzling and confusing fish, befitting its remote high-Arctic environs. It is a distant relative of trout and Pacific salmon, a closer relative of brook trout, lake trout, Dolly Varden, and bull trout. It is not just a char, but an Arctic char. Its cousins should have been renamed: 'brook char' for 'brook trout,' 'lake char' for 'lake trout.'

Arctic char are found all across the North American Arctic, although they are pursued by relatively few anglers annually, and then only for a few weeks. The largest appear to come regularly from Victoria Island and the Tree River, both in Canada's Northwest Territories. Geographically these locales are not far from one another, yet their char are distinctly different. Tree River char in their spawning colors have a dark back and are not fully swathed in red or orange. They have a humped back, too, and often a more pronounced kype (protruding lower jaw).

Arctic char are renowned for their beauty and for their sporty virtues. Their pinkish, orange, and bright red coloration is only found when the fish are migrating inland to spawn, as they are silvery otherwise. They are as royal a fighting fish as is found in freshwater, known for blistering runs and salmon-like leaps, especially in river environs, and their vivid pink flesh is coveted when fresh.

Char are found in both sea-run and landlocked forms. They are anadromous, and the larger fish are those that migrate from Arctic oceans into freshwater rivers and lakes. No Arctic char remain in the ocean during the winter. In late August and early September they run up the rivers and into holding lakes, where they stay through winter. When ice leaves the rivers, most of the char descend rivers and return to the ocean for the brief summer. Fish that don't make the seaward journey are those that will be spawning; they change color and inhabit the rivers and lakes, eventually to spawn beneath the winter ice.

Arctic char angling can be a feast or famine affair. Char sometimes are clustered so thickly that a river seems full of these fish, or they can be scarce. Fishing is sometimes fast, with continuous action, but these are spooky fish; when a school is spooked, it will move off, and it will be necessary to rest the locale for an hour or two.

River fishing is more dependable, with the fish often holding at the head of a pool. Where current drops over a gravel bar and dumps into a deep pool is a particularly good location. In lakes, concentrate on inlets, where the river dumps into a lake. Light to medium spinning tackle, using spinners and spoons all or partly colored red, is used, with 6- to 10-pound line standard. Fly fishermen need a reel with ample backing, and use streamers on sinking or sink-tip 7- or 8-weight fly lines.

A fish of tundra waters, Arctic char are one of North America's most elusive species.

COBIA

Cobia are a fine sport and table fish that roam both inshore and offshore environs. They are found in warm, tropical waters from the mid-Atlantic coast south and in the Gulf of Mexico; larger specimens are more likely to be found in the Gulf.

These fish are also known as 'ling,' 'lemonfish,' and 'crab-eater,' the last of which is derived from their preference for eating crabs and shrimp. However, they also consume various fish. They feed near the surface at times, on the bottom often, and in between, and as a result are caught in many places and by a variety of means.

Actually, the dark brown colored cobia is sometimes mistaken for a shark or remora because of resembling features. While it may swim with these creatures it is not related to either.

Cobia are exceedingly object-oriented, and cluster around pilings, sunken wrecks, buoys, and other floating or stationary objects, including anchored boats. They are taken by trolling with lures or bait, but more fishing is done near the bottom, with cut or live bait or with jigs tipped with meat (and sometimes when chumming). There are opportunities for sight fishing and casting to cruising cobia, as well.

Beach anglers roam the water's edge searching for a pod of cobia to cast to, and may work them near the surface. When this happens, fly rods may be used, but spinning or bait-casting tackle is more likely. Spoons, large plugs, and heavy jigs are used for casting, attached to a wire leader. Bait consists of small live fish, such as pinfish or menhaden, or live crabs; cut or strip baits and squid are also used.

Cobia strike hard and fight vigorously. They are grudging, determined fighters that make long runs, and sometimes jump out of the water. They seldom give up easily, and often have to be horsed away from the very obstructions that cause their presence, so tackle is often fairly stout, except when smaller inshore fish are to be encountered. Lighter spinning, bait-casting, or fly tackle may be used for the smaller fish, but in open water, a 6-foot boat rod, large-capacity reel, and 15- to 20-pound line is standard.

Caught by a variety of methods cobia are often found around some type of object.

COD

Cod are one of the most sought-after commercial fish in North America, and a popular species with party boat anglers and private boaters in both Atlantic and Pacific Oceans. Their flesh is highly valued and is used in a variety of ways in the commercial marketplace. There are a variety of fish that are related, or similar, to cod, including pollock, hake, tomcod, and haddock. Many of these species are caught using the same fishing techniques, but here we will focus just on cod, or 'codfish' as they are also widely known.

Cod are a favorite with the party boat fleet, and are caught in intermediate to deep water.

A distinctive-looking fish, cod have three separate dorsal fins, two anal fins, and a noticeable barbel under their chin. The Atlantic cod species is found in the north Atlantic waters and the

Pacific cold from mid-Pacific states north to Alaska. These are a bottom-dwelling species exclusively, living in cold offshore environs. Cod are found at great depths and are seldom caught in water under 60 feet deep. Their wide-ranging diet includes many small fish, plus crabs, clams, and worms.

Not surprisingly, the bulk of fishing is done with bait, fished on heavy sinkers on or near the bottom in deep water. Sinkers weighing from 4 to 10 ounces or more are necessary, depending on the current, wind, and depth conditions. Bait may be assorted fish or clams, and bait hook sizes range from 5/0 to 8/0. Deep fishing with heavy jigs, sometimes festooned with a chunk of fish, is also employed, being fished vertically. If conditions allow, the boat drifts, if not, an anchor is dropped.

Cod fishing is primarily a winter activity, because these fish come into shallower water at that time and are more accessible. Longer boat runs aren't necessary then, but, of course, fishing conditions can be stiff.

Although cod can be caught up to 60 or more pounds, most fish run in the 3- to 20-pound range. Because of their size and the fishing conditions, however, a stout boat rod and a heavy-duty conventional saltwater reel are necessary. Line should be 30 pounds or so.

Some cod are occasionally caught by trollers, and a few are taken when they venture shallow enough to be targets for jetty anglers. Some of the related species may come shallow and be possible to catch by casting, too.

Cod are a major target for party boaters, who often fish with bait on the bottom, sometimes in extremely deep water.

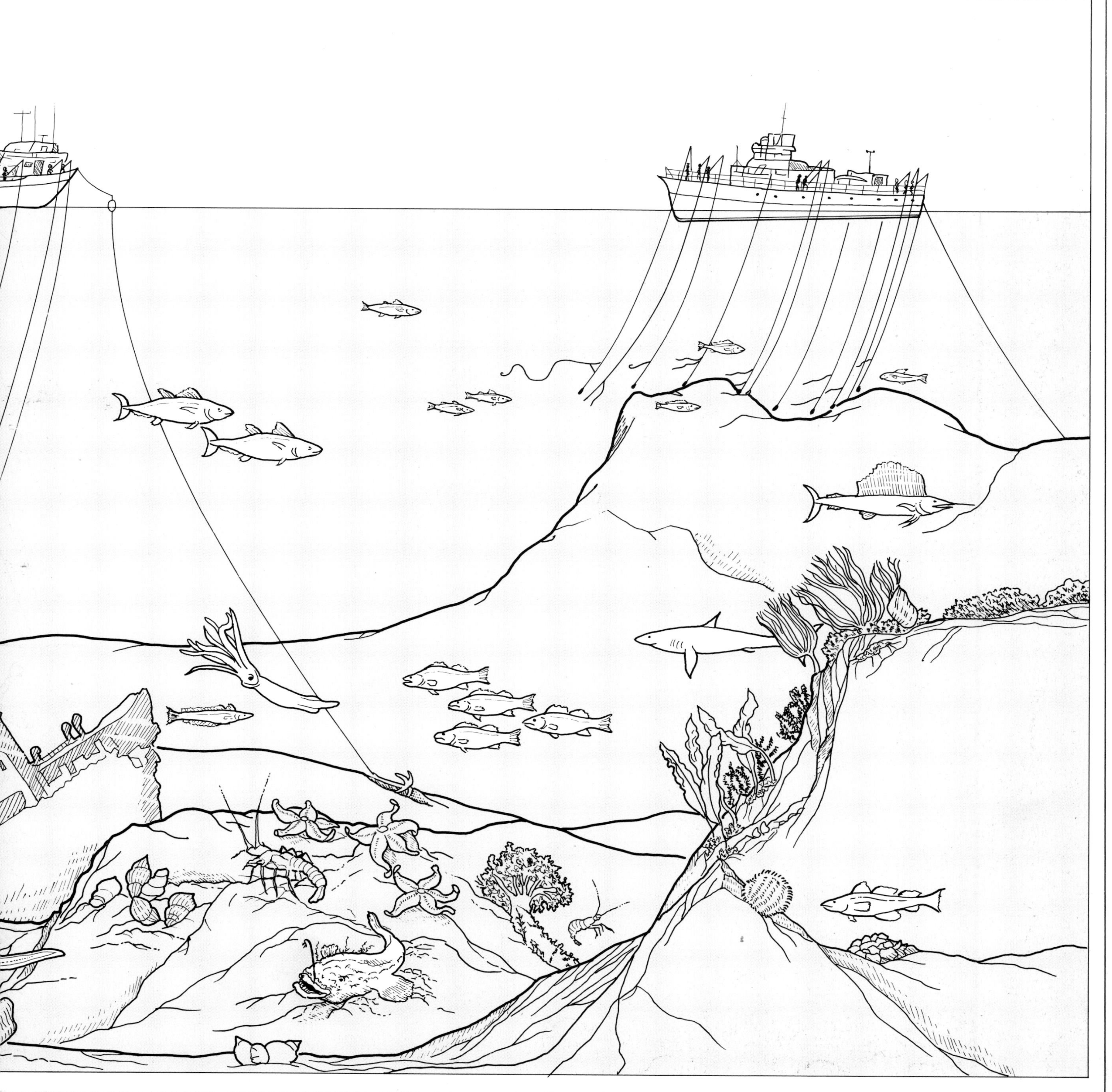

CRAPPIE

Among the most popular freshwater fish in the U. S., and resembling sunfish in shape, crappie are widely distributed and intensely pursued. They are known regionally by an assortment of names, including 'calico,' 'speckled perch,' 'strawberry bass,' 'barfish,' and '*sac-à-lait*.' Actually, there are two species of crappie, the white and the black, but they look very similar and their range overlaps. The black crappie prefers cool, clear lakes and slow-moving rivers. It is a little more particular about its environment than the white crappie, which flourishes in warm and more silted water.

A bottom dropoff, especially if it has some form of cover, is a good place for crappie to congregate from summer through mid-fall.

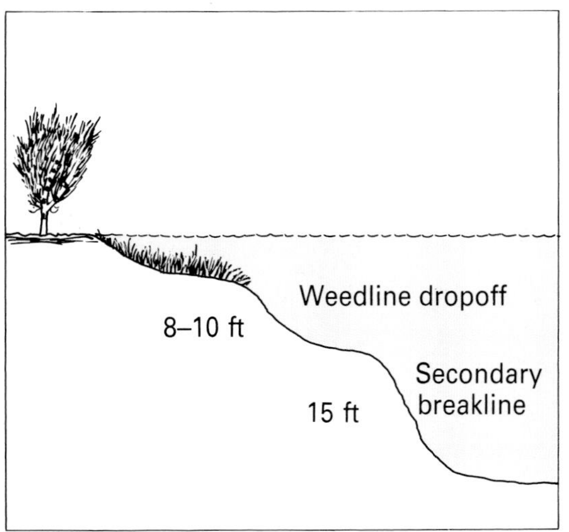

Crappies feed primarily on insects and small fish. In southern reservoirs, gizzard or threadfin shad are major forage and in northern states, insects are more dominant. Crappies also consume the fry of many species of game fish.

In the spring, when water temperatures reach about 60 degrees, crappies move shallow to build nests and spawn, and this is a particularly favorite time for angling, much of which is done around some form of wood or brush. Spawning-time crappies are reasonably predictable and easy for anglers to catch. After spawning, crappies move to deeper water and gather in schools. They congregate tightly in sunken weed beds, dropoffs, offshore brush piles, flooded timber, and sunken cribbing. Massive schools of crappies form at different levels of the lake, and usually are situated horizontally.

In the fall, crappies may move into deeper water to gather around underwater structures such as old channels, rocky ledges, or weed beds. Though they will move around a bit, they generally remain in deep water until spring. Crappies also offer a prime opportunity for winter fishing, and many northern ice anglers make these fish their number one pursuit.

Although some trolling is done for crappies, the vast majority of anglers drift or anchor, and either jig or stillfish with minnows. Small marabou jigs are the favored artificial, sometimes tipped with a tiny minnow. Crappie have tender mouths and strikes are often delicate, and the most regularly successful anglers are those who develop a fine jigging motion and subtle feel.

Crappie fishermen primarily use ultralight spinning reels equipped with 4- or 6-pound-test line and 5- to 5½-foot-long rods. Fly rods, spin-casting rods, telescoping fiberglass rods, and cane poles are used as well. Cane poles or telescoping glass rods play a large, traditional role in crappie fishing. Eight- to 12-foot poles work well for boat anglers, but bank fishermen prefer 16- to 20-foot-long rods. The line is seldom longer than the length of the pole. Live bait is used, and dabbled in place after place.

Crappies are delicious fish, which is a prime reason for their popularity. In many places crappies are quite plentiful, and creel limits are liberal, so it does no harm to keep a batch of these fish for the table.

Crappie are usually found in schools, and primarily caught with small minnows or small jigs.

DOLPHIN

Dolphin are a highly prized game fish of the open sea. Nonanglers confuse this fish with certain porpoises, however, which are mammals and unrelated to the dolphin species; porpoises are commonly referred to as 'dolphin,' but are not pursued by sportfishermen. For this reason, anglers often refer to the game species as 'dolphinfish.' Known also as 'dorado,' dolphin are superb table fare, and often appear in restaurants under their Hawaiian name, *mahi-mahi*. They are distinctively shaped and colorful, though their brilliant color fades rapidly after capture.

Dolphin are pelagic and primarily found in the blue-water environs of warm seas. The Gulf Stream of the Atlantic, the Caribbean, the Gulf of Mexico, southern California, and Hawaii are dolphin grounds, and the fish feed primarily on such fast-swimming species as flying fish and squid, but also on small tidbits clustered around floating sargassum weed and kelp. Dolphin roam the near-surface waters of the open ocean, but are commonly found around objects. Floating debris, buoys, weeds, and even boats can attract and hold these fish, and such objects are searched by anglers specifically looking for dolphin.

Most dolphin are located by trolling, usually while fishing for other blue-water fish, primarily marlin and sailfish. Rigged trolling baits on large hooks are usually used, with flying fish, squid, mullet, and balao as the common offerings, as well as offshore trolling plugs and feathers. A quick trolling speed is employed, as dolphin are very fast swimmers. Heavy big-game tackle is the norm, primarily for larger quarry, and while big dolphin fight well even on this tackle, their fight can be enjoyed much better if they are caught on light big-game outfits or spinning equipment.

Trollers often keep spinning tackle handy in case a school of dolphin is found while trolling. When this happens, they stop and cast to the fish, using surface or diving plugs, bucktail jigs, spoons, and even streamer flies. Live bait may also be used. Dolphin run hard, leap often and rather spectacularly, sometimes tailwalking across the surface, and this fight is especially enjoyed when a fish has been caught on light tackle and played from a drifting boat. A 7-foot spinning rod and 6-to 12-pound line is ideal, as most fish don't weigh more than 20 pounds. The strike, when casting or trolling, is usually savage.

Sometimes anglers keep a hooked dolphin on the line near the boat to encourage a school to stay around, and this may result in catching several fish out of a school. Some anglers will also chum when a school is found to keep the fish in the vicinity.

An excellent battler, especially on light tackle, dolphin leap high and thrill many anglers.

DRUM

There are scores of fish in the drum and related croaker families. The most significant of these in North American saltwater fishing are the black drum and red drum, which are similar in many respects and which overlap in their range. Found inshore from the northern mid-Atlantic south through the Gulf of Mexico, these species are respectively the largest and second-largest drums. They are bottom feeders and schooling fish that possess strong throat teeth which they use to crush mollusks.

Black drum have a shorter, deeper body than the more elongated red drum. Blacks possess barbels under their chin; reds have a clearly distinguishable large black spot on both sides of their caudal peduncle. Red drum are reddish in color and are commonly known as 'redfish' and as 'channel bass.' Both are schooling fish, found close to shore and sometimes in estuaries or brackish environs, and are commonly caught near breakwaters, jetties, pilings, channels, sandy and muddy shorelines, inlets, and shellfish beds.

Drum are migratory and seasonally abundant in northerly areas. The better fishing is usually in the spring, especially near shore off mid-Atlantic barrier islands and beaches. Surf fishermen often catch large drum then, as they move in to spawn near the mouths of rivers and bays.

For surf casters as well as boat anglers, the most common technique is bottom fishing with live or dead bait. Boaters drift or stillfish. Such bait as shrimp, clams, crabs, squid, cut or strip bait, and mullet are used. Metal and leadheaded bucktail jigs are used by casters, and trolling with diving plugs and spoons may be effective. Lures have to be worked slowly, however, as drum do not strike aggressively and don't run down a lure.

They are tough fighters, however. Drum don't jump but they wage a heavyweight tug-of-war, with sustained runs and a steady pull. Bait casting tackle or medium-action boat rods with 15- to 20-pound line is appropriate, with long rods being used by surf casters.

In some southerly waters, red drum can be stalked on the flats by sight fishing, angling for them as one would for bonefish, i.e., watching for tailing fish and casting ahead of them.

Also known as a channel bass or redfish, the red drum is a good fighting saltwater fish.

FLATFISH

There is actually no such species as 'flatfish' per se, but the term is used to refer to an assortment of flounders and halibut that populate coastal North American waters.

Summer and winter flounder are the two most abundant members of the flounder clan, and are found along the Atlantic coast only, with winter flounder having the more northerly range. Winter flounder are primarily a cold-water species, predominant in late winter and early spring and in the fall, while summer flounder, which are also widely referred to as 'fluke,' are a warmer-water species, and one that grows larger. Both are popular with sport fishermen and are highly valued as table fare.

Flounder have both eyes on one side of the head, and this upper side usually blends in well with the ocean floor. Flounder conceal themselves there, motionless, and wait to pounce on unsuspecting prey. They can feed at all levels, but primarily feed on the bottom, and virtually all angling efforts are focused at that level, whether in shallow or intermediate-depth water. Flounder feed on an assortment of small fish and small shellfish.

The primary place to find flounder is on a sand or mud bottom, or a mixture of both, in bays, harbors, estuaries, creeks, and canals, and in the proximity of bridges and piers. Drifting is highly popular, provided the boat doesn't move too rapidly. There are sometimes a lot of flounder in a given area, so repeated drifting over productive locales is commonplace. Drift fishermen do some jigging, with bucktail jigs tipped with a piece of fish, but more bait fishing is done. Flounder baits include strips of fish, worms, and shellfish. Some chumming is done for flounder, too, as well as a little bit of trolling.

Inshore flounder fishing is best on a moving tide; a slack tide is very poor. Flounder are daylight feeders, and early morning is often a highly productive period. They strike lightly, but fight actively. In shallow water, a 6-foot spinning rod with 8-pound line is adequate, but in deeper water, quick tides, and where heavy weights are used, a sturdier boat rod with heavier line is more appropriate.

Halibut are found in Atlantic and Pacific waters, and are primarily a cold, deep-water fish. The Atlantic halibut species is found in portions of the Atlantic and inhabits extreme depths. California and Pacific halibut are found in Pacific waters, with the former being more southerly in range and more abundant, and the latter being a larger-growing fish and one that closely resembles its Atlantic brethren.

These fish feed on a variety of creatures, including small fish, crustaceans, squid, and mollusks. They may be found shallower in the more northerly regions, deeper to the south. Like flounder, they feed at different levels, but are mainly caught while fishing on the bottom, drifting or jigging. Heavy tackle and large bait are used for the bigger specimens, some of which weigh in the hundreds of pounds.

Above: Since flounder are primarily caught on the bottom, a rig such as this is a good bet. Leader length needn't be long, and baits can be varied.

Below: Most fishing for flounder is done with bait, worked close to the bottom.

GRAYLING

Arctic grayling are an outstanding game-fish known to comparatively few anglers. Found primarily in the northern part of the continent, these distinctive-looking fish with the sail-like dorsal fin are seldom the primary quarry of distant-traveling anglers, although they serve as a desirable secondary attraction to anglers primarily seeking lake trout, walleye, northern pike, or char.

Although these fish are also known as 'American grayling,' there are few grayling to be found in the continental U.S., primarily in Rocky Mountain waters. Grayling are most abundant in clean, cool, swift-flowing streams and rivers from southern to Arctic regions of Canada and Alaska, and in many cold Arctic lakes.

Grayling are a member of the salmon family, but they don't attain typical salmon sizes. A 3-pounder is a large grayling, and most are in the 1-pound class, although some waters are noted for large average-size fish. They are routinely found in groups, and feed heavily on aquatic insects in all stages of development. Grayling are most commonly observed in flowages while dimpling the water and feeding on surface insects; they often do this very daintily, but occasionally feed dramatically by clearing the surface and coming down on the insect.

Primarily caught by fly fishing, grayling provide a challenge and thrill. Dry-fly fishing with 5- to 7-weight lines is most practiced and certainly preferred. When not rising freely to insects, grayling may better be pursued with a wet fly or nymph. A floating fly line is used most of the time, but a sink tip line may be necessary. Grayling can be leader-shy, and they pursue flies and often strike at the end of a drift, so attention to detail is sometimes important. Fly size ranges from No. 12 through 18, and the general rule is skimpy and dark. Exact representations aren't usually critical, but a black or brown color is.

Grayling are an excellent fish to catch on light or ultralight spinning tackle, too, using 2- through 6-pound-test line. Small spinners and spoons are often used, but the best artificial is a small dark jig. Black or brown marabou or soft-plastic-bodied jigs in 1/16-to 1/8-ounce sizes produce very well, in flowing and still water.

While most grayling are caught in the slick water of rivers and streams, and sometimes where it flows quite fast, they can also be found in lakes near river inlets, usually along small-rock-studded shores. There, in calm water, they may be seen cruising and inhaling surface insects, and caught with flies, jigs, or spinners.

Grayling have small mouths and many fish that strike are lost. They are scrappy, feisty fish that jump and fight to the end, but they must be handled gently, as they die quickly when held out of the water or if manhandled.

A sail-like dorsal fin is found on the scrappy grayling.

GROUPER

Groupers are a very popular and important tropical-water fish for saltwater anglers. There are literally hundreds of groupers, however. In North America, there are few groupers in Pacific U.S. waters, yet many in the southeastern Atlantic, with more than fifty varieties found in Florida waters alone.

Groupers are actually members of the sea bass family, and bear the characteristic broad head and thick body shape of those fish. In form, groupers look much like the largemouth bass of freshwater, though there is no relation. They are found in all sizes, most commonly being caught in the 2- to 5-pound range, but some of these fish grow exceptionally large in the extreme, including such notable gargantuans as giant sea bass and jewfish.

Some of the more prominent members of the grouper clan include the following: speckled hind, red hind, red grouper, yellowedge grouper, Warsaw grouper, Nassau grouper, snowy grouper, gag, scamp, coney, black grouper, marbled grouper, rock hind, tiger grouper, and yellowfin grouper. Certain species are deeper dwellers than others, though generally smaller fish are usually found closer inshore and larger fish are found in deeper water. Some species can be targeted by sport fishermen based on depth and locale, but the catch of others is often usually by chance.

Groupers are strictly bottom-dwelling fish. Their habitat includes reefs, sunken wrecks, rocky outcrops, bridges, and piers. Many of these fish hide in holes or crevices along the ocean floor, and ambush their prey, which includes squid, crabs, shrimp, and assorted small fish. They are a favorite and most commonly caught quarry of deep-jigging aficionados, who use leadheaded bucktails adorned with a strip of bait or with a soft plastic curl tail in shallow and intermediate-depth waters. In shallower reef habitat, some trolling is done, mainly with deep-diving plugs.

Live or dead bait is popularly used, of course, too. Grouper have large mouths, so big hooks, in 4/0 to 10/0 sizes, are employed. The deeper the water, the heavier the weight used; at the greatest depths sometimes 1- to 3-pound weights are necessary.

These are strong fish, and the bigger grouper often surge for the bottom and some obstruction immediately after being hooked, so it takes effort to keep them out of cover and to prevent them from breaking the line. With really large grouper caught in very deep water, fairly stout tackle, including conventional reels equipped with an ample supply of heavy line, are used as a result.

Grouper fishing lacks the glamour that is associated with angling for some other more accessible species, particularly those taken on light tackle, but these fish lack nothing as table fare, and in this regard are more prized than most saltwater species.

Using a live butterfish for bait, this angler caught a reef-dwelling grouper.

JACKS

There are a host of jack species in North American waters. Some, such as amberjack and permit, are notable enough to receive separate review elsewhere in this section. Others, such as roosterfish, pompano, and crevalle jack, are detailed here.

Roosterfish

These are an exciting and popularly sought Pacific Ocean fish that are mainly found seasonally from southern California south. This inshore species inhabits moderate depths of water and fights particularly well. They jump several times after being hooked, dive deeply, and engage in a slugfest.

The roosterfish looks, in fact, very much like an amberjack in general body shape. The most distinguishing feature of a roosterfish, however, is its unusual first dorsal fin, which looks like the raised comb of a cock bird. There are seven spines in this fin, and when the fish is aroused while chasing forage or fighting an angler, the spines are raised.

Roosterfish may be found in loose groups, and are often spotted under working birds. They are caught by boaters who drift and troll, but also by casting anglers and surf fishermen. Sandy-bottomed locales are good, as are bays and sections of mild surf. Smaller fish are usually closer to shore. Trolling with strip bait, live bait, plugs, and feathers is popular; casting and live-bait drifting, particularly when a group of roosterfish is located, may be very effective.

Tackle is often quite stout, but medium-action gear with 15- to 20-pound line has merit, and fly rods and light spinning or bait-casting gear can be used as well.

Most members of the jack family are strong, stubborn fish; these anglers have landed a crevalle, one of the more popular jacks.

Crevalle jack

Another excellent fighting fish in this fraternity, crevalle jack are found along the Atlantic Coast and in the Gulf of Mexico. A close relative, the Pacific crevalle jack, is found in similar western environs. These are different fish, but they look and behave the same.

Crevalle jack tolerate a wide range of environs. Primarily an inshore species, they are found in harbors and bays, on shallow flats, and around brackish river mouths, but may also inhabit offshore reefs. They forage actively and almost voraciously, charging hard after schools of fish, and they strike a lure or bait with gusto. As a result, they are prized as a light-tackle quarry, and can be taken by casting with spinning, bait-casting, or fly tackle, as well as by trolling or live-bait fishing. Lures or flies are usually retrieved quickly, and the trolling pace is rapid. Mullet and pinfish make good baits.

Crevalle are sometimes mistaken for horse-eye jack in Atlantic waters. Horse-eye jacks are found in small schools around islands and reefs, in holes, in channels near flats, and in brackish water. They are also a good light tackle species that are taken in various manners. In southwest Pacific waters, anglers occasionally encounter bigeye or bluefin trevally. These are tropical-water jacks found near reefs and rocky areas, and are caught by trolling, casting, and bait drifting.

The distinctive roosterfish is equally impressive on rod and reel.

Pompano

A highly valued food fish, pompano provide fine light-tackle action for sport fishermen. Although they inhabit Atlantic waters from New England south, they are more commonly found from Virginia to the Bahamas. They are caught primarily in inshore waters, ranging from shallow water out to depths in the 100-foot range, by small and large boaters as well as surf fishermen and shore-based anglers fishing from bridges, piers, and jetties. These fish migrate in schools; spring and fall are better times to find them in southerly waters, summer and early fall to the north.

The primary tactic is fishing with bait, on or close to the bottom, although casting and trolling will yield fish, too. Pompano feed on clams, crabs, shrimp, and mussels, so bait should follow similar lines. Small jigs, in yellow, pink, or white, are good for casting in shallow water.

Although relatively small, pompano strike hard and fight vigorously. They are caught on light- to medium-action spinning or bait-casting tackle, and will make several line-peeling runs before being overcome.

MACKEREL

There are a variety of fish in the mackerel family that are pursued by North American anglers and valued for both sport and food.

Atlantic mackerel

Among the smallest fish in this group, but popular on the East Coast, Atlantic mackerel is recognized by its wavy black lines that run down each side to the lateral line. These schooling fish are highly mobile and often found close to shore, sometimes in harbors and bays. Averaging about a pound in size, they are a fun light-tackle fish, usually caught on a spinning outfit with 6- or 8-pound line.

Atlantic mackerel are caught with a variety of methods and with many lures and baits. Trolling, drifting and jigging, casting, and fly fishing are all possibilities when a school is found, and they can be attracted to a chum slick, too. A traditional ploy is to use a mackerel rig, which sports a chrome jig at the bottom below several smaller teaser jigs; this can account for several fish at a time when the action is hot.

Spanish mackerel

Running a little larger, Spanish mackerel are caught in a similar manner, and are more abundant southerly on the East Coast than Atlantic mackerel. These are a good food fish and are found in large schools. They are often caught close to shore by boaters, and by land-based anglers around piers, bridges, jetties, and the like.

King mackerel

This is the largest of the mackerel group. Although they are sometimes caught around inlets and from piers, they are also taken in inshore waters and around wrecks, reefs, buoys, and the like. King mackerel prefer warm waters, and are mostly located in tropical and subtropical environs. They are highly migratory, and feed primarily on migratory schooling fish. King mackerel can reach up to 100 pounds,

Wahoo are one of the larger members of the mackerel clan, and are usually caught while trolling.

although they are rarely caught that size. The bigger fish, however, are usually landed by trollers. Trolling, drifting, and fishing with bait while chumming are common tactics.

Wahoo

The hardest fighting and most well respected member of the mackerel clan, however, is wahoo, which grow fairly large and fight like fish even bigger, often being mistaken for other fish when caught while trolling for biggame species. These fast-swimming fish are noted for peeling a lot of line off a reel after striking, and will make a long run.

Inhabiting Atlantic and Pacific waters, wahoo usually are caught well offshore in tropical and temperate environs, and found singly or in small groups, sometimes around wrecks and reefs. They feed on flying fish, herring, mackerel, and other schooling species.

Wahoo are steel-blue in color, with bright vertical markings, and are good eating, but are primarily caught incidentally by high-speed trollers, on rigged whole or strip baits as well as trolling plugs and feathers.

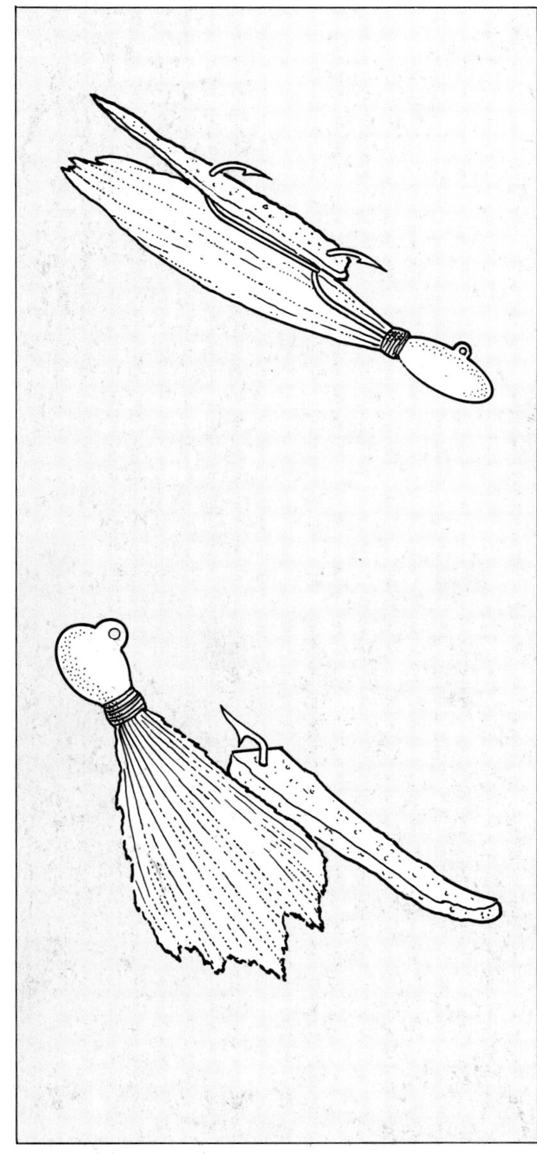

Above: Mackerel and wahoo are sometimes caught on a jig tipped with a strip of bait or a baited trailer hook.

MUSKELLUNGE

Muskellunge are generally harder to catch than any other freshwater species, and are quite unpredictable. The subject of many legends, they are fervently pursued by a coterie of devoted admirers, most of whom release nearly all the muskies that they catch. Musky fishing is the one form of freshwater angling in which it is highly regarded merely to see the quarry; a 'follow' –when a musky trails a lure to the boat – is as meaningful as tossing a horseshoe close to the peg.

Muskellunge are coolwater fish that are close relatives of pickerel and northern pike. They are most abundant in Upper Midwestern states, southern Canada, and Great Lakes drainages, but have been stocked in mid-South reservoirs. Hybrid muskellunge, which are a sterile offspring from pure musky and pike parentage, have been introduced widely.

Although some muskies are caught in open-water locales, the majority are found in or close to some form of cover where food is abundant and where they can ambush prey. Muskies are not generally a wide-roaming fish nor one that will swim long distances to obtain a meal. Walleyes, ciscoes, suckers, perch, golden shiners, and bass are their primary foods.

Submerged vegetation is a likely musky lair, and many of these fish lie in the midst or on the edge of weed beds. Points with a long underwater slope adjacent to deep water are good places to seek musky, as are islands, sand bars, and gravel bars, especially if they are washed by strong current.

Muskellunge prefer water temperature that ranges from the mid 50s to low 70s. They spawn in very shallow near-shore water in the spring, usually before the fishing season opens in northern states, and stay in near-shore shallows for a while after spawning, then move to a permanent residence. Most muskellunge are caught quite shallow throughout the season, usually in less than 30 feet of water and primarily under 20 feet. Casting is the foremost method of pursuing them, with a bucktail spinner being the premier lure for shallow- to mid-depth casting. Diving plugs, shallow-running minnow-style baits, 1/2- to 1-ounce jigs, and just-under-the-surface plugs referred to as 'jerk baits' are the other principal types of musky casting lures. For trolling, an assortment of 5- to 8-inch-long floating/diving plugs get the nod in straight or jointed versions. Good lure colors include black; black-and-white; chartreuse; silver-and-black; perch, walleye, largemouth bass, and musky patterns; and yellow with red or black stripes.

Trolled lures are fished, incidentally, on short lines. There is seldom much reason to put out more than 75 feet of line. Muskies are not spooked by boat noise, and some trollers catch them right in the prop wash, within 10 to 25 feet of the boat and just a few feet below the surface.

Most musky anglers use heavy tackle. Twenty-five to 40-pound line and a stiff rod is standard, but some anglers are very successful with 12- to 20-pound line and a 6-foot fast-action bait-casting rod.

Muskies fight well but not laboriously, although they can provide some spectacular jumping action. They are noted for being hard to drive a hook into, and for escaping from anglers who thought they had a well-hooked fish. The use of a steel leader is advised because of a musky's formidable dentures.

Below: A point is a prime place to fish for muskellunge; if trolling, maneuver around the point in a figure-eight pattern.

Right: The muskellunge is perhaps the hardest freshwater fish to catch with regularity.

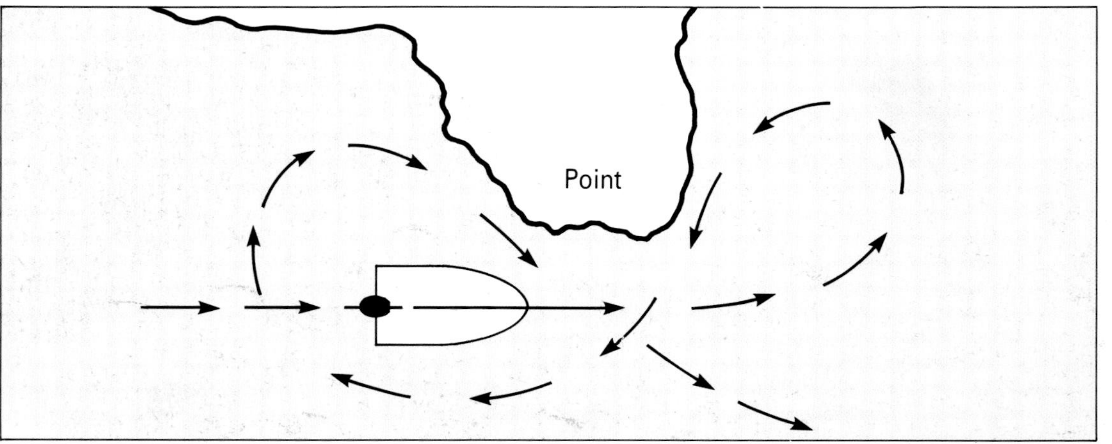

PANFISH

Bluegill, also known as bream, are the premier panfish species and are caught on bait, small lures, and flies.

There is no such fish, *per se*, as a panfish, but freshwater anglers refer to a host of creatures, primarily of the sunfish clan, as 'panfish' because of their general size and edibility value. Most of the so-called panfish are very abundant in their respective environments, sometimes detrimentally so, and although these fish collectively are quite popular, in many locales there is not nearly the fishing pressure that there could be and which would be beneficial for the population of these as well as other species.

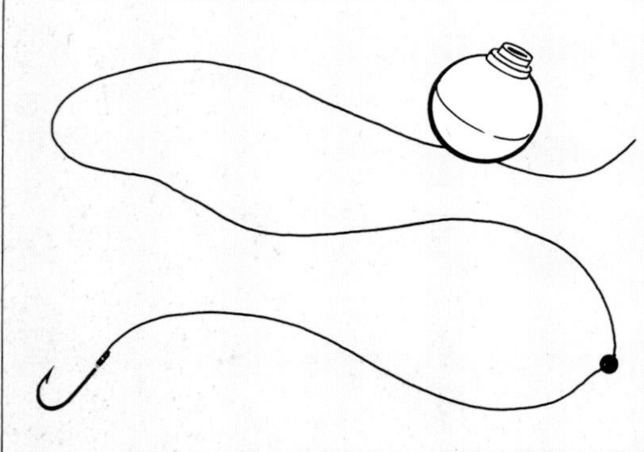

The time-honored terminal tackle for panfish consists of a bobber, small split shot, and hook.

Sunfish

Known as 'bream' in many locales, bluegills are the most widely distributed panfish, and are found with, or in similar places as, such companion and related species as the redbreasted sunfish, green sunfish, pumpkinseed, shellcracker, and longeared sunfish, all of which are similar in configuration but different in appearance. These species, collectively known as 'sunfish,' are highly respected fighters even though they are diminutive fish. They are most commonly pursued in the spring and early summer while they are spawning in shallow water and where their round clustered nests are readily visible along the shoreline of ponds and lakes. Vegetation is a prime place to seek sunfish, followed by stumps, logs, and fallen trees.

A popular sunfish family member that has a bit different demeanor is the rock bass. This fish inhabits both lakes and rivers, spending much time around rock and wood structures, preferring to feed deep below the surface on such forage as crayfish, insects, and a variety of small minnows. These are schooling fish and can be found in substantial numbers at times, perhaps near deep-water rocky ledges, rocky river pools, deep-water gravel beds, and beneath overhanging willow trees along a river or lake shoreline.

A lot of fishing for sunfish is done with live worms and bobbers in relatively shallow water, although the bigger fish are usually found deep. A long-shanked No. 8 or 10 hook is employed, since sunfish don't have very large mouths, and is used unweighted or with just a small split shot. Other baits include crickets, tiny minnows, and meal worms. Small jigs are a fine lure, and small spinners and spinnerbaits can be productive, as well as dry flies, nymphs, and popping bugs used with a fly rod. A slow retrieve is best. Sunfish are popular in winter, too, where small jigs, flies, and meal worms are used.

Yellow perch

Predominantly a northern coolwater fish, yellow perch are among the most favored panfish for edibility, tasting much like their walleye relations. Not a member of the sunfish family, yellow perch are in fact a true perch. They are schooling fish, and while they are caught in open water they are most avidly sought through the ice in winter and while in the midst of their spring spawning runs in which they ascend tributaries and seek warm shoreline areas in bays and back eddies. Primarily, yellow perch like cool water and will school deep in places where surface temperatures get warm, although they will move shallower to feed.

Perch are caught on a variety of baits and lures, with live worms, small minnow-imitating plugs, jigs, spoons, and spinners being among the best attractors. Bobbers are frequently employed with live bait; nightcrawler rigs, sporting a No. 2 hook and No. 2 spinner, are also effective.

The tackle used for panfish needn't be stout. Light spinning or spin-casting outfits are more than adequate, and in many areas, long cane poles without reels are used to dabble bait into selected pockets for various sunfish species. Four- to 8-pound-test line is ample. Fly fishing is also an excellent way to pursue panfish, particularly bluegills and other sunfish species, and even perch when they are in shallow water in the spring. Floating and sinking flies, small streamers, and poppers are the terminal items.

Light tackle is appropriate for panfish, such as this rock bass.

PERMIT

Permit are one of the more elusive, coveted, and heralded saltwater fish. They are renowned for being difficult to approach, difficult to entice to strike, difficult to set the hook in, and difficult to land. The fact that they are a warm-water fish not available to most North American anglers, and that angling attention focuses on south Florida, the Florida Keys, and the Bahamas, enhances their mystique.

These fish with the high blunt forehead are closely related to pompano, and are confused with them in smaller sizes. They can achieve weights exceeding 40 pounds, however, although they are commonly caught in the 10-to 20-pound range. The Pacific permit, known as 'palometa,' is a close relation that looks similar but does not grow as large. Permit inhabit sandy flats and reefs, and feed on mollusks, crustaceans, sea urchins, and small fish.

Some angling is done by bait fishing or jigging in intermediate-depth water over reefs, wrecks, and the like, but the vastly favored practice is to stalk the same shallow flats as would be angled for bonefish, and to sight-fish for permit and cast a jig, fly, or live bait to them.

Small permit travel in schools, which are occasionally large. Big fish are usually solitary, however. Permit venture onto sandy flats on a rising tide to scour the bottom for food, and are often seen cruising or tailing while feeding on the bottom. They feed much like a bonefish does, rooting in the sand for shrimp or crabs.

On the flats they are skittish creatures, and fishermen stalk them carefully in a boat or by wading. It is usually critical to make a precise presentation, although this is made easier and less critical if a school of fish is located because the competitive instinct may prevail. Nonetheless, it should be noted that relatively few fish are hooked, and fewer still landed, in comparison to the number of fish seen, so the tasks of stalking and presentation should not be underestimated.

Many permit are caught on live crabs or shrimp. Small jigs produce a fair number of fish. Streamer flies are the more challenging offering, and therefore less effective but no less enjoyable. No matter what is used, the hook must be sharp, and it is advisable to set the hook forcefully several times to effect penetration, since a permit's mouth is extremely leathery. Similarly, if slack is created during the fight, chances are good the hook will drop out.

When the hook is set, however, permit bolt off like a streak of lightning, zooming over the flats and heading toward deep water on a long, sustained run. They might seek obstacles to cut the line on or to try to dislodge the hook, so you must keep the rod high and be using a reel with ample line capacity and an excellent drag. Permit have superior stamina and will fight for a long time. They are often caught on light- to medium-action 7-foot spinning rods and 8-pound line. Fly rodders use a 9-foot rod and floating line.

Predominantly caught on shallow tidal flats, permit are wary and make long runs once hooked.

PICKEREL

Long, slimy, toothy, camouflaged, and sporting cold-blooded eyes, the pickerel is a smaller but equally villainous-looking version of its northern pike and muskellunge cousins. This freshwater fish is referred to affectionately and derisively as a 'snake,' 'jack,' 'jackfish,' and 'pike,' and is sometimes confused with walleyes (to which it is unrelated), particularly in southern Canada where the walleye species is widely known as 'yellow pickerel.'

Pickerel range from Nova Scotia south to Florida and from Texas through most of the easterly states, though their primary abundance is in the northeastern U.S. and Florida and Georgia. Chain pickerel, with a distinctive network of broken chain-like lines along its body, are the larger and most common pickerel; grass and redfin pickerel also exist but are caught by few anglers.

These fish have fine sporting values and are able battlers when caught on light tackle. The best all-around gear for pickerel fishing is a spinning outfit with 4- or 6-pound-test line. On light tackle or fly rods, they'll run, jump, and cavort in a pleasing manner. Only the large pickerel put up a really good fight on medium to heavy tackle.

Pickerel are a favorite quarry of springtime open-water anglers as well as ice fishermen, and their flesh, though bony, is sweet and delicious.

A notoriously gluttonous fish, pickerel have a wide-ranging diet. Their primary forage is small minnows and fry, yellow perch, and other pickerel. They may consume nearly anything that invades their domain, including frogs and other fish that are one-half to two-thirds their own size, and it is not uncommon to catch pickerel that have tooth-like scars on their back, courtesy of a relative. Their habitat is primarily the vegetated and abundantly covered shallow areas of ponds, bogs, tidal and nontidal rivers, streams, lakes, and reservoirs.

Pickerel are particularly attracted to movement and flash. Standard spinners and small spoons are traditionally effective pickerel lures, but spinnerbaits, weedless in-line spinners, and weedless spoons in white, chartreuse, and silver colors are preferred in thick cover. Worms and jigs are also taken by pickerel, although many of these lures are lost when the sharp and abundant teeth of a pickerel cuts the fishing line. Surface and shallow-running plugs have merit, too, with silver, gold, and perch colors being preferred. A moderate to fast rate of lure retrieve is best, but it often pays to start a retrieval slow and then quicken it, as pickerel frequently follow and chase.

Fly fishing is also worth while for pickerel, streamer flies and popping bugs being especially ravished. Live bait is popularly used, particularly in cold weather and through the winter. Minnows or shiners up to 6 inches long are the preferred baits.

Chain pickerel, shown here, are the largest and most abundant fish in the pickerel clan, and are aggressive predators.

PIKE

Northern pike don't get much respect from people who catch them accidentally while pursuing other species of freshwater fish. If they did they wouldn't be called 'water wolves', 'hammer handles', 'jacks', or 'snakes', or likened to barracuda. Yet, there are sportsmen who recognize that pike are a worthy angling quarry, one that can grow quite large, fights well, and is fairly accommodating.

Well-camouflaged fish that usually inhabit weedy environs, northern pike are caught on many types of tackle.

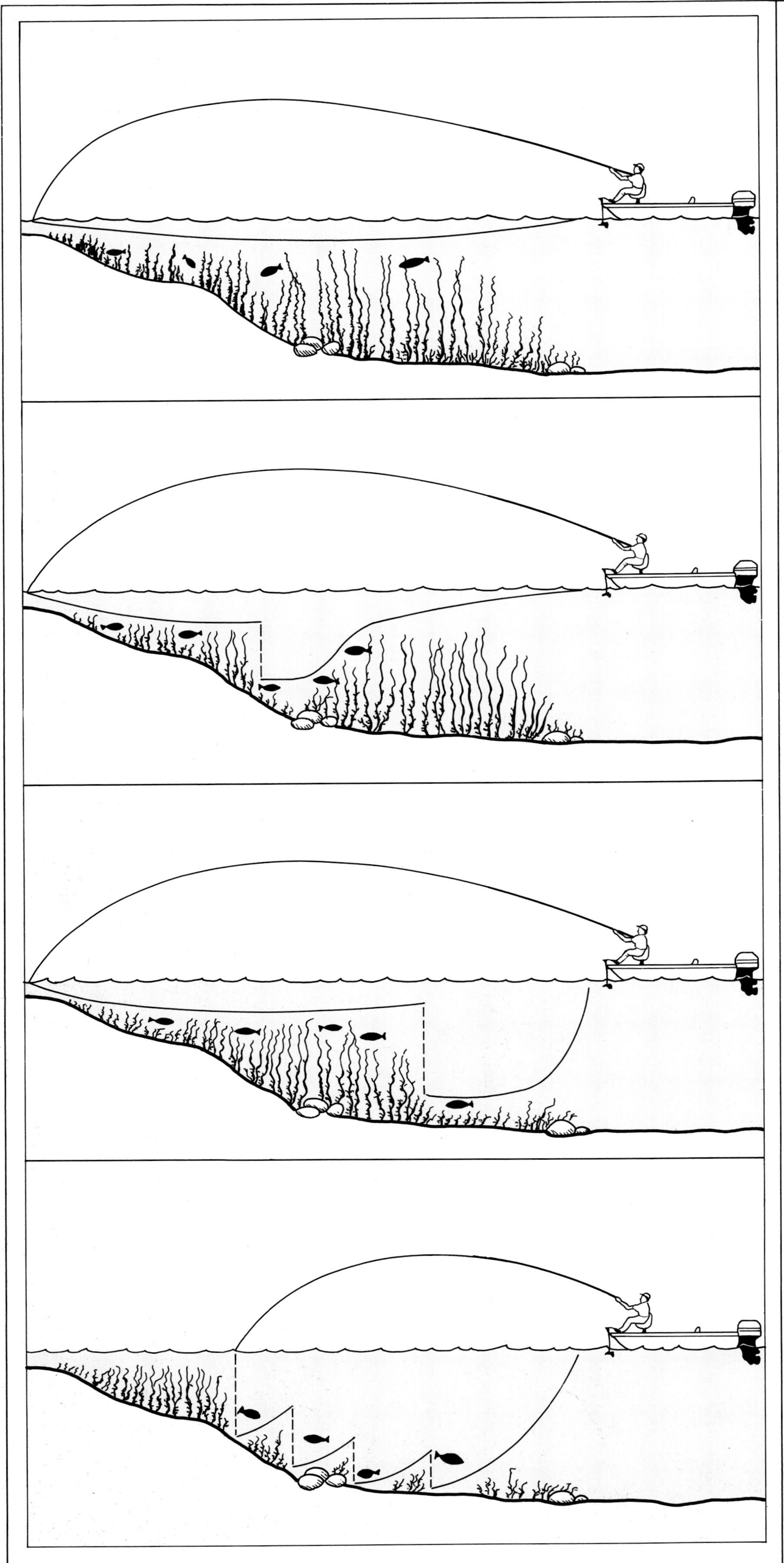

This toothy, slinky, coolwater fish is most prominent in the northern U.S. and across Canada, with the majority of larger, trophy-size specimens coming from mid to northern Canadian rivers and lakes. They have a wide-ranging diet made up of small- to large-sized fish, but will take other fare.

Born in weedy waters in the spring, pike spend much of their life in similar environs, holding motionless in the vegetation, camouflaged to suddenly strike passersby. Prominent pike habitat includes weedy bays and river inlets, shoreline points with beds of cabbage weeds on their open-water sides, reefs with coontail weeds, marshy shorelines, lily pads, reedy pockets along sandy and rocky shorelines, the juncture of small streams with rivers, shallow river backwaters, shorelines just below riprap or wing dams, the inside of large eddies, the back side of bridge pilings, under docks, and downstream from a river island.

Not all of these environs may have some form of vegetation, but vegetation is often a key factor. This is often found shallow, but as the season progresses, better action is had in deeper weeded locales, often where the water goes from 6 or 7 feet in depth down to 15 feet.

Although there is some trolling done deliberately for pike, casting is vastly preferred, and there are many good pike lures. The more popular ones include a standard and weedless red-and-white spoon, fluorescent-orange-bladed spinnerbait or bucktail spinner, an orange-/yellow-backed minnow imitation plug, a yellow Five-O-Diamonds pattern spoon, a black bucktail spinner with a single fluorescent blade, and some large diving plugs. Bright, flashy colors are the rule. Live and dead bait, as well as strips of fish, are also used.

Bait-casting, spin-casting, and spinning gear are all suitable, though bait casting is most preferable where large lures or bait are used. Some fly-rodding, using large streamers, is also done. Line capacity is not a big factor with reels in pike fishing. Rods should be $5^1/_2$ to 7 feet, with a stiff butt and midsection and rather fast tip. Most pike fishermen prefer heavy line, with 12- to 17-pound-test favored, but many opt for 6- to 10-pound line where the cover is not thick.

Pike aren't hard to subdue. They do a lot of thrashing and short-distance darting, and some don't really fight until they eyeball the boat or fisherman. The one difficulty with light lines is the heavy weeds in which these fish are found. Big pike tend to make long, steady runs through thick vegetation.

Probe the holes, edges, and surface of vegetation when fishing for pike. As the water warms, the bigger pike are more likely to be on the deep edge.

PORGY

Porgies are the proverbial panfish of saltwater. Like their counterparts in freshwater they are eagerly sought by some inshore anglers, and caught accidentally and with some disappointment by others.

There are several fish that are known as 'porgies', and this group of fish also includes sheepshead. Porgy are known as 'scup' in some places, mainly in New England. They are usually caught in the 1-pound range, but may grow larger, although sheepshead will grow considerably bigger.

These slightly hump-backed fish are bottom dwellers, and are caught on or within a foot or two of bottom. Most porgies are caught in relatively shallow water, often 10 to 30 feet deep. Larger fish are often taken deeper, however, and some species are located in deep offshore water.

In bays or inlets, look for porgies over a sandy or hard bottom. They are also found on shellfish beds and the edges of reefs. Most anglers fish a two, and sometimes three, hook bait rig, using sand worms, blood worms, squid, clam, and grass shrimp as bait.

A saltwater panfish, the porgy is usually caught by anglers using bait rigs fished on or near the bottom.

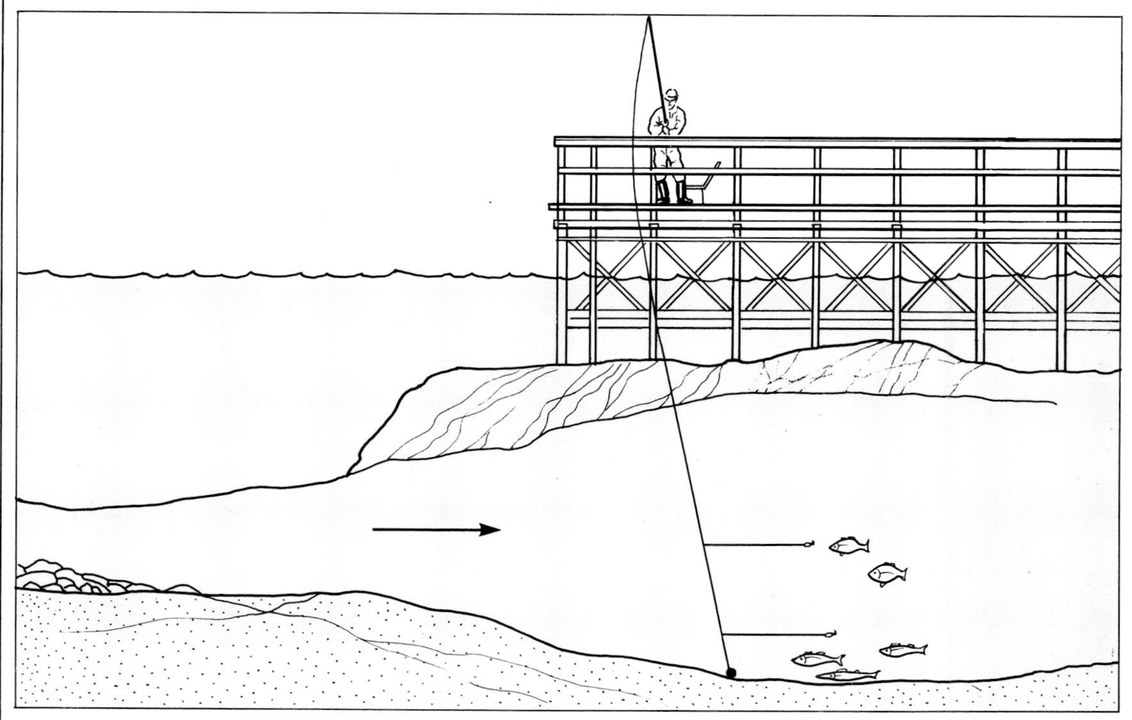

A pier fisherman using a double bait rig fishes for porgy or flounder on the bottom, and might catch a different species on the upper hook.

Porgy are notorious bait stealers; fishing a small piece of bait, usually just enough to cover the hook, is sufficient to curtail nibbling and bait loss. Chumming, incidentally, is sometimes helpful for increasing the catch.

Porgies put up a good fight for their size, and are respectable battlers on light tackle. Where light sinkers are used, a light to medium spinning outfit, with 8- or 10-pound line provides good sport. When heavy weights are needed, because of tide, current, or depth, a boat or bay rod may be required.

Porgies are sometimes quite plentiful and can be caught in good numbers. Other times the reverse is true. In northern environs they usually become available in spring, and fishing lasts through summer. Many porgies are caught by anglers fishing the bottom for some other species.

SALMON

Salmon are anadromous fish, spending their lives in open water and returning to their tributaries of birth to spawn. Open water has traditionally meant the ocean; for some species, however, saltwater environs have been replaced by large inland lakes. In either instance, salmon have a relatively short life, characterized by wandering, rapid growth through extensive feeding, and an inborn instinct to return to spawn in their natal water.

Taxonomically, there are six species of salmon in North America. These fall under the categories of Atlantic or Pacific. Chinook, coho, sockeye (kokanee), pink, and chum salmon make up the Pacific grouping, although only chinook and coho figure very prominently in North American sport fisheries. The seagoing Atlantic salmon is the sole species in that grouping, and it is also found in a 'landlocked' form. All Pacific salmon die after spawning. Some Atlantic salmon live to spawn more than once.

All of the salmon species have differing life expectancies, size ranges, and behavioral patterns, and they have played dissimilar roles in the history of sportfishing in North America. However, all of these salmon begin their life in the fall in the upper reaches of streams and rivers, where, as eggs, they are buried under gravel. The fry hatch in late winter or spring. Young fish, called 'parr', remain in the river until they are roughly 6 to 8 inches long, at which time they are called 'smolts'. Smolts eventually migrate to sea. Some return after one year and are called 'grilse'. Most return after several years, and all cease feeding as they enter spawning tributaries.

Atlantic salmon

Despite its relative scarcity today, this is still considered the premier salmon. Dubbed 'the leaper' by Romans, this salmon is revered for its sporting quality, succulent flesh, general tenacity, and mysterious lifestyle. Today there are fishable runs in only a portion of their original range, mostly in eastcoastal Canadian provinces.

These fish migrate great distances from their wintering grounds in the Atlantic to their natal tributaries. It is during their limited spawning run period that seagoing Atlantics are pursued by sport fishermen in rivers; there is virtually no ocean sport-fishing done for this species. The average fish weighs less than 15 pounds, and one over that is considered quite large,

Left: Salmon are born in rivers and return to them, and some of the finest angling experiences in North America are had when salmon are migrating upstream.

Above: This landlocked salmon is a relative of the seagoing Atlantic salmon, though it does not usually grow as large.

though even the smaller fish fight extraordinarily well.

Although 'landlocked' is a poor term that is used to describe the nonseagoing Atlantic salmon, it is one with which most anglers are familiar. For descriptive purposes we'll clarify this by saying that landlocked salmon are Atlantics that do not, or cannot, run to sea and return to freshwater, thus living their entire lives in freshwater environs. These are the progeny (natural and stocked) of seagoing Atlantic salmon, and though they are not anadromous in the true sea-run sense, they utilize a large lake as if it were the ocean, and they also return to their natal tributaries to spawn. 'Freshwater' salmon or 'lake' salmon are two names that have been suggested for these fish, and in eastern Canada they are known as 'ouananiche'.

Landlocked salmon are found primarily in the Northeastern part of the continent and the Great Lakes, and then not in great abundance. In the U.S., most of the landlocked salmon population is supported by stocking efforts. They are, however, a highly desirable fish, known for long runs and superior fighting ability, and they are widely sought by anglers in lakes and rivers.

The life history of landlocked salmon is quite similar to that of the seagoing Atlantic, the principal difference being that the latter will enter tributaries from summer through early fall prior to spawning, while the former don't enter tributaries until September. Landlocked salmon in relatively small inland waters generally do not grow quite as large as their seagoing brethren.

Right: Transplanted from the West Coast, chinook salmon have become enormously popular and prized fish in the Great Lakes.

Chinook and coho salmon

Also known popularly as 'king salmon', chinook salmon are the largest members of either salmon genus, are extremely strong-fighting fish, and are the premier salmon quarry in both the Northwest coastal region and the Great Lakes. Along with coho salmon, they were introduced to the Great Lakes and have been a key factor in the revitalization of sport fisheries in those waters, and both species use those lakes the same way that landlocked Atlantic salmon do.

There are spring and fall runs of seagoing chinooks; the former stays in the river for a year or more before migrating to the ocean, while the latter generally leaves after a three- to four-month period. The spring-run fish may enter the rivers from mid- to late winter, spawning late in the spring; the fall-run fish typically enter the rivers from mid- to late summer, spawning in the fall. In inland lakes, there is only a fall run.

Cohos are a popular sport fish in the West as well as in the Great Lakes. Though much smaller on average than chinook, they are able fighters, known to be active jumpers. Their coastal range parallels that of the chinook. Like chinooks, coho populations in the Great Lakes are supported almost entirely by hatchery production. They have brightly colored silver sides when they are in open water, and are widely referred to as 'silver salmon'. Both coho and chinook salmon are intensively sought by boat fishermen in the ocean and the Great Lakes, and by boat, bank, and wading fishermen in the rivers.

Fishing techniques

Since coho, chinook, Atlantic, and landlocked salmon are found in various environments, there are many fishing methods utilized for them, most of which overlap by species. None of these techniques are exceedingly difficult in principle, and while one might infer from this statement that salmon are quite easily caught, such is not true either. Identifying habitat, structure, and so forth – as one might do for bass, walleyes, pike, or muskies – is less of a problem than either enticing nonfeeding river fish to strike through careful presentation, or locating the right depth and temperature of open water in which salmon schools will be located. Essentially, then, there are open-water and river-fishing techniques.

Turning is an important part of trolling, especially for salmon; lures rise or fall as the result of a turn, and often trigger a strike.

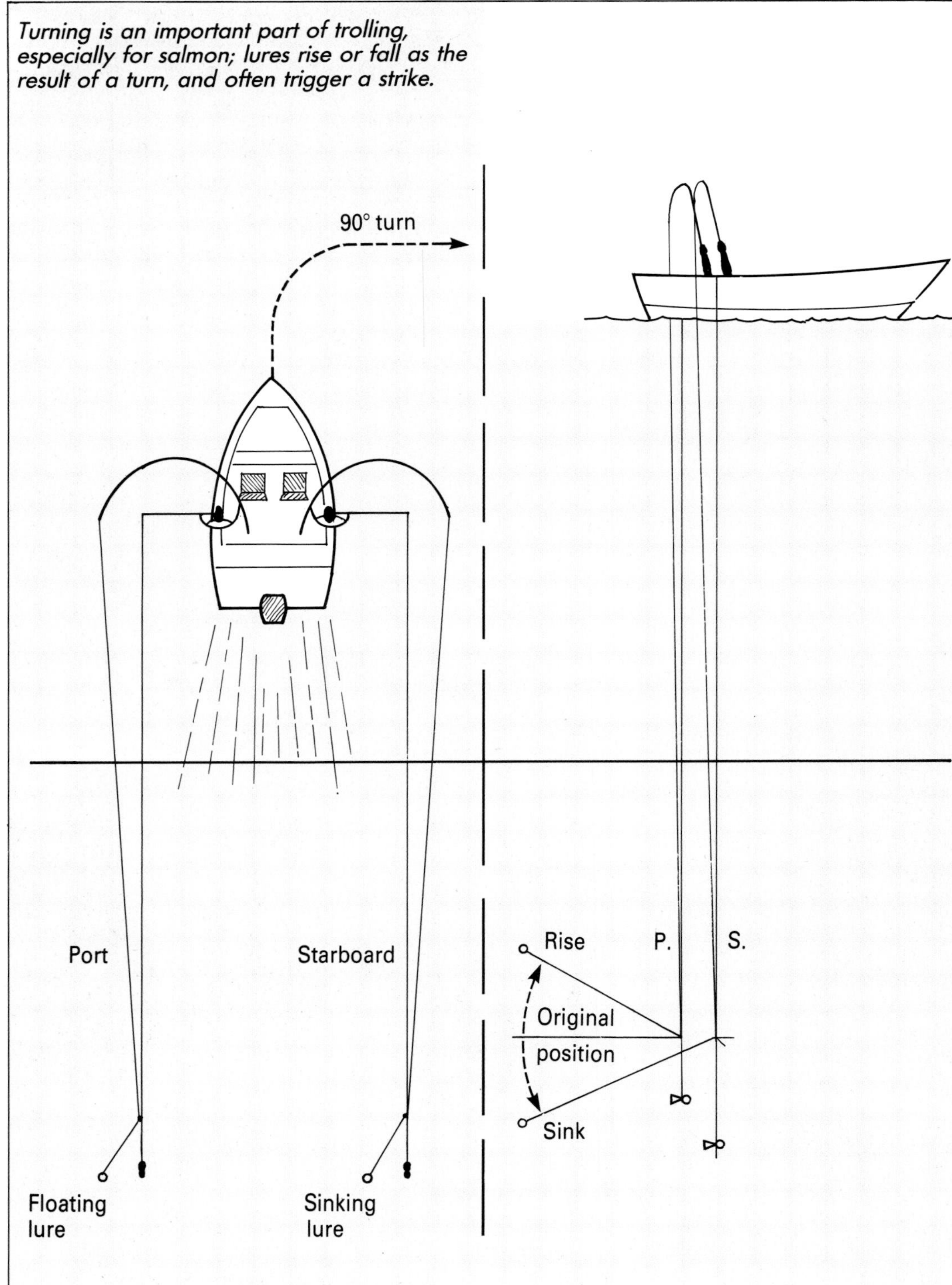

A coho salmon, shown here, is a spunky fish, known for its wild dashing and thrashing and occasional leaps.

With the exception of seagoing Atlantic salmon, there is a significant open-water sportfishery for salmon, the extent of which varies with locale and species. Landlocked salmon are generally perceived to be the most difficult species to catch. After ice-out in the spring, landlocks may be shallow and near shore. Warmer water takes them deeper and further out in the lake, where they seek a cool water temperature, ranging from the mid- to upper 50s. They forage mainly on smelt, alewives, and various minnows. Spawning fish migrate to certain tributaries in the fall and may be caught prior to ascending the streams in the vicinity of tributary mouths.

Coho and chinook in the Great Lakes follow a somewhat similar pattern of behavior. They are inshore early in the season and ultimately seek out a water temperature of 52 to 55 degrees, which occurs at the thermocline. The thermocline is usually deeper as summer progresses; however, due to shifting winds, its depth changes. Coho tend to be found closer to shore than chinooks, though the depth and location of each is a highly variable factor. These fish gather in schools and traverse great distances as they seek out desirable water conditions and alewife or smelt forage.

In the Pacific, once salmon leave a river system and head for the far-off feeding grounds, they are not much of a factor in sportfishing activities until they return a few years later to spawn. When massed along the coast prior to entering their natal rivers, they are a big factor in the sport fishery, and are relatively near the shore, though at varied depths, depending on the water temperature and current conditions.

Since salmon do a great deal of migrating and are found at varied water levels in open water, particularly beyond 30 feet and as much as 70 to 100 feet deep in the summer, it is necessary at most times to search and fish deeply for them. A variety of trolling techniques are primarily used, with downrigger fishing being most popular. Some drift fishing and a limited amount of jigging is also done.

Salmon in the Great Lakes grow darker in late summer as they venture closer to shore and prepare to run up the tributaries. The bigger fish, like this chinook, are usually caught then.

Depending on locale, river salmon fishing can be done by wading or boat anglers, with most fish taken from pools and deep runs.

While open-water salmon fishing is essentially a boating proposition, the land-bound angler can score on open-water salmon in the spring and fall, and occasionally in the winter. Spring is the best all-around time for both salmon and trout in the Great Lakes. When the fish are in close to shore seeking out the most comfortable water temperature (influenced by wind direction and the introduction of warm tributary waters) they are just as accessible and vulnerable to shore-based fishermen as they are to boaters. The only edge that boaters have at this time is mobility – being able to cover a large expanse of water. Shore fishing close to the tributaries is generally best, as this is where the warmer water is. Breakwaters, piers, beaches, and other access points become jammed with long-rodded casters at this time. As the fish move out, shore fishing becomes markedly less productive. It increases in productivity again in late summer and early fall when many salmon return to migrate upriver.

Live bait fishing is a seldom-practiced technique among all salmon anglers, except when ice fishing for landlocks, principally due to the wandering nature of the quarry and the fact that a prodigious amount of natural forage (alewives, smelt, anchovies, etc.) makes it difficult to get a hooked offering recognized. In Pacific waters, cut bait fishing is extremely popular, and anglers 'mooch' by using cut herring for coho and chinook. Salmon eggs are very effective bait, and are used for drift fishing in coastal rivers and Great Lakes tributaries.

Tributary fishing is the predominant Great Lakes method of catching chinook and coho salmon each fall. It is the only sportfishing ground for seagoing Atlantic salmon from summer through fall.

Fish that have just entered rivers or have only been in them a short while may still exhibit a feeding urge in the sense that they may strike a lure or fly as a conditioned, reflexive act. But the longer they are in the river the less this is so. Often it can be difficult to get these fish to strike any offering and it is usually vital to present the offering right in front of the fish. A precise presentation, therefore, is of foremost importance.

Long rods, medium-heavy lines, and small offerings are the elements in coho and chinook river fishing. Salmon eggs, fished singly on a hook or clustered in a spawn bag, are very popular, and spinners, spoons, and wobbling plugs have devotees as well. Fly fishing is more popular in the West than in the Great Lakes, primarily because the rivers in the former are bigger and longer than those in the latter, affording a greater expanse of fishing opportunities and somewhat less crowding.

Salmon hug the bottom, resting in pools and deep-water sections. They are not usually caught in the fast-water reaches. Regardless of technique, lures must be cast slightly upstream and across, drifting with the current to the end of the swing. Whatever the offering, it must bounce or swim along the bottom, and the right size sinker is critically important. Too little and the offering never reaches the bottom and is totally ineffective; too much and it drags in the current, acting unnaturally or hanging up repeatedly.

Presentation and depth factors are similar in seagoing Atlantic salmon fishing, though fly fishing is the angling method by law or tradition in most of North America. Atlantics are, however, usually found shallower than other salmon and are almost always caught by sight fishing, i.e., casting to a specific fish that has been seen, rather than casting blindly for unobserved fish as is usually done in coho and chinook angling.

Wet flies in various colorful patterns and sizes are the norm for Atlantic salmon fishing, with the larger flies generally reserved for fast, high rivers. Dry flies work at times, too, which is an anomaly considering the nonfeeding disposition of these fish. Atlantics may take on the first, fiftieth, or one-hundredth cast, acting out of reflex or annoyance, and they may be put down easily or be relatively undisturbed by the angler's presence and activities. Unlike other salmon, in the river they are prone to jump high and often, in addition to making long, demanding runs. Long rods and reels with plenty of backing are required.

Much river salmon fishing is done by bank or wading anglers, but in large rivers, angling from boats for coho and chinook is not only practical but effective. Non-fly fishermen usually use wobbling plugs in the river more than they do other hardware, or they use salmon eggs or spawn sacks. Trolling here is not a popularly utilized tactic, and is not often practiced due to boat and angler traffic. Anchoring or controlled drifting are the primary boat-fishing methods. Those who anchor do so in or above selected pools, setting their lines out 50 to 75 feet behind the boat and allowing the plugs to work constantly in current.

Salmon are among the most highly regarded game fish in North America, and are intensively pursued for sport and for virtues that any chef could extol.

SEATROUT

Seatrout really aren't trout at all, but they do somewhat resemble freshwater trout. Weakfish and spotted seatrout are the principal species known as sea-trout in North America, and they are both highly popular inshore schooling fish that provide good sport and fine eating.

The range of these fish overlaps, and they are similar in many ways. Weakfish are more northerly, found along the Atlantic coast with major abundance in the mid-states region. Known also as 'squeteague', 'gray trout', and 'tide runners', they are more migratory than the other species. Spotted seatrout are called 'weakfish' by some, but are most commonly referred to as 'speckled trout', or simply 'specks'. They are found along the Atlantic Coast and through the Gulf of Mexico, but are most common in the southerly portion of the range, where they are a year-round resident. Weakfish and spotted seatrout are similar in form, but color varies, and they are distinguished by spots. Both have black spots on the body; on the spotted seatrout these spots extend to the fins, but are not on the fins of weakfish. Both also have a tender mouth.

Seatrout are primarily bottom-feeding fish that consume crustaceans, but they will feed through the water column as well, and also take such small fish as mullet, menhaden, butterfish, and killifish. Thus, there are a variety of ways to fish for them.

Drifting or stillfishing with bait is very popular, using an assortment of live or dead baits, sometimes chumming while bait fishing. Jigging with metal jigs, grubs, or bucktail jigs garnished with a plastic worm body is also a favorite method, again either drifting in a boat or anchored. Trolling with plugs and spoons is another technique, although shore fishing, from the surf and by wading, or by casting from piers and jetties, is just as effective. Some casting is also done with surface or deep-running plugs or with streamer flies, usually when the fish are fairly shallow and in bays and estuary environs.

Seatrout will move into brackish water, and the shallow bay areas of estuaries is a common hangout, particularly along grassy bottoms and in brackish rivers or creeks. They will move onto shoals in schools to feed, and concentrate around oyster bars, bridges, and inlet jetties. Anglers should focus on structure and edges to locate seatrout, including such places as a channel in a shallow bay; a slough, cut, or trough in the surf; the edge of a tide rip, flat, and dropoff; deep holes in a bay; and along a sand bar.

Light to medium spinning or bait-casting tackle is usually just right; seatrout are able fighters but a lot of line capacity isn't necessary, and there's fun to be had by using ultralight gear and fine line. Six- to 12-pound line is commonly used, often on standard freshwater tackle. Boat anglers don't need as long a rod as shore fishermen, and it's a good idea to have a net along.

A proud angler displays two large weakfish. These and other seatrout are popular inshore saltwater species.

SHAD

Shad are a delightful springtime phenomenon on both the East and West coasts of the U.S. These fish, not to be confused with the shad (threadfin and gizzard) found in southern and western reservoirs, which are baitfish, live most of their lives in the ocean, then return to major coastal rivers to spawn, returning to the sites where they were born. American shad, which are the favored and more plentiful species, generally weigh in excess of 2 pounds; 3- to 5-pounders are the norm, and an occasional 6- to 8-pounder is caught. Hickory shad run smaller and are only found on the Atlantic coast, and not as far north as American shad. The males (called 'bucks') of both are usually smaller than the females ('roes').

Praised as the 'poor man's salmon,' the derring-do of the shad is not to outdone by any other fish. Drag-screeching runs, a broadside-to-the-current fight, and frequent aerial maneuvers are common. Shad are a good-eating fish, with fine-tasting roe that is considered a delicacy. While not well known outside of the major river systems, they are hotly pursued by a devoted corps of anglers.

Shad are here today and gone tomorrow, however. The upstream migration only lasts for approximately six to eight weeks, and they can be scarce one day and plentiful the next, especially in the early stages of the run before the main body of fish has migrated by. Shad also aren't much for mid-day activity; the early and late hours of the day are usually most productive.

A light-action spinning rod, 6- to 8-pound-test line, an appropriate spinning reel with a good-quality drag, and a mixed supply of shad darts are the only tackle requirements. Darts, which are a lead-bodied, buck tailed form of jig with a tapered body and slanted nose, are the vastly favored lure, though some anglers also use tiny spinners and spoons. Fly fishermen enjoy success using an 8-weight, sink-tip line with a weighted streamer.

Whatever your offering, you usually must get it down near the river bottom, a task that is influenced by the depth of water, strength of the current, and weight of your lure. Shad apparently strike out of anger or reflexive action and thus don't seem to go out of their way to chase a lure. Your offering has to get down in front of a fish's nose to be effective.

Shore fishermen or waders should cast across and upstream, allow their lure to sink to the bottom, then, with line tight, let the lure swing downstream with the current until the lure reaches the end of its sweep. Boat fishermen either troll into the current or anchor and stillfish their lures by letting them swing in the current. In either case, let out approximately 75 feet of line, using a heavy enough lure (or weighting it with a sinker) to get just off the bottom.

Shad basically stick to the channels, preferring the deeper water to the swift, riffling sections. The primary place to fish for them is in the pools. This is slower, calmer, and deeper water than the rest of the river sections, and shad primarily rest in such spots before continuing upriver. Sometimes, when success tapers off in a given spot, you merely need to move slightly up, down, or across the river to be back in action.

American shad are seasonally available in coastal rivers, but are an excellent light-tackle quarry.

SHARK

Sharks have become a hotly pursued saltwater quarry in recent years. There are over two hundred different species, but the more voracious and predatory ones have been the focus of angling attention, as they tend to be easier to catch and vigorous fighters. Popularly-sought sharks in North America include mako, dusky, spinner, thresher, porbeagle, white, blue, tiger, and hammerhead, some of which are wide-ranging and which also grow quite large.

Some sharks are found in shallow water and close to shore, and present opportunities for flats fishermen or shore-bound anglers, but most are pursued away from shore and they are usually caught from a boat. The most common method of fishing for sharks is to use bait, live or dead, and drift for them while chumming. This is usually done over deep water, even though the sharks are usually caught in the upper 50 feet.

With the boat drifting, a considerable amount of chum is ladled out, using oily fish to create a slick. Several hooked baits are fished amidst the chum, set at different levels. One might be close to the surface, another 15 to 20 feet deep, and a third even deeper. Sometimes you will see shark cruise through the slick and be able to cast a lure or fly to them. This presents an opportunity for light-tackle use, although generally sharks are caught on fairly stout equipment. Depending upon the size of quarry likely to be encountered, shark tackle ranges from medium boat rods to big-game gear, from 20- to 130-pound line, from 4/0 to 12/0 reels, from 6/0 to 16/0 bait hooks, and also long wire leaders. Many shark anglers like to fight their fish using stand-up tackle that is placed in a belt gimbal.

A lot of sharks are caught while trolling, sometimes when they have been seen finning but more often incidentally while trolling whole or strip bait for larger quarry, including billfish. Smaller sharks are caught on the flats by casters who sightfish for them.

Of all sharks the makos are the most coveted and renowned fighters. These blue-gray, streamlined, solitary, and pelagic sharks leap very high, fight doggedly, make strong runs, dive deep, and even charge the boat. They are also excellent eating (like swordfish), and are usually found offshore and taken while trolling for billfish.

Some other sharks are known for occasional leaps as well, including threshers and porbeagles. The latter resembles a mako but inhabits generally colder water. It is known for following migrations of such fish as mackerel, herring, and bonito. The thresher is distinguished by the long upper lobe of its tail, and is usually found alone or in pairs. The most abundant shark may be the blue, which is often found in packs.

Some of these sharks, of course, can be dangerous to humans, both in and out of the water, and should be treated with care when landed.

This mako shark was aggressive enough to grab the bait offered by two anglers, and struggles mightily even while being captured.

While some shark are caught by trolling, most are caught on live or dead bait drifted in or near a chum slick.

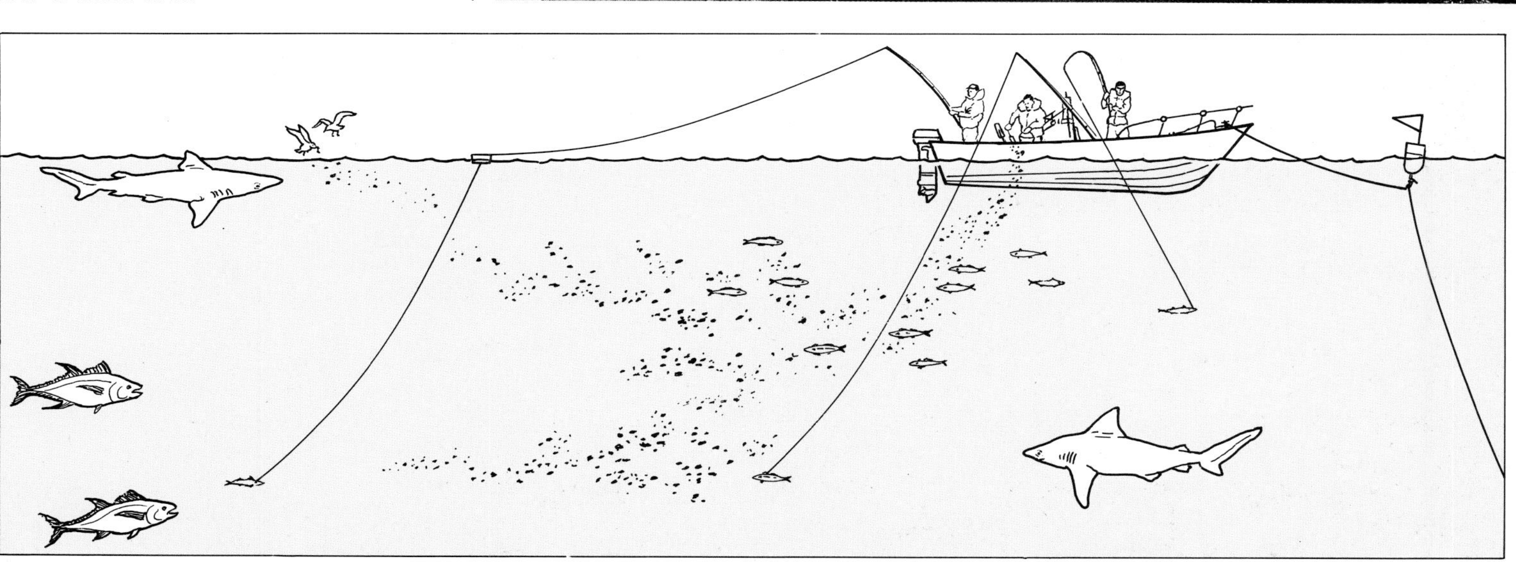

SNAPPER

Like most fish in the snapper family, red snapper are found on the bottom around reefs, wrecks, and rocky outcrops.

There are over two hundred species in this broad category of fish. Some of the more prominent ones among sport fishermen include red, lane, gray, cubera, yellowtail, mutton, longfin, blackfin, vermilion, and silk snapper. Many snappers are found in tropical environs, and are especially plentiful in southeastern U.S. waters. Most weigh from a pound to several pounds, although a few get quite large. Some are warier than others, and most fishing is done with bait, on or near the bottom. Snappers are schooling fish that dwell on the bottom, often around reefy habitat; sonar and Loran may be used to locate schools and appropriate habitat. However, a good number of small and medium-sized snappers are caught by shore fishermen, primarily around piers and bridges.

Snappers have sharp strong teeth, and are often active at night. They are scrappy fighters in small sizes, and strong, hard-fighting battlers when large. Light-tackle usage provides a lot of fun where appropriate. In deep water, and where heavy weights are used, stouter tackle, such as a boat rod with 4/0 reel, is employed.

The most prized snappers, in terms of fighting ability and size, are the cubera and dog snappers. The cubera is found in southeastern waters, while the dog snapper, which is also referred to as the 'Pacific cubera,' is found in southwestern waters. The cubera is the giant of snappers and can exceed 100 pounds; the dog snapper may reach 80 pounds. Both may be caught in shallow water inshore and in intermediate depths, and are sometimes confused in appearance with the gray snapper in small sizes. They are excellent, hard-fighting fish that anglers are delighted to encounter, and are good eating. Cubera and dog snapper are caught in a variety of ways, including live-bait fishing, trolling with diving plugs or feathers, and jigging.

Although most snappers are good table fare, none is more renowned in the culinary department than red snapper. These reef dwellers are found along the East Coast and Gulf of Mexico, usually in 150- to 300-foot bottom depths. They are primarily caught by bait fishing with squid, small fish, or strips of fish that are slowly fished on or near the bottom, sometimes on multi-hook rigs. A similarly colorful and good-eating relative is the vermilion snapper, although it feeds in mid-water as well as on the bottom. Vermilion snapper can sometimes be attracted to the surface for casting by lowering and raising a chum bag.

One of the most commonly caught snappers is the gray, which is also known as 'mangrove snapper.' This small species is found around reefs, wrecks, and rocky outcroppings in the southeastern U.S., and feeds on crustaceans and fish. Smaller gray snapper are taken inshore and shallow, and provide fun light-tackle sport.

Yellowtail snapper, distinguished by a prominent yellow lateral stripe, are another popular species; they are often caught from bridges and piers inshore by anglers using cut bait. Mutton snapper are popular, too, growing as much as 25 to 30 pounds, and providing good light-tackle angling; they are found around reefs, holes, channels, wrecks, and the like, and sometimes on the flats, and can be caught in a variety of ways.

SNOOK

Snook are a coastal saltwater fish that are primarily found in warm, tropical waters. Sporting a distinctive black line that runs laterally along the body, they are one of a few saltwater species that can also do well in freshwater or brackish water, and they are often found in the far reaches of freshwater rivers, as well as in lagoons and canals, often in the same cover-laden places where anglers catch largemouth bass. Their most common habitat, however, is inshore saltwater areas, particularly along mangrove-lined banks as well as around such objects as bridges, docks, pilings, oyster and sand bars, along dropoffs and island edges, and in deep holes.

A renowned fighter, snook jump, run, dive deep, pull very hard, and are generally tough to land, especially in larger sizes. Many snook are lost by anglers. These fish have a penchant for heavy cover; when hooked, they repeatedly try to reach cover and get free by cutting the line, and they are often successful. While an angler must have a good-working reel drag, he also must be able to apply pressure to the fish to turn it and force it away from objects. The bigger the snook, the more of a challenge this becomes.

Snook feed on various small fish and crustaceans. They are primarily caught by casting or live-bait fishing. In the latter, small bait, such as mullet, is livelined by stillfishermen or while drifting. Casters primarily work shallow near-shore areas, often casting into thick mangrove stands and up under the bank.

Accurate casters who can pitch a plug into an opening or back under the brush will usually fare better than those whose casts repeatedly land on the edge of the cover and are always working away from, rather than through, it.

Although small spoons and flies or poppers are used, the favored snook plugs are stick baits that are worked rapidly on the surface, or darting shallow-running plugs that are worked in jerky, erratic motions just under the surface. A moving tide, usually the high ebb, produces well.

Some sight fishing is done by anglers drifting and looking for cruising fish on cover-laden flats or shores, but most angling is blind prospecting in likely places. Fly fishing is most prudent when fish can be seen, but is also done in known snook-holding cover where fish aren't visible. Popping bugs and streamer flies are the terminal items.

Snook may be found singly or in groups, with larger fish tending to be loners. Some fishing is done in deep holes with jigs or by trolling, too, although this is often in the winter when cold water makes snook sluggish. The better fishing time is during the June through November spawning period. Some night fishing, primarily around bridges and piers, is also done for snook in the summer.

Although a stiff-tipped rod is needed for properly working snook plugs, the tackle may be similar to that used in largemouth bass fishing. Bait-casting gear is better for accuracy and fish control, with 12- through 17-pound line the norm.

Typically found along brushy banks, snook are strong fighters and are popularly caught on shallow-running plugs.

TARPON

If tarpon were found in all North American coastal waters, they'd probably be enshrined as a national fish. As it is, although their North American range is virtually confined to Florida, the Keys, and the Gulf of Mexico, they are among the premier saltwater fish, and certainly are one of the most thrilling battlers an angler could hope to encounter. Their high, frequent jumps are surpassed by no other fish, and delight fishermen, many of whom are happy simply to get a few jumps out of a tarpon before it shakes the hook.

Tarpon are primarily an inshore coastal fish ideally pursued in warm shallow water. The better fishing is in spring and fall, but they are caught in all months in some locales. Their preferred habitat is slow rivers, bays, lagoons, shallow flats, passes between islands, mangrove-lined banks, and the like. Small, or 'baby,' tarpon – those up to 20 pounds or so – are usually located in estuaries and river mouths, even considerable distances up freshwater rivers and in sloughs and canals. They feed on crabs, shrimp, and assorted small fishes, and often patrol shallow water in small groups and in a daisy chain arrangement.

They are frequently spotted in these groups when rolling on the surface. This is not a feeding maneuver, and rolling tarpon are often hard to catch. They are rolling then to take in air, which they do in water that is too low in oxygen content for their gills to function properly.

Casting to fish in shallow water, however, is probably the most preferred angling technique, using plugs, flies, and bait. Anglers usually sightfish for tarpon, staking out a shallow-draft boat near a channel or hole; there, they wait for tarpon to come within casting range, or try to spot cruising fish and then move to intercept them.

Growing to large sizes and known for extensive aerial displays, tarpon are among the most prized saltwater gamefish.

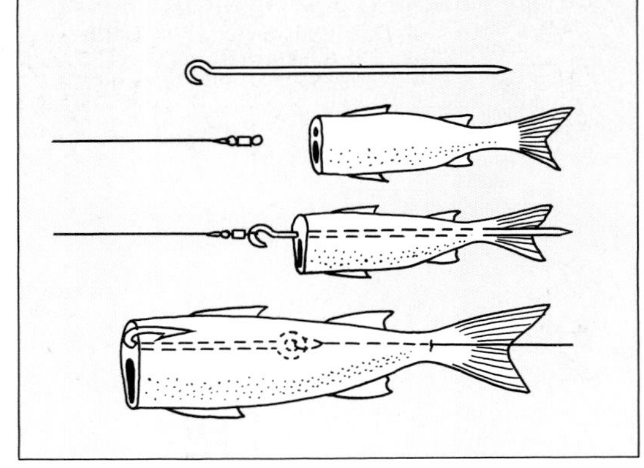

This is a very effective dead bait rig for bottom fishing for tarpon. Use a 10/0 hook at one end of a 6-foot 120-pound-test monofilament leader, and a barrel swivel at the other end. Insert a bait needle the full length of a beheaded mullet, attach the swivel to it and pull the entire leader through the mullet and out the tail.

A variety of plugs are cast for tarpon, with shallow runners fished in a whip or jerky pull-pause retrieve being most effective. Surface plugs are also fished, and fly casters mainly employ large streamer flies on 2/0 to 5/0 hooks. Lures and flies are cast just ahead of a passing fish. Often casters only get one chance at a cruising fish or school. Sometimes tarpon strike seadily, and other times are quite finicky. But they seldom take a lure or bait with great authority.

Live bait fishing is also widely practiced for tarpon, with anglers drifting or anchored and still fishing with a float. Such live bait as mullet, pinfish, crabs, and shrimp are used. Some jigging is also done in deep-water holes and passes; slow trolling, using big spoons, plugs, and feathers, is attempted along the edges of flats near deep water.

Sharp hooks are an absolute necessity for tarpon fishing; these silvery fish have a tough, bony mouth that is hard to penetrate, and you usually have to set the hook firmly several times in order to make a good connection. Even so, many tarpon are lost during one of their many jumps. They also have a tough gill plate that can cut the fishing line readily, so strong leaders are used.

Standard tackle is a 6-foot bait-casting rod and reel filled with 150 to 200 yards of between 12- and 20-pound line. Fly casters use a 9- to 10-foot rod with backbone and a fly reel that has plenty of strong backing line. Tarpon have to be thoroughly played out before being landed, although they revive well for release. Most tarpon are released because they aren't a highly valued food fish.

TAUTOG

Most people have never heard of the wrasse family of fishes, but they are abundant throughout the world, and the tautog, which is also known widely as 'blackfish,' is one of its most popularly sought members.

Populating the inshore areas of the Atlantic coast, the bottom-feeding tautog are most abundant from Massachusetts to the Carolinas. They migrate from deep to relatively shallow water in the spring, and the reverse in the fall as cooler weather sets in.

The place to look for tautog is around rocks. These fish are almost always found on a rocky bottom, and on or within a foot of it. Key areas include reefs, jetties, breakwaters, and boulders. The more extensive the area, the better. Shellfish beds are a popular locale, too. The edges of these structures is often the focal point, and early morning is a particularly good time of day to catch these fish.

Tautog don't school as such, but they will cluster in small areas. It's important to note the location of fish when they're caught, so you can place your bait back in the same spot. Being off a few feet may result in not catching any more fish.

As with most bottom-feeders, it is common to use bait with tautog. Crabs and softshell clams are mostly preferred, although worms are sometimes used. Tautog normally feed on shellfish and they have tough mouths with which they crush their food. Well-sharpened hooks are necessary as a result, and a quick, hard hook-setting action is also needed. A two-hook rig is commonly fished.

Tautog are stubborn battlers that often dive for rocks when they have been hooked. Although the average fish only weighs a few pounds, fairly stout boat rods are used to keep them from digging in behind a rock. That tackle is also employed because weights up to 6 to 8 pounds are used to get and keep baits down near the bottom, sometimes in heavy current. Tautog fishermen lose a lot of terminal tackle, however, hanging it in the rocks, but that is to be expected.

These fish are seldom found in more than 60 feet of water, and may be much shallower and close to shore if the right bottom terrain is available. In shallow water they are wary fish, and keeping the bait away from the boat, instead of directly below it, is a better presentation. They also do more nibbling than hard striking in shallow water, and you may have to give them a little time to move off with the bait before setting the hook.

Blackfish, or tautog, are caught on the bottom around rocks, usually by fishing with bait.

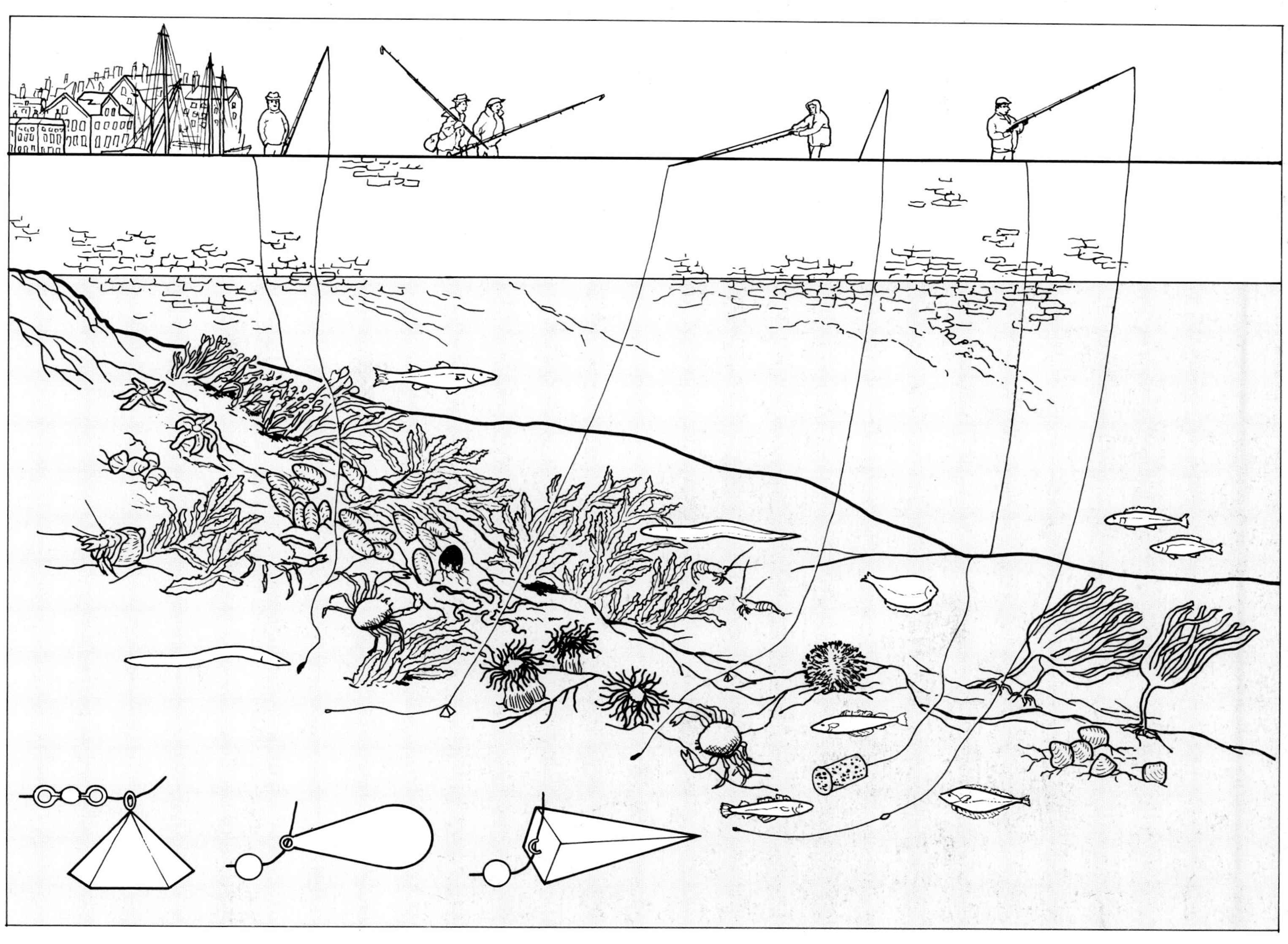

While blackfish are apt to be caught at this pier locale, so are some other inshore bottom-feeding species. A fish-finding rig that allows a fish to move off with the bait without feeling the sinker is appropriate. Three such rigs are a swivel and sand sinker (1), split shot and bank sinker (2), and split shot and pyramid sinker.

TROUT

Collectively and individually, trout are the foremost coldwater fish in North America. They exist naturally or through stocked introduction in mountain creeks, highland reservoirs, glacial lakes, beaver ponds, meadow streams, swift-flowing rivers, and other locales, and are found in a host of species, sizes, colors, and dispositions.

From the viewpoint of distribution, abundance, and angling importance, the foremost fish of this classification are brown trout, rainbow trout, steelhead, brook trout, and lake trout. Some of the habitats and angling approaches for these fish overlap, but lake trout differ enough to be treated here separately. Other trout species of some interest in North America, and found mainly in the western regions, include cutthroat trout; golden trout; and bull trout and Dolly Varden, both of which are actually char and found in the Pacific Northwest.

Brown trout

This type, which were imported to North America from Europe over one hundred years ago (they are still called 'German browns' by some anglers), and which closely resemble their Atlantic salmon relation, are widely distributed fish, with a fair tolerance for intermediate-temperature water. They are cunning fish, often more difficult to catch than other trout. Browns grow large in some environments and they spawn in rivers in late fall or early winter.

Brook trout

On the other hand, Brook trout are a more diminutive, native fish, less widely distributed and preferring cooler waters than brown trout. A colorful fish that spawns in late fall or winter in flowing water, the brookie is actually in the char family and more likely to be found in less fertile, elevated environs.

Unlike other trout, the rainbow is a springtime spawner; it can grow to large sizes.

Rainbow trout and Steelhead

Rainbow trout are a native North American fish that are as, if not more, widely distributed than brown trout and which have a higher tolerance for warm and/or lesser-quality water than the other trout. They can grow large, are known for acrobatic fighting, and spawn in the spring. These fish are also found in a more streamlined, silvery, anadromous version known as a 'steelhead'. Steelhead grow large and fight well enough to be rated very highly for sporting values; they are found mainly in Pacific coastal rivers and Great Lakes waters.

All four of these fish are found in flowing water as well as in the so-called still waters of lakes, reservoirs, and ponds.

Left: Brook trout, which are less widely distributed than other trout and less tolerant of warm or pool quality environs, are a sentimental favorite of fishermen.

Angling in rivers

To some anglers, the thought of fishing for river trout brings to mind a gentle flowage and small fish dimpling the surface during a profuse insect hatch, and using a light fly rod and fine-tippet leader to daintily drop a tiny imitation fly among the rising fish. To others it means tossing a flashy spinner in a roily cold flow and prospecting for an intermediate-size fish that will mistake the lure for a darting minnow. And to still others it means flipping a gob of fish eggs into a deep pool with a long rod and setting the hook into a 30-inch-long ball of silver fury that rockets out of the water and heads for the next county.

Each of these is a classic view of some type of river trout fishing, and this points out the extremes that exist in this facet of angling. Fishing for trout in rivers – and by 'river' we refer to all forms of flowing water – is a diverse activity, one that requires proper presentation, a knowledge of the habits of the species, and an ability to analyze the water and determine what places will likely hold fish, to be consistently successful.

There are a number of different-size flowages in which brook, brown, and rainbow trout, and steelhead exist, and portions of these can be extremely fast or dramatically slow. There are some excellent trout-holding areas which can be found in nearly any flowage, however, and these fish may all be found in some of the same waters.

Brown trout tend to lie in slower and warmer waters than brookies, yet they will both inhabit pools and slicks in rapid-flowing waters. Both primarily feed on various stages of aquatic insects, but also on small minnows. Rainbows and steelhead tend to stay in deep, main-flow water, and feed on aquatic insects as well as fish eggs and small fish. Yet, all of these trout are often found in some similar locations, such as pockets behind rocks; fishing the so-called 'pocket water' is a standard river fishing ploy, especially in low water and where smaller fish exist. Other such places include the slick water downstream from an eddy or pool; dark, swift water just above a falls or rapids drop; the sanctuary beneath a falls; and spring holes.

Trout rivers vary from mild to raging flows and from brooks to major waterways. This is a typical river trout fishing scene in mid spring.

Fly fishing A great many river trout are caught by fly fishing. Fly anglers usually use a light outfit (7- or 8-foot rod for 4- to 7-weight line) in order to fish small streams, using perhaps an outfit on the upper end of this range for larger or more open waters and/or places where big fish might be found. Leader length should be about 7 feet long for small waters, slightly longer elsewhere (equal to the length of rod is often a normal measurement), tapering to a 2X or 3X tippet. Flies must be selected according to the type of minnow or aquatic insect that needs to be imitated. There is an enormous assortment of dry and wet flies, nymphs, and streamers to use on trout, depending on the circumstances.

Spring and summer insect hatches particularly attract river trout. In the spring these hatches may occur during

To help a fly drift naturally even though the belly of the fly line is in mid-current, you need to 'mend' the line. As current puts snake loops into fly line (1), leading to midsection bulge (2), lift and toss the fly line upstream with a high quick flipping motion (3), which will prolong the effective drift (4).

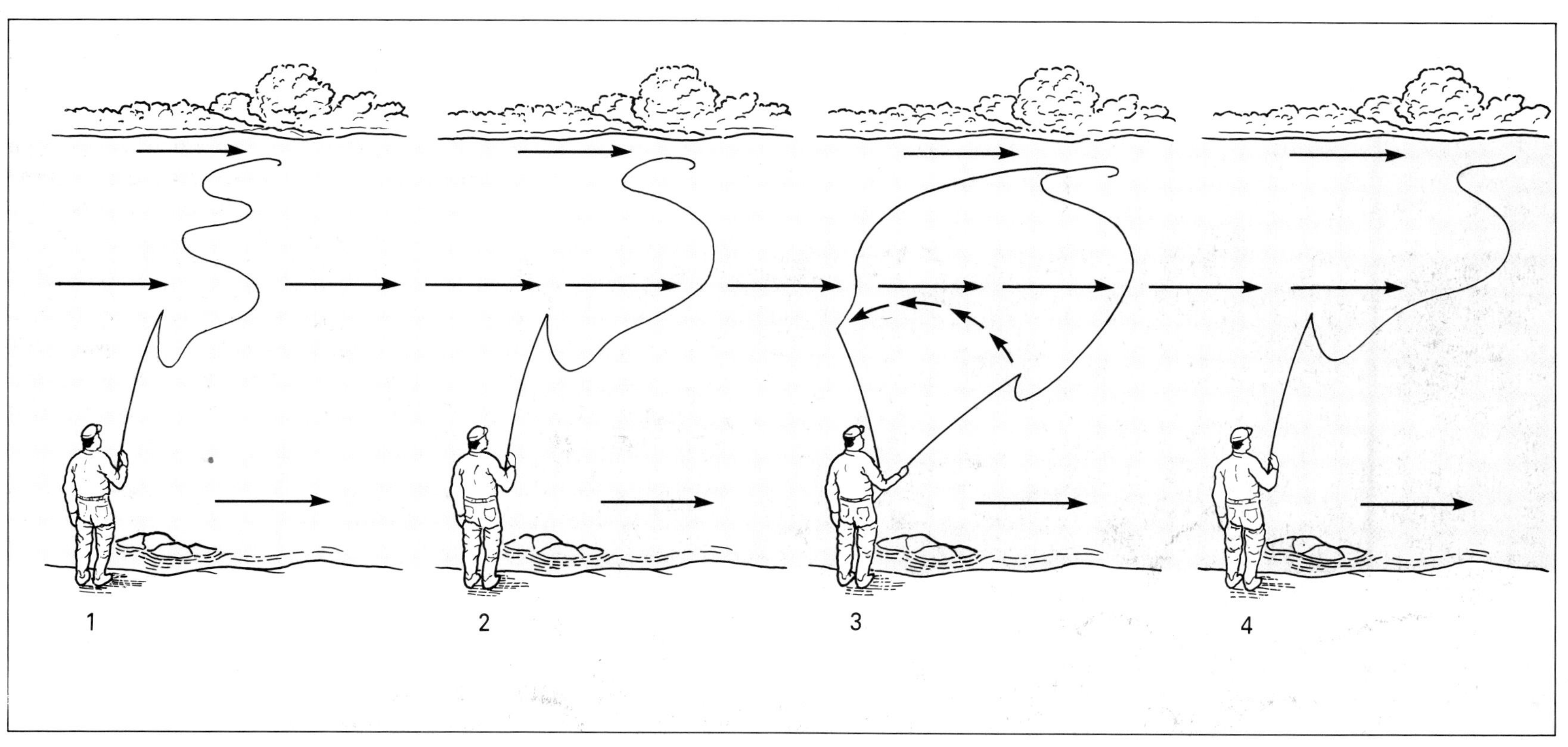

A hatch of aquatic insects, such as stoneflies here, is usually quite evident and a signal for trout fishermen to use an imitating fly.

the day, but later in the season they may be most evident around sundown and last long into the night. Trout, especially browns, will feed on meatier forage in the night as well. Small fish are often preyed upon in a long, shallow, gravel flat above a deep pool.

Fly fishing tactics vary, of course. Nymphs must be retrieved in short jerking movements, and at an angle downstream. Streamer flies, which represent minnows, are retrieved at a steady pace across or upstream in rivers. Dry flies are cast upstream and float naturally downstream while the angler gathers line rapidly. To work a fly across stream or retrieve upstream causes your offering to drag or move in an unnatural fashion, and fish will seldom strike a fly presented this way. In a very slow pool or a midstream beaver pond, a dry fly should sit motionless and drift with a breeze if there is one. Give the dry fly enough slack by mending line so it drifts without line pull.

Spinning Spin fishermen have a lot of success with river trout also, using small spinners, small spoons, occasionally a light jig, and sometimes minnow-imitation plugs, as well as live worms and salmon eggs where bait fishing is legal, and large spoons and spinners in big, swift-flowing waters. Spinning equipment should be light or ultralight, with lines ranging from 4- to 8-pound strength. In some smaller streams you might use 2-pound line and a 5-foot ultralight rod. Line capacity and drag is seldom a factor with reels used in spinning for trout. Where big steelhead are to be encountered, line capacity and drag are more crucial.

Drifting and backrolling Steelhead, rainbow, and brown trout are sometimes targets for big-river drifting or backtrolling presentations, too, which were described in the previous section (see pp.102 and 92 respectively). Most of this is done with diving plugs or bait; winter-run steelhead, for example, are caught with pencil- lead-weighted spawn sacks or single-hook salmon eggs. Many attractions — plugs, spoons, spinners, flies, and bait — are used.

Spin fishermen use this bait rig (1) for drifting worms, single eggs, and egg sacks for trout and steelhead in rivers. Split shot or pencil lead is attached to a short dropper line, and the baited hook is attached to a longer leader. Note methods of hooking single egg or gob of eggs (2).

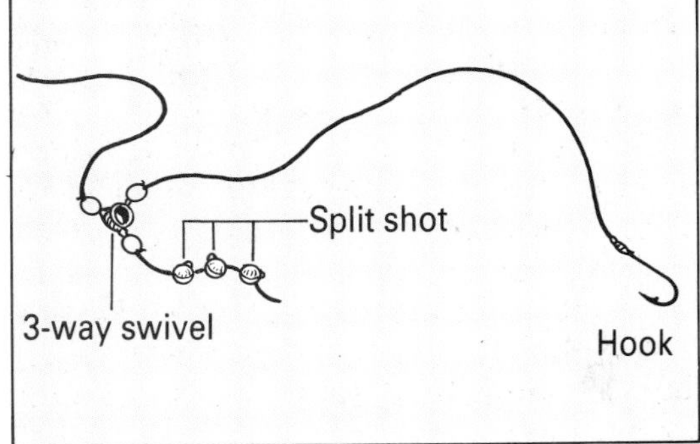

Angling in Lakes

Using the term 'lakes' generically to include reservoirs and ponds, angling for trout in lakes is a completely different sport than angling for trout in flowages, not only because lakes usually harbor larger fish, but because such waters often provide suitable year-round water temperatures, have abundant forage-fish opportunities, and their trout aren't readily accessible.

Trout in lakes move a lot and aren't always confined to readily identifiable terrain. Primarily they move in search of food, which is not made up principally of aquatic insects but such forage as alewives, smelt, ciscoes, chubs, sculpin, assorted species of shiners and darters, and even yellow perch and crayfish. It is usually a certainty that the prominent forage species in any environment constitutes the major part of the diet of a trout.

Temperature plays a large role in the location of trout, including steelhead such as this, in lake environs.

Not all river trout, including this brown, are caught by wading anglers; fishing from boats is possible depending on the size and nature of the flowage.

After ice-out or in late winter and early spring, trout lakes begin to warm on the surface. Trout may be found at any level at this time, and are often within the upper strata (20 feet or less) of a lake or in shallow water close to shore. Thermal discharges, tributaries, rocky shorelines, and the like contribute to warmer water locales. In large lakes, a vertical surface distinction between water temperature may exist until the weather warms. Known as a 'thermal bar', and found offshore in the spring, it is particularly attractive to steelhead.

Trout seek preferred temperature zones in lakes as they get warmer. Brown and rainbow trout prefer water in the upper 50s and low 60s, and once the water warms on the surface, they usually are found in this temperature water, whatever depth it may be, provided that there is ample oxygen at that level. Often, their forage is found at or close to the same level. With brown and rainbow trout, the place where those temperatures meet with the bottom of the lake can be a very strong locale for catching fish, especially if they are prominent aspects of underwater terrain, such as a point or near-shore ledge.

An ideal situation in large lakes is to find a place where temperature, forage, and shore structure coincide. If you are looking for schools of baitfish, and monitoring preferred water temperature, try to find both of these where the thermocline intersects the bottom. This would be a prime place to begin looking for trout in the summer on large lakes. Trout may be more concentrated, incidentally, along a sharply sloped shoreline than a moderately sloped one.

Trout orient to objects and edges. By identifying physical terrain, from depth contours to irregularities in the shore or bottom, you can get an idea what places attract baitfish as well as trout and pinpoint possible ways to fish them. A good locale is where baitfish get funneled, or where they might routinely pass by. The deep-water/shallow water interface near islands can be similarly productive. The edges of long underwater bars or shoals are places where bait migrate naturally by, and logically present feeding opportunities for trout. In midsummer, deep trout may cruise over a large area, so in big lakes you may have a lot of scouring to do.

Fishing techniques

Fishing for trout in lakes is like blind prospecting. To have regular success means covering a lot of water. When trout are shallow and near the surface they can be caught by trolling, casting from shore or in a float tube, or drifting with bait. Although casting is the most fun, trolling is often more popular, because it allows you to cover a lot of ground and look for active, aggressive fish, particularly trout that perhaps have not been spooked or otherwise bothered by other fishermen and boaters. Drift-fishing with a boat usually is a live-bait proposition, but it is slow and, where motors are permitted on lakes, less productive than lure trolling. If you cast from shore, you may simply be limited to one spot, such as a pier or breakwall, and must cast repeatedly in hope of attracting a moving,

Most fishing for trout in lakes is done by trolling; these brown trout were caught on small plugs that imitated the prominent natural lake forage.

incoming fish to strike your lure. This can pay off in tributary areas where warm river water attracts a significant number of fish. In most lakes, however, it is better to be mobile, concentrating shore-casting efforts near prominent points, inlets, steep banks, rock- and boulder-studded shores, shorelines with sharp dropoffs to deep water, and warm bay and cove areas. Try casting spoons and plugs (crankbaits or sinking minnow-style baits) from shore.

Once the trout are deep, it becomes tough, if not impossible, to catch them from shore, and here the boater with the ability to get his lures down, to scout for fish with some type of sonar, and with the ability to ply a lot of water by trolling, has a distinct advantage.

In fishing for trout in lakes, once you have established some idea of where and how deep to fish, the consideration becomes what type of lure to fish, what color, and at what speed. Spoons, plugs, and spinners all catch trout, as do jigs at times. Many flat-line trollers use fairly heavy spoons to help them get down, but light spoons are preferred on downriggers. Fly fishing is predominantly done in small, shallow lakes and ponds, to rising fish with dry flies or to near-shore fish with streamers and sinking lines.

There is seldom any reason to use heavy tackle for trout in lakes, although large browns and steelhead can be powerful fish and line capacity may be a factor. Spinning and bait-casting tackle is used for trolling, and spinning and fly equipment for casting. Rods are usually long, in the 7- to 9-foot range for all but brook trout fishing, and line strengths from 4- to 10-pound are usually adequate, although big-water anglers who troll simultaneously for trout and chinook or coho salmon may use heavier line.

Lake trout

Lake trout are generally one of the least accessible freshwater game fish, frequenting the cold, dark, and mysterious nether depths of northern lakes and reservoirs. Called a 'trout', they are really in the char family and a relative of Arctic char and brook trout, although they grow much larger than either of those species, and behave quite differently from other char and trout.

Their range is limited in the U.S. outside of the Great Lakes, but they are widely distributed across Canada, seeking out cold water. Although lakers

A popular steelheading technique on large rivers is backtrolling, primarily with plugs but also with bait, controlling downstream momentum so that offerings get down into pools and stay in front of fish much longer than they would for a cast-and-drift angler.

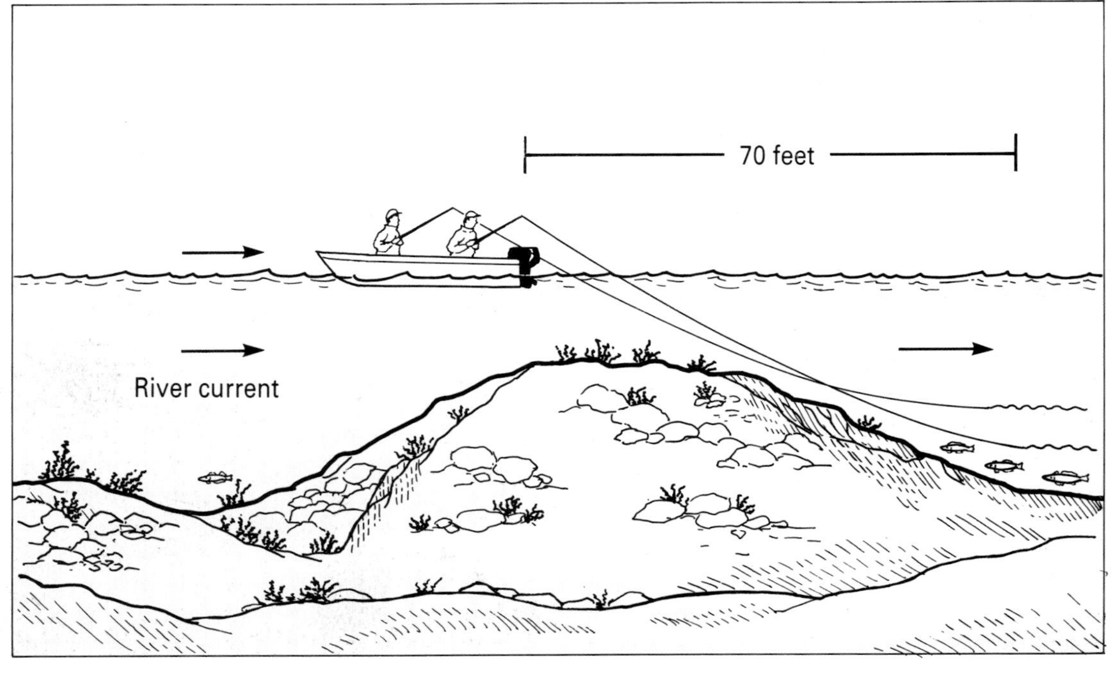

Lake trout can grow larger than other trout, especially in far northern waters.

do not have the reputation of being an exciting sportfish, this is partially due to the heavy tackle many anglers traditionally use, the depths from which they are often dredged, and the nature of the lakes in which they are found. There is a distinct difference, however, between north-country lakers, which reside in waters that seldom warm up enough to establish a thermocline, and those which live in lakes where the upper strata becomes quite warm. Fish in the former are strong-pulling, head-shaking runners who give an able account of themselves in all sizes.

Since lake trout are denizens of open water, where they feed on sculpins, smelt, alewives, ciscoes, and similar bait, they are primarily pursued by trolling. In most places in the southern part of the lake trout's range, trolling for these fish is mainly done at relatively deep levels. This is because lake trout are attuned to very cold water (mid 40s to low 50s) that is situated below the thermocline, and because they are often near bottom and some form of hard structure (primarily shoals or reefs) from late spring through early fall.

Not all trolling for lakers is done at decompression depths. Rocky islands and reefs are prime foraging grounds for lake trout, which move into such spots to feed (even in the summer and even if the water temperature is higher than they generally prefer), then retreat to deep water. Also, early and late in the year are good times to find lake trout in the upper 20 feet of a lake or reservoir if the water temperature is favorable. Thus, trolling methods are quite varied (although downrigging is most popular), with spoons being heavily favored. Lakers basically like a slow presentation, quite slow, in fact, compared to salmon and other trout. They are also curious fish that follow lures a considerable distance. As a result, changes in lure action often prompt strikes.

Jigging, both in deep and shallow water with either heavy or light lures, is an overlooked and very successful fishing method in northern lakes, especially at river mouths and to the side of heavy current where a major tributary dumps into a large lake. In casting, light jigs, spoons, spinners, streamer flies, and occasionally a dry fly will catch near-shore lake fish and those in northern rivers.

Tackle runs the gamut from deep-trolling hardware to fly, spinning, and bait-casting equipment. Lakers give the best account of themselves on light line, which, because they inhabit open water, is very feasible.

TUNA

Tuna are among the most important of all saltwater fish, both for commercial and recreational fishermen. To the latter, they are revered for their fighting stamina, size, and flesh, and are pursued with fervor seasonally up and down both North American coasts.

These fish are actually members of the mackerel family; they are migratory, pelagic fish that primarily inhabit tropical, subtropical, and temperate waters. They are usually found well offshore in North America, but tuna may at times venture closer to shore and into cooler water.

Tuna grow quite rapidly, which is not surprising because they are voracious feeders. Their diet is usually whatever is most abundant in their present location, but characteristically includes squid, crustaceans, flying fish, mackerel, small tuna, sardines, herring, whiting, and other fish. They usually forage close to the surface.

Tuna of all sizes are exceptionally streamlined; they are often described as 'torpedo-shaped'. They do not jump out of the water when hooked, but no fish fights harder, pound for pound, in either freshwater or saltwater. They strain the heaviest tackle, and have awesome endurance, often diving deep and often able to recoup some of their expended energy even in the midst of a tussle. The largest tuna may be battled for many hours, and even small tuna provide a powerful, though briefer, struggle.

Small tuna, in the 5- to 100-pound-range, are referred to as school tuna, and are characteristically found in large groups. The smaller the tuna, in fact, the larger the school, and vice versa. These fish provide outstanding angling, often with light tackle, and sometimes extremely frenzied action. Not only are they more plentiful than their larger brethren, but they are usually easier to fool. Large tuna, particularly bluefins, are known as giants. Some fishermen refer to a giant as a fish over 100 pounds, but many veteran big-game anglers don't consider a tuna to be classified as a giant unless it exceeds 250 or 300 pounds.

Yellowfin tuna are one of the strongest of North American fish, usually caught offshore by chumming and trolling.

The major tunas of interest to North American anglers include albacore, yellowfin tuna, blackfin tuna, bigeye tuna, and bluefin tuna.

Albacore

These have longer pectoral fins, which extend all the way to the anal fin, than other tunas. Occurring in both Atlantic and Pacific environs, they often mix with schools of other tuna, and are very highly desired as food, since they are the only member of the group classified as 'white meat' tuna. They are sometimes difficult to distinguish from small bigeye tuna, and are favored for relatively light-tackle fishing.

Yellowfin tuna

Also found on both coasts, yellowfin tuna don't range as far northward as the other tuna do and evidently don't travel as widely as such species as albacore and bluefin tuna. Also called 'Allison tuna', yellowfins grow to intermediate sizes and are more colorful than other tunas, although smaller ones look a lot like blackfin or bigeye tuna. Large yellowfins usually have long second anal and dorsal fins.

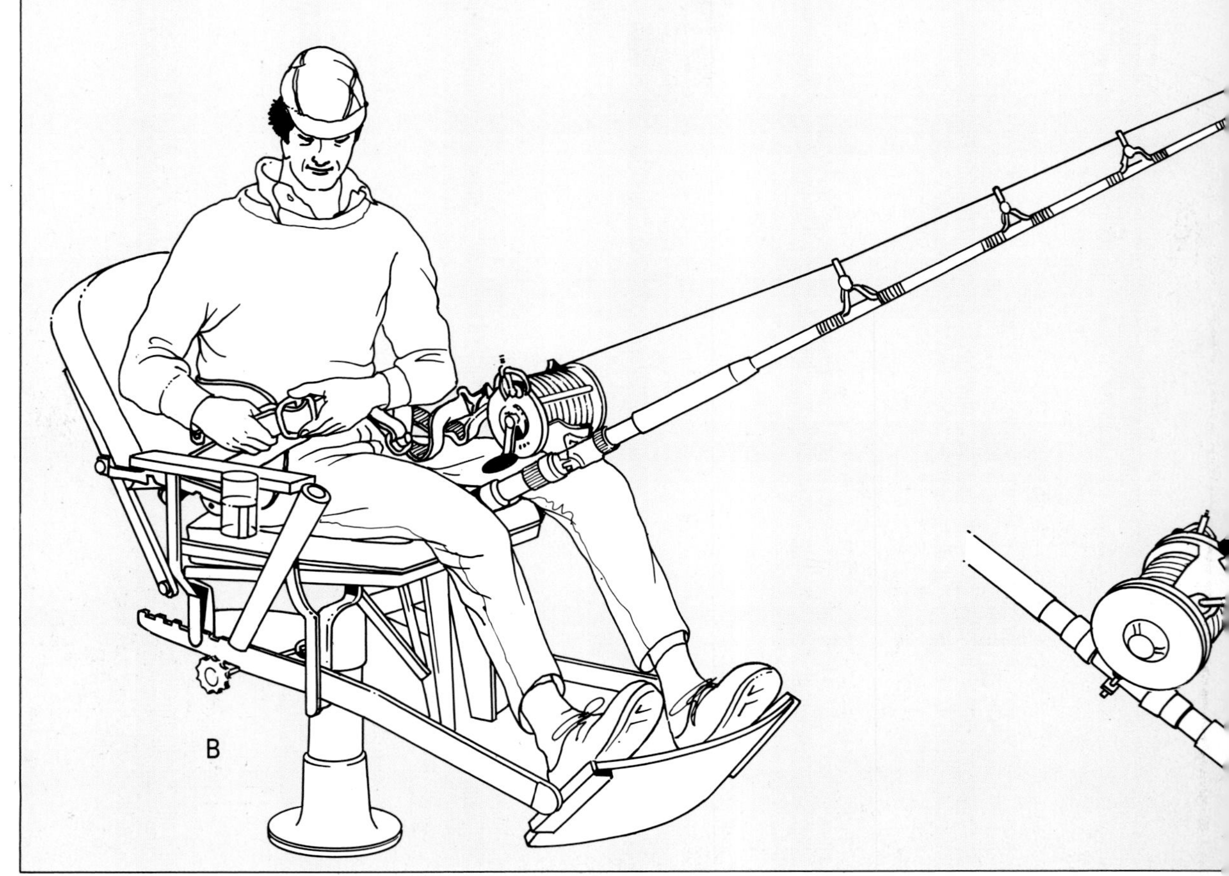

For a grueling battle with a giant tuna, you need a harness for back and kidney support (A), and an adjustable swiveling fighting chair with sturdy rod gimbal (B). The fish must be fought with constant tension, and by pumping (C). To pump, start at position 1 and bring the rod all the way to position 2, and as you lower the rod downward again (position 3), crank the reel handle furiously to gain line until you reach position 4. Repeat until the fish is to the boat.

These anglers have caught a blackfin tuna, which is a good light tackle fish and the smallest of the tuna species.

Blackfin and bigeye tuna

Blackfin tuna are only found in the Atlantic waters of North America. They are a small, football-shaped tuna, but a spunky fish good for light-tackle angling. Bigeye tuna, however, grow to sizes similar to yellowfins, and are found on both coasts. They tend to roam deeper than the other tunas.

Bluefin tuna

These are the VIPs of the tuna clan. They migrate more extensively than the other fish, they grow larger, and their speed and strength is unparalleled. Giant bluefins can grow to weights exceeding 1,000 pounds and a length of 10 to 11 feet. The biggest fish are pursued with the heaviest of big-game tackle and can take hours to subdue. Bluefins are found in both Atlantic and Pacific waters, sometimes quite far north.

Fishing Methods

The primary methods of tuna fishing include fishing with bait, and trolling with lures or rigged baits. Trollers cruise at a fast clip, often 6 to 12 knots. Lures are trolling plugs, feathers, and spoons, including daisy-chain rigs, as well as whole rigged baits such as balao, mackerel, and mullet, or strip baits. Tuna are often spotted feeding or cruising on the surface, which gave rise to the use of flying bridges ('tuna towers') for observation while running the boat. When tuna are spotted, the boat is maneuvered to bring the baits or lures ahead of them without spooking the fish.

Chumming and fishing with live or cut bait is a highly popular technique for big tuna, especially for yellowfins and bluefins. Mullet, squid, herring, and other fishes are used. Anglers anchor in deep water on a hump or shelf and put a large buoy on the anchor rope. They ladle chum out to set up a slick or chum line and wait for smaller fish and hopefully tuna to be attracted to the smorgasbord, drifting hooked bait in amidst the chum. If small tuna are hooked they are played with the boat at anchor, but large tuna are played with the boat unhooked from the buoy so the fish can be followed and the boat can be used to help with positioning and fighting. Sometimes fishermen locate schools of tuna by trolling, then stop and fish live bait in the vicinity of the school.

As bluefin tuna go, this 70-pounder is a small one; no fish fights harder, however, pound for pound.

Big tuna take a lot of line immediately after being hooked, and many line-losing surges are likely to be experienced in the course of a fight. Only reels with the best drags are used, and the tackle for big tuna is rather specialized, ranging from light 20-pound outfits all the way to 130-pound class equipment. While smaller tuna can be caught with conventional stand-up tackle, bigger fish are fought with rod imbedded in the gimbal of a swiveling fighting chair. Tackle, from knots to rod guides, must be of the best caliber, and able to take extraordinary punishment.

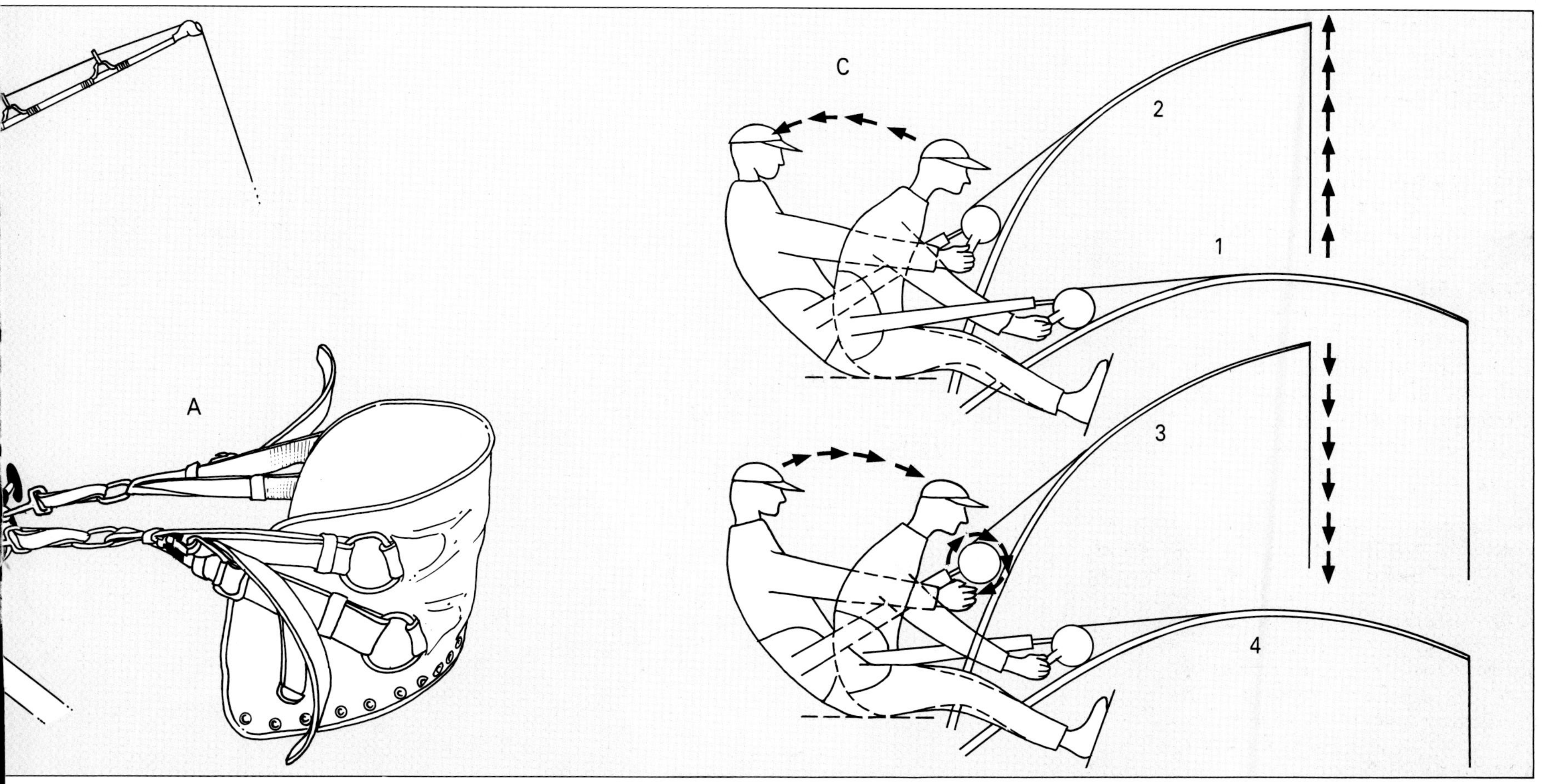

WALLEYE

Not the spunkiest of fish, but certainly one that gets extremely high grades as table fare, the walleye is an enormously popular coolwater species of fish that is widely spread from the mid reaches of the U.S. north through the mid reaches of Canada. Smaller in size and less widely distributed is its similar looking cousin, the sauger.

Walleyes generally relate to structure, have light-sensitive eyes that make them primarily active in low-light and dark situations in many environments, are not particularly aggressive feeders, and do not usually inhabit extreme deep-water environs. They are schooling fish, so you can expect that when you catch one, more are near by. They mainly forage on small fish, primarily minnows, perch, shad, and shiners, but also crayfish.

Often the fastest angling and the biggest walleyes are caught when these fish are making their late-winter, early-spring spawning run. Walleyes begin spawning when the water temperature reaches the mid-40s. In some lakes and in big rivers, walleyes have sufficient spawning areas and water conditions and don't make an official run, but nonetheless are in very shallow water. In natural lakes, casting or stillfishing with bait may be a better technique at this time, but in large river systems and impoundments, trolling has merit. After spawning, walleyes inhabit areas adjacent to spawning grounds, like a shallow bay or the mouth of a stream.

For most of the season, from late spring through summer and into fall, walleyes are attracted to specific types of cover. These include rock reefs, sandbars, gravel bars, points, weeds, rocky or riprap causeways or shorelines, and creek channels. Walleyes are particularly known for congregating in or along the edges of vegetation. Weeds attract small baitfish and larger fish in the food chain, such as perch, and thus provide a food supply for walleyes, and they also offer protective cover. Walleyes are often situated where the weeds end and the bottom begins to drop off to deeper water.

Walleyes usually hug the bottom around favored haunts, too, and it is almost a tenet of all kinds of walleye fishing that you have to get down to the bottom with your offering to be successful. This is especially true on natural lakes with a lot of cover, and in rivers, but walleyes do suspend off the bottom in some environments. They are also known to be active in the evening and at night, moving shallower to the edges of a bar or a rock or gravel point that breaks sharply to deep water.

The most prominent conventional methods of walleye fishing include casting jigs (with and without bait); casting or drifting with weight-forward spinners; and stillfishing or drifting live bait. Additionally, some people cast crankbaits, and cast and slowly retrieve live-bait rigs. Many walleye anglers use a controlled wind drifting technique – employing an electric motor to keep the boat in proper position – when conditions warrant, or backtroll to precisely position jigs, live-bait rigs, and spinners. Lures and bait are almost always fished slowly. Light to medium tackle, mostly spinning outfits with 6- to 10-pound line, is the norm.

A fish of both river and lake, the walleye is usually caught on or close to the bottom, and is highly esteemed for food value.

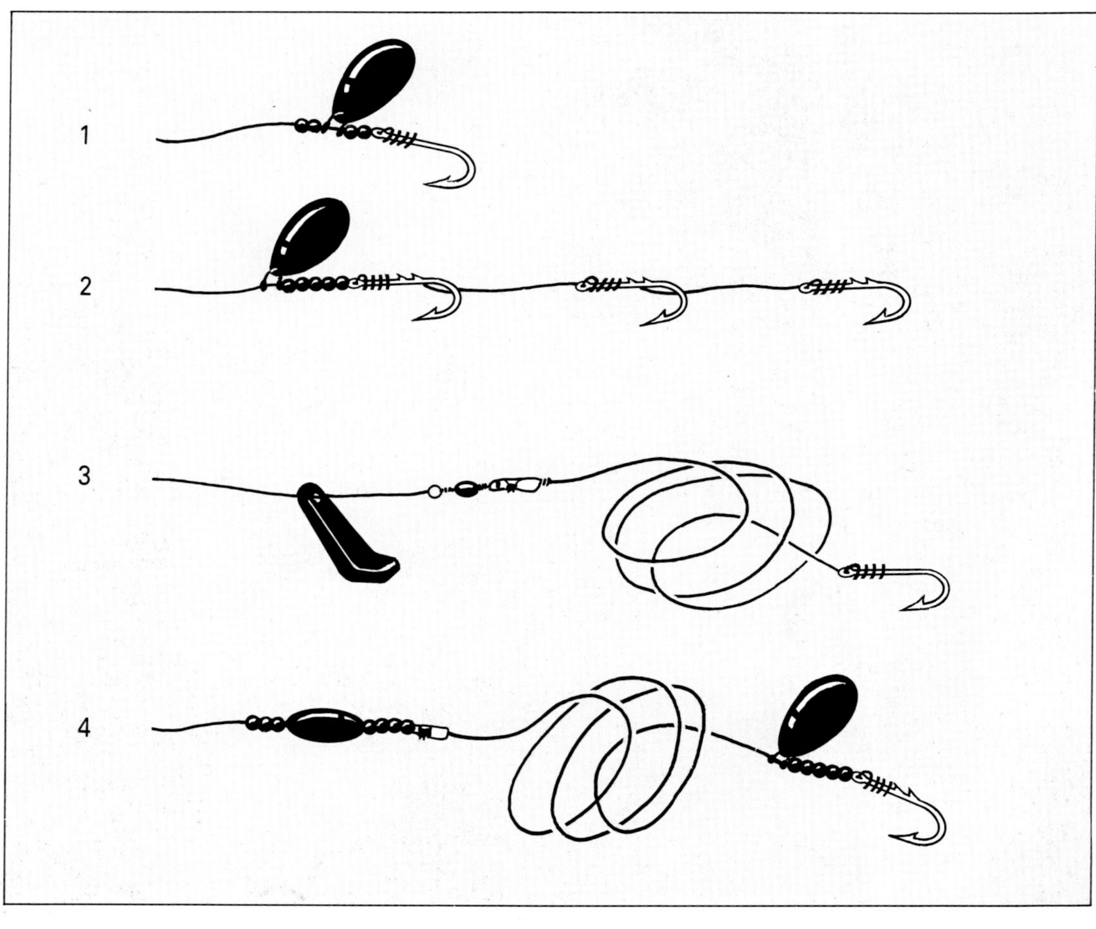

Common worm rigs used for exploring the bottom for walleyes include: (1) a standard spinner rig; (2) spinner-and-worm-harness rig; (3) a walking sinker rig; and (4) a leadered spinner rig attached to a bead chain sinker.

WHITEFISH

Whitefish are not as well known to American anglers as they are to Canadians. Three species of whitefish – round, mountain, and lake – are found in North America, with the lake whitefish being most abundant. They are generally found throughout Canada and Alaska and the extreme northern parts of the U.S., and are respected for game as well as gourmand values.

The average whitefish caught by anglers is in the 1- to 2-pound range. Fish of 4 or 5 pounds, and even larger, are sometimes caught. In lakes, whitefish are readily taken when schooled and when rising to flies, but are often hard to catch otherwise. Though many open-lake fishermen catch them accidentally while seeking other game, they are successfully pursued through the ice. In rivers where they are abundant, they are routinely caught by fly fishermen, sometimes being a nuisance rather than a pleasure, and they will be found in slow pools, beneath waterfalls, and along back-switching bank eddies.

Whitefish are principally an insect-feeder, although they also eat mollusks, leeches, fish eggs, and the like. They are most likely to be caught on nymphs or dry flies, the latter especially in lakes when these fish rise to the surface in large schools which travel along the shores of a deep-water bay.

Whitefish rise gently when feeding upon floating insects, and often one sees the dorsal fin cutting through the surface momentarily. A dry fly presented slightly ahead of the cruising fish will usually be taken, but the hook-setting motion need not be vigorous. The whitefish has a soft mouth, so a smooth rod-lifting action will set the hook without tearing it away from the fish.

These fish can be caught in other manners besides fly fishing, although not usually as reliably. Once in a while a whitefish will strike a spoon or small plug, though a jig is far more likely to be effective. A small dark jig is best; it can be fished plain or can be tipped with a small insect or grub, with the latter popular when ice fishing.

Whitefish fight well, occasionally jumping and characteristically making a diving run and shaking near the surface. They are a fine light-tackle fish, with light or ultralight spinning rods equipped with 2- through 6-pound line very suitable, as well as light, medium-length fly rods for 5- through 7-weight fly lines.

Though not a prime quarry of most anglers, whitefish provide good sport on light spinning or fly tackle.

INDEX

Figures in italics refer to illustrations.